FINDING

The Utterly Useless
Part II – The Farce Contin

\g

By Bob Newbury

(Still shamelessly plagiarising the diaries of Liz Newbury)

Two naïve liveaboards and a cat blunder their way around the Eastern Mediterranean.

Preamble to the kindle edition:

The paperback version of this book makes copious (some would say unnecessarily and self-indulgently copious) use of footnotes. Footnotes don't work in e-books as there is no real bottom of the page, so they seem to self-convert to endnotes. To keep you on your toes, though, they still refer to them as footnotes.

Using them is not entirely intuitive so, at the risk of being deafened by the sound of grandmothers sucking eggs, there follows a quick Dummies' Guide to using endnotes on a kindle:

1. They are marked in the text by a number in superscript in square brackets, like this: [23].

2. To view the note in brief, tap once on the number. A footnote box will open at the bottom. To return to the main text, tap on the X in the top right corner of the box.

3. If all of the note is not displayed in the box, tap on 'Go to Footnotes' in the bottom left of the footnote box. This will open the footnotes page.

4. To return to your place in the text, tap on the number of the footnote you opened. It is usually at the top of the page.

With regard to point (4), if you've got fat fingers like me the kindle has an irritating habit of bringing up the navigation bar at the top, instead of returning to your place in the text. Worry not; just hit the back button (between 'home' and 'settings'.

Got that?

Good. Off you go.

Preface

This book is a mish-mash of cod-anthropology, half-baked philosophical ideas and cynically misrepresented social science, all wilfully taken out of context. These sit uneasily with ineptly researched historical analyses and totally unsubstantiated political and cultural prejudices, with the whole sorry, ramshackle edifice masquerading as a travelogue. Its real subject is the social, cultural, psychological and linguistic quirks of the yottie tribe, and its real purpose is to facilitate the author's egotistical desire to impose his splenetic, ill thought out and internally inconsistent views on the unsuspecting general public.

Don't say you weren't warned.

An anthropologist, even a cod one, needs a subject. Early in the development of the field, most anthropologists studied obscure, small, exotic societies such as Amazonian hunter-gatherers, nomadic Bedouin or Samoan fishing villages. This had several advantages; the sample sizes were small, making it easier to get your head round, and the exotic subject matter made the pop-anthropology books that span off from it popular with the general reader.

This latter advantage was reinforced by the opportunity to pad the books with photographs of lissome young women with unrestrained breasts and muscular men prancing around in nothing but penis gourds. The anthropological label gave the works a veneer of academic respectability that would have been difficult to justify in back copies of Parade, Health & Efficiency or Harrison Marks figure studies.

In keeping with the less judgmental mores of the internet age, the dirty photos for this particular work are available in a special online edition protected by a paywall. This can be found at www.boatsboobsandbums.com

As the field matured, anthropologists started to turn their attention to larger and more familiar groups, eventually to the point of undertaking detailed studies of nation states, including their own native cultures. This had advantages and disadvantages. On the plus side, you have easy access to, and detailed knowledge and experience of, your subject matter. On the downside, the sample size is large enough to challenge a Cray supercomputer and familiarity with the subject matter can easily lead to the glaringly obvious being blindly overlooked.

In this *magnum opus* I get the best of both worlds. I am reporting on my native culture, the Yottie Tribe, but the risk of familiarity breeding oversight is reduced by the fact that I'm not really a proper yottie. I am to yotties as the yottie is to proper big hairy sailors.

In addition, the sample size is quite small, with estimates of the total number of liveaboard yotties ranging from around 15 000 to around 50 000 over the whole planet. Although this is considerably bigger than the six hundred or so in a Samoan fishing village, common cultural beliefs and social patterns and rules can nevertheless be discerned. Take, for example, the matter of greeting rituals and the establishment of a social pecking order.

This is both simple and complex. It is simple in that status among yotties is determined by only two criteria, namely liveaboard experience and proficiency in the many and varied skills essential to successful cruising. It is complex in that it is considered very bad form to brag about ability or experience in any fashion. Relative status is therefore established by a delicate verbal dance of reticence and self-effacement, garnished with a *jus* of understatement and litotes.

References to any life prior to cruising are also subject to the same rules. Enquiries regarding previous occupations are shrugged off with a dismissive wave of the hand and the implication that it was all a period of rather tedious and pointless inconsequence. Thus, you will hear airy affectations such as "*Oh, I used to do a bit of work in retail.*" (I was the CEO of a major supermarket chain), "*I used to help out the local bobbies*" (I was a world-renowned forensic scientist, consulted by police forces and governments across the globe), "*I daubed a bit of paint about*" (I've just had a major retrospective at The Tate), and "*I was just a bean-counter*"

(I was recently awarded the Nobel Prize for economics for single-handedly preventing global financial meltdown in 2008).

Don't let that fool you though, this game is played for high stakes and the yotties taking part play to win. It follows similar ritual formalities to those found when animals such as bull elephant seals confront each other over territory, food or mates and that is because it serves the same purpose; namely to establish the appropriate rank and privileges whilst, as far as possible, avoiding unnecessary injury. Should such injury occur in animals it is often real, physical and occasionally fatal. Among yotties the injury is primarily to the pride, but it hurts all the same.

So, when two yotties meet for the first time, the game is on. It begins with a wary conversational mutual circling, the verbal equivalent of a couple of strange male dogs meeting for the first time on neutral territory. The opening gambit involves the selection of the subject. This usually comes down to either a comment on the type of boat, the weather, or (and this is probably the favourite) anchor types and anchoring techniques. Let us look, then, at a stereotypical I.C.E. (Introductory Coded Exchange) between two yotties (let us call them East and West) meeting for the first time:

East eyes the anchor on West's bowroller.

East: *"How do you find the Rocna?"*

West: *"Yes, it is similar to the Rocna, isn't it, but it's actually a Manson"* (Love 15)

"Which have you got?"

E: *"Oh us - we've got three, one for rock, one for sand and one for weed."* (15 all)

W: *"Which do you use for weed?"*

E: (warily) *"A fortress"*

W: *"We tried one of those but found it damaged the coral in the Red Sea"* (15 - 30)

E: *"Funny that, we found it fine on the Barrier Reef"* (30 all)

W: *"We always wanted to go to the barrier reef but*

had to divert to Vanuatu when we were caught out in Typhoon Emily. All a bit of a bore, really." (30 - 40)

E: " *Oh Dear, Poor you. Make an unlucky call on the weather and find yourself in the wrong quadrant of the storm?"* (Deuce)

W: "*No - we were outrunning it but were hit by a sperm whale in the middle of the night. It took me two days in the water to fix the steering gear while we lay a-hull."* (Advantage W)

E: "*Well good on you. In all our quarter-century of living aboard we've never even seen a sperm whale, let alone been hit by one"* (Deuce)

E: "*No, the most annoying thing we experienced was having to fight off the polar bears with a Stanley knife and a pair of nail clippers when we were ice-bound in the Bering Straits overwinter."* (Advantage E)

W is speechless and double faults (game, set & match to E)

Henceforth, West is East's bitch.

All that follows will make marginally more sense if you have read its predecessor *An Idiot Aboard*. This chronicles the misunderstandings, misadventures, misconceptions & mishaps encountered during stage one, the three-year voyage from the English Channel to Turkey on *Birvidik*, a 12 metre sailing boat. In fact, if you haven't read it yet, stop being such a tight-fisted git and buy it now.

Turkey

The trouble with limited horizons is that there is a greater chance of reaching them. Anticipation being a large component of the joy of travel, getting to your destination can come as a bit of an anticlimax. Fortunately, the cruising lifestyle has sufficient distractions to take the edge off this potentially dispiriting existential disappointment.

Our limited imaginations had originally planned only as far as Turkey. Much to our surprise (and that of many of our friends and acquaintances) we had achieved this goal in a mere three years – time enough for proper sailors to sail around the world several times.

We may have got to Turkey, but we had seen very little of it. There was a whole indented coastline to explore, bedecked with bays and peppered with islands. On top of that there was the pressing matter of finding a winter mooring, preferably one that met the exacting criteria described in the previous book,[1] so we set ourselves the onerous task of cruising up and down the southern coast of Turkey checking out possible winter moorings on the way.

We had been to Turkey several times before; by motorcycle in the early seventies, on one of the first package holidays there in the eighties and then on a couple of flotilla holidays. We were now back some 30+ years after our first visit. It had changed dramatically.

Turkey has been a nexus for travelers for millennia; the Silk Road ran right across the 1000 miles of the country from East to West. From around 1660 to around 1840, the Grand Tour served as a fore-runner for mass tourism[2], but only the most adventurous of those on a Grand Tour detoured as far as Greece, let alone Constantinople, Ephesus or Izmir, and tourism as an industry didn't really start to take off in Turkey until the second half of the 20th century.

The seeds were probably sown by the overland expeditions of the 1950s. In these, students, complete with regulation Manfred Mann beards, Hank Marvin glasses and Three Stooges haircuts would pile into beat-up Land Rovers or Dormobiles and head off East. On their way they would climb mountains and undertake such wildly sexy and depraved activities as carrying out geographic surveys and writing up reports for dissemination on their return. These reports inspired another cohort of travelers who were far less interested in scientific and geographical data than they were in the perceived exoticism and mysticism of the countries *en route*. That and the ready availability of cheap dope. Thus was born the Hippie Trail, and with it the bus companies – *Indiaman* (1957), *Swagman* (1960) and multitudes of others too numerous to mention. Ironically, *Magic Bus*, possibly the best known, was merely a booking agency and never ran any busses of its own.

So it was that hordes of stoned, chillum-toting, straggle-haired, beard-sporting hippies blundered, lurched, mumbled and drawled their way toward the chemical nirvana to be found in the major cannabis producing areas of Asia. Most travelled by bus, but significant numbers took public transport, some travelled in private cars or vans and there were even a few foolhardy and deranged individuals on motorcycles.

Unfortunately, many of them failed to make themselves acquainted with the fact that the Turkish authorities were somewhat less than tolerant of dope. As a result, many found themselves in sağmalcılar prison and the like, with only one of them managing to turn a profit on the whole enterprise by writing *Midnight Express*. The irony is that by the 1980s it was Turkish gangs that controlled most of the heroin distribution in the U.K.

The hippie trail ended in 1979 when the Islamic Revolution took place in Iran and the Russians invaded Afghanistan. These events effectively closed the overland route, which had already been mortally wounded by the advent of cheap air travel. Interestingly, the hippies did not completely go away but decamped by air to places like Goa. Well, some did. The rest shaved their beards off, rediscovered the joys of showering and got jobs as accountants along with wives called Emily or Samantha and houses in Surrey or Chipping Norton.

Three years later the Turkish government introduced massive changes in law and infrastructure in order to promote tourism. They worked. Mass tourism exploded, especially along the southern and Western coasts. This led to dramatic changes to Turkish society and culture that persist to this day, a phenomenon that we will come back to in more detail.

The Lycian Coast – Ecinçek to Antalya.

(and back a bit)

July 10th 2009 – October 19th 2009.

"The next morning, I awoke to the gentle sound of wavelets lapping softly on the hull. The goat bells' random song, clear and soft like distant wind chimes, drifted across the water. Sunlight danced off the sea and dappled the ceiling of the cabin with flickering reflections. I turned over and watched Liz sleeping next to me. The reflected light flickered across her face and her soft breathing blended effortlessly with the soundtrack of birdsong and cicadas playing in the background. We were now, truly vagabonds. Of no fixed abode. Birvidik was our only home. I had never felt so utterly content and so full of time. My tribe had shrunk to just two people and no other tribe had offered and supported me so much. My tribal range was as small as a suburban living room and as large as the ocean."[3]

My reverie was disturbed by the realisation that *Birvidik* was not only lying to her anchor, but was also tied to a bloody great tree by her stern. This in turn meant an early morning swim. There's no better way to start the day than swimming to shore, scrabbling up a rocky beach, untying a rope, swimming back to the boat, clambering back on board, hauling in and coiling up the rope and finally heaving up a 35 kg anchor and 50 metres of 10-millimetre chain.

We intended to go to Skopea Limani, which we

remembered from charter holidays in the early 90s as an enclosed bay with myriad islands and sheltered anchorages. These anchorages, going by such evocative names such as 'Wall Bay', 'Ruin Bay', 'Tomb Bay', 'Deep Bay' and 'Cleopatra's Bay' were isolated, peaceful spots with clear blue water, goats grazing amid the marquis and the occasional primitive restaurant ashore.

The first 20 miles or so was along the coast with a lee shore a mile or so to port and nothing to starboard until you got to North Africa. As a result, and despite the lack of wind, there was a nice rolling 1½ metre swell hitting us beam on and setting *Birvidik's* mast swinging like a pendulum. This was sufficient to get us both a bit ratty. How soft we'd become. We had conveniently forgotten how we spent eight weeks coming down through Biscay and along the West coasts of Spain and Portugal with a constant three to five metre swell on the beam.

There was virtually no wind and so the sails had little steadying effect. Things improved somewhat when we rounded the cape and set off up towards Skopea Limani, putting the swell on the stern.

The entrance into the bay is through a narrow channel between two islands, which we pottered through under motor, with all sail set. We intended to sail gently across to Wall Bay and anchor there for the night, soaking up the atmosphere and perhaps going ashore for a cheap rustic meal at a cheap, rustic beach restaurant. We managed to dismiss from our minds the fact that the last time we did this on one of our flotilla holidays all four of us on board were laid up with gutrot for two days afterwards.

The channel was about 100 metres long and 20 metres wide. We left a smooth sea with a low swell and no wind. We came out the other end to a force seven wind on the beam, which promptly laid us down on our side. Heaped seas chopped against the boat and spray and spume streaked across the sea and lashed into the cockpit. Where the Hell did that lot come from?

We rapidly reefed our sails and took stock. It seemed that there was a local topographic effect funnelling the wind between the mountains and into the bay. Our intended anchorages were taking the brunt of this. The wind was screaming out of them and just getting to them would have been difficult enough, let alone trying to anchor and row a line ashore. Attempting to do so would most likely have ended up with my having a crash lesson in paragliding in the inflatable dinghy. We turned and ran north, downwind under genoa alone. Even then we were doing seven knots.

Our reasoning, such as it was, went along the lines of the wind strength easing as it spread out in the bay, and our then anchoring in somewhere like Tomb Bay, which should have been sheltered from the SW.

Well, we were sort of right. The wind did ease, but it slavishly followed the contours of the land and so wherever you went, at whichever point you tried to anchor and run a line ashore, it was beam on. On top of which it was busy. Fiendishly busy.

Since we'd left the Ionian it had become noticeable how fewer and further between the boats had become. This became even more pronounced the further east we went, right up as far as Ecinçek. We had obviously discovered the reason why - all the boats were in Skopea Limani. After trying five different anchorages, all of which were jam-packed with gulets[4], gin palaces, speedboats and yachts, we did manage to squeeze into a space in Boynuz Buku between two gulets. We dropped the hook and ran a line ashore, but we weren't very happy with it.

All the bays here are very deep until you get right up close to the shore. As a result, you have to drop your anchor in 15 to 20 metres of water. The rule of thumb for anchoring is that you let out chain equal to three to five times the depth of water, in order to ensure a nearly horizontal pull on the anchor to keep it from dragging. That would, by the rules, have required letting out 60 - 80 metres of chain. We had dropped anchor about 20 metres from the shore. Any further off than that and we'd have been dropping in 50 metres of water.

So, we ended up with a line ashore and a scope of less than twice the depth of water. I wouldn't have minded if I'd been able to dive and see if the anchor had bitten, but the water was too murky, and I was a bit out of practice to free dive to 20 metres. We sat there for a bit, but couldn't relax and so pulled up the anchor, only to find that it had bitten beautifully in sand and mud.

We decided to go to Goçek at the northern head of the bay. The pilot book said that this had good anchoring in about eight metres on mud and sand. We remembered it from the charter holidays as a charming little village with a ramshackle quay and pontoon and a few local bars and restaurants. So off we went, weaving our way between the ever-increasing numbers of boats, augmented by swarms of small speedboats and RIBs, hacking in all directions at high speed, almost all of them showing no understanding of the collision regulations whatsoever. It was bedlam.

The Goçek anchorage didn't exist anymore. There was a fuelling berth in the middle and pontoons around the outside with notices saying *'Private - piss off'* in eight different languages. Anywhere not occupied by the pontoons had been buoyed off and festooned with similar notices. The ramshackle little quay was now a sodding great marina jammed to the gunwales with charter boats (and we'd hit changeover day).

This was getting beyond a joke. Under other circumstances we might have retained our usual sanguine attitude, but we were now getting seriously pissed off, possibly because we'd built up our expectations for this area. We'd started at 6:30 in the morning. It was now 6:30 at night and we were tired and hungry, so we decided to take our ball back and go off in a sulk. We executed a 180 degree turn and headed the 12 miles across the top of the bay to Fethiye.

By this time the wind had dropped to almost nothing. The swell, however, came back with a vengeance and started throwing the boat from side to side and its contents all over the place. I was getting fed up with it, but Liz had a complete sense of humour failure. I tried to jolly her out of it and had just got to the point where I thought I'd succeeded when a particularly badly timed swell threw the boat violently on one side then the other, and an ominous crashing sound came from the saloon.

At Liz's retirement do, one of the surgeons remarked in his speech that he'd never seen her in a bad mood. There was general agreement with this sentiment. Reconcile that with the following verbatim, if slightly bowdlerised, quotation:

"Right! That's it! I've had enough. We've just rolled so much that the f-ing eggs have just f-ing flown from a place they've never f-ing moved from before and smashed all over the f-ing carpet!"[5]

I was shocked. And amused, but my laughter was probably not the most politic of responses under the circumstances.

Never mind. By eight o'clock that night we were snugly anchored in a bay off Fethiye and, with my having fed Liz a vodka and soda, a sense of perspective had slowly returned.

After the trials of our leg from Ecinçek we decided to spend a few days relaxing at anchor. Said relaxation, however, was somewhat compromised by a combination of human physiology, Turkish environmental regulations and plumbing constraints.

Liquid waste discharge from boats is divided into two categories; grey water and black water. Grey water is relatively innocuous – bath water, shower water, washing up water and the like. Black water, on the other hand is seriously unpleasant, being mainly urine and faecal matter.

Traditionally, boats were equipped with sea toilets and grey water drains. These discharge both categories of nasties directly into the sea. In a situation where there are very large bodies of water and very few boats, this poses few problems. A combination of the huge dilution factor and the rapacious appetite of all forms of sea life ensure that everything is mopped up by the ecosystem before you can say biomagnification[6]. Sticking large numbers of boats in small, mostly enclosed, non-tidal bays such as are found along the Lycian coast, however, is an entirely different kettle of coprophages. Large amounts of nutrients disrupt the ecological balance, favouring a few species and seriously disadvantaging many others. Biological diversity plummets.

On top of all this, who wants to swim in not very diluted shit?[7]

In theory, Turkish regulations regarding the disposal of liquid waste were among the most stringent in the Western hemisphere. No waste, black or grey, is allowed to be discharged at sea. Draconian fines, running into several thousand pounds, have been imposed for breaches of these regulations. It is unfortunate, then, that the authorities failed to install anywhere near enough pump-out stations to cope with the demand. Our yotties are therefore condemned to either a life of chronic constipation or to playing Russian roulette with their bank account.

When we were equipping *Birvidik* back in Jersey, this problem had exercised my mind considerably, and I had come up with a cunning system involving a spare water tank. five diverter valves, two pumps, six sea cocks and about 20 metres of 80-millimetre piping. This enabled almost anything to be pumped almost anywhere. Grey water and/or black water could be pumped directly to sea or into a 200-litre holding tank which, in turn, could be pumped back out to sea or vacuum-extracted by a shore based pumping station.

There was one slight hiccup with this cunning plan and that was the previously mentioned fact that although the Turkish authorities had, very reasonably, banned any discharge, grey or black, in the area, they had signally failed to provide anywhere near enough pumping stations.

Up to this point we had discharged grey water directly to the sea and diverted black water to the holding tank, where it festered until we moved into deep open water where we could discharge it at great dilution. On black water alone the tank capacity would last around a fortnight with two people aboard. Mind you, another yottie wouldn't want to moor his boat near the holding tank breather pipe if there was about a fortnight's worth bubbling away in there.

We now found ourselves in the unenviable position of having to divert all the grey water into the holding tank as well. We had no idea how long this would give us, but it was a dead cert that it would be a lot less than two weeks. A boat produces a lot more grey than black water, even if you scrimp on showers and the like. We had no real idea how long it would last before it started overflowing through the breather pipe, rapidly followed by the roar of a coastguard RIB and an officious and probably expensive rapping on the hull.

Apart from the abovementioned, there was one other potentially distasteful phenomenon, one which we had incidentally discovered while still in Jersey. Here we had inadvertently left the diverter valves from the shower tray to the holding tank partly open.

At first nothing of note happened. Over the next few days, though, the holding tank gradually filled up. On the third day I had my shower and pumped it out. The pump made its usual gurgling, sucking noise, indicating that the shower tray was empty, and I switched it off. There was a further, *un*usual, gurgling and bubbling noise in the shower tray, followed by the most God-awful, sulphurous, mephitic, nausea-inducing stench.

I pumped the tray out again and was rewarded with a repeat performance. I made my excuses and left the shower. Having dried off and donned the tattiest clothes I could find, I gingerly lifted the shower grating, to be confronted with the sort of stuff that middle-eastern despots dunk their political prisoners in. Head first.

The shower tray was fractionally lower than the top of the holding tank. As a result, once the tank was full it back-siphoned into the shower tray. I dug out bleach, bucket, sponges and rubber gloves and proceeded to mop it all out. The problem was, how to dispose of it once I *had* mopped it out?

Luckily, I had some 20-litre, water-tight plastic containers. These are highly desirable and expensive items in Yottie Land. My original intention had been to use these as reserve fuel containers, but priorities had changed. I was still faced with the problem of how to dispose of their contents once I had filled them, but I decided to cross that bridge when I came to it. The first priority was to get the damned stuff off the boat.

It took two containers to mop it all up. These I wiped down with bleach and carried to the top of the pontoon. I went back to pick up the rest of the unpleasant detritus associated with the job and returned to pick up the containers and visit the marina office to try to find out the best way of disposing of them and their contents.

It's funny, isn't it, how problems just sort themselves out sometimes.

When I returned, they were gone. Some thieving git had seen the containers and thought *'There's handy. I'll have them"*

I'd have loved to have seen his face when he opened them.

After a couple of nights at anchor off Fethye, nervously sniffing every time we washed up a mug or cleaned our teeth, our nerve broke and we moved into the marina. This saved on the holding tank as there were toilets and washing facilities provided. In addition, it offered shopping and dining opportunities. We stayed for five days.

This part of Turkey is known as the Lycian coast after the bronze age Anatolian peoples who lived in the area from around 4 000 B.C. to 500 A.D. or thereabouts. They were the first civilization known to have developed a working federation of democratic states. They also followed a cult of ancestor worship and the whole area is peppered with sarcophagi and rock-cut tombs. In most ancient civilizations (and most modern ones for that matter) the dead are disposed of outside of the main areas of habitation. Current thinking is that this was driven by aesthetic and hygiene reasons. I can go along with that. You couldn't really savour your breakfast with full appreciation if it was accompanied by the delicate fragrance of great-uncle Kheriga's suppurating corpse impersonating a volcanic mud pool just outside the kitchen door. Especially if you knew he'd died of plague.

The Lycians, however, were made of sterner stuff. In keeping with their ancestor worship, tombs and sarcophagi were integrated into the inhabited areas and could be found at roadsides, squares and even next to houses and in gardens. The Lycians were, in effect, always living cheek by jowl with their departed. Must have been fun on a 40 degrees C summer's day.

Although modern Turks do not have quite such an intimate relationship with their forebears, they live with the legacy of Lycian custom and practice. Four-thousand-year-old tombs and monuments litter their public areas and homes. Children grow up scrabbling in and out of the bronze age sarcophagus next to the chicken coop in the back garden. As the Turks grew up with it, they take it as perfectly normal. They park their cars between them. To the outsider it jars – an anachronistic mismatch of the sublimely exotic and the tediously mundane.

Despite this perceived exoticism, some things never change, as became apparent when we climbed to the heights above Fethiye to view the castle and the Lycian rock tombs.

On the way up, we were befriended by Elgin who gave us a guided tour and a plausible history of the region. He also showed us the Lycian 'prison' from about 3000 years ago. Well, I say 'prison' but it was really more of an oubliette. This was an interconnected series of small caves and cramped tunnels, accessed via small vertical holes. Prisoners were lowered (or thrown) down one end and only pulled out the other end when they were suitably dead.

No parole there then.

The tombs were fascinating, especially as you could get right up to and inside them. Their public aspects, from the outside, were huge, impressive and elaborate structures, carved out of the rock in the form of temple frontages. Bas-relief columns supported equally faux beams, arches and gigantic triangular pediments. They implied the continuation behind of large rooms and imposing spaces. In reality, the business end, where the actual job of sticking leftover Lycians took place, was a tiny little hole just big enough for a couple of stiffs - 98% of effort and expenditure on image and PR and a mere 2% on actually doing the job. Human nature hasn't changed that much in three thousand years.

Another thing that probably hasn't changed all that much in three thousand years is the climate. We were there in July and August and by the cringe[8]it got hot.

Afternoon temperatures averaged over 40 degrees in the shade, and even by ten at night they were still up in the mid-thirties. Bedclothes were dispensed with except for a thin sheet pulled over between 04:30 and 06:00 when the temperature had, on rare occasions, been known to drop as low as 25 degrees.

These conditions require some adaptation, physiological, behavioural and environmental.

Physiologically, our gradual move south and east meant that we had become acclimatised to higher temperatures and could probably cope more with the heat than we would have been able to have done a couple of years before, but it didn't feel like it, certainly when compared with the locals.

Take, for example, our walking through Antalya city centre one warmish afternoon. We were dressed in light shorts, sandals and thin, short sleeved, loose-fitting shirts. All effort was made to keep in the shade, even though this meant zig-zagging from one side of the street to the other and skulking in and out of doorways like Clouseau at his most incompetent trying to tail a suspect. Air-conditioned shops (i.e. almost all of them) became strangely attractive, irrespective of the wares on offer within.

Despite all this we were drenched in sweat. Dark stains spread over shirts, armpits, backs, chests and stomachs. Shorts developed damp patches in embarrassing places. Hair became lank and slicked back. Sweat dripped off noses and earlobes and ran through sodden eyebrows into the eyes, carrying sun-tan lotion with it, stinging and blurring vision. Now what are the locals like when they have to walk, and work, under exactly the same conditions? Cool, relaxed, airy and what's more, dry that's what. They stroll elegantly down the street in dresses, headscarves, shoes (and socks!), long trousers, shirts and ties, even jackets and hats. Some had vests under their shirts as well.

How do they do that? Do they have a sheep dip full of antiperspirant in the front garden through which they're poked with sticks on their way out every morning? "*Mehmet!*

*Make sure uncle Ibrahim's head goes right under this time -
you missed behind his ears yesterday."* And compare them
to us. We might as well be carrying a bell and a placard
announcing *'Unclean! Tourist of dubious personal hygiene'*.

Environmental changes mainly involved modifying the
internal environment of the boat. Sunshades are great at
cutting out the heat of the sun (the clue's in the name), but
they also drastically reduce airflow. So we had to increase
ventilation.

This leads us on to a minor ripple in the pool of
domestic harmony that is *Birvidik*.

Not to put too fine a point on it, Liz became jealous.

Of the fridge.

She considered, with some justification, that I had
become obsessed. She argued (forcefully) that every time she
turned round I would be on my knees before the fridge,
gently spraying its delicate inner workings with water. *"It's
the heat"* I would cry in concern, *"The poor thing can't cope -
it needs help."* Liz reckoned it wasn't the only one.

She kept buying fans (which I would argue we didn't
need) but when she went to use them, she'd find they had
disappeared. Then she would come across them lovingly
arranged around the bloody fridge! She's convinced that
even if she bought a hundred fans, I'd still have them all
focussed on the fridge. I had even been known to set a timer
to make sure that, should I be engrossed in a really good
book for example, I wouldn't forget to check that the fridge
was doing OK. Bags of ice were bought and stuffed in to help
it. If she was very lucky, I would let her have a couple of
lumps in her vodka and soda, but she reckoned that the
pained expression on my face when the ice cubes were
sacrificed in this way took away from the enjoyment
somewhat.

Still, it's all worth it as long as my beer's chilled.

The plethora of fans did help in other ways, especially
in bed if one of them could be left on all night in the aft
cabin. This made it just about cool enough to enable sleep
and had the added benefit of stopping our slumbers being
disturbed by mosquitoes. Our new *'Megawatto*

Typhoonerama' fan created such a blast of air that any mosquito attempting a bit of vampirism either died from exhaustion trying to fly against it to get to us or, if trying to go with the flow, ended up slamming terminally head first into the headboard. Of course, the combined wattage of all these fans meant that the wind generator and solar panel couldn't cope so we had to buy a petrol generator to replace all the lost amps. If things go on like this we'll have a carbon footprint the size of Luxembourg.

In behavioural terms, the obvious thing to do is nothing, especially in the hottest part of the day. Which is most of it.

The real peak temperatures, though, are between one and six in the afternoon. In the height of the summer, afternoon temperatures in the high thirties Celsius are looked upon as a minimum. Low forties are seen as normal, the high forties as not uncommon and a drift into the fifties is not without precedent.

Most cultures that are exposed to temperatures like these very sensibly evolved the phenomenon of the afternoon siesta. Behavioural patterns such as these are ingrained from a very young age and they are a bugger to shift. The two of us grew up in Britain, which is not known for its blistering summers. In our culture, having a nice snooze in the afternoon was one those strange habits that Foreigners have; a marker of innate idleness and almost certainly an indicator of Lack of Moral Fibre and a predilection for suspicious foodstuffs.

We Brits, by contrast, are strongly imbued with the protestant work ethic. Working hours, especially between the hours of nine and five, are sacrosanct, reserved for the holy obligation of Work. Here we stand in stark contrast to the French. They are, at least nominally, Catholic and will have nothing to do with Perfidious Albion and her frightfully uncivilised puritan work ethic. They sanctify Lunch. As you would already know if you had read the first book.[9]

Because of our cultural background, we have trouble with siestas. We recognise their logic and practicality on an intellectual level, and we appreciate that it verges on the impossible to do anything productive, physically or mentally, in temperatures such as those. What we can't do is shake off the nagging guilt that we should really be working at three in the afternoon, not lolling around in an enervated slump, flicking half-heartedly through some cheap, lurid novel and dozing intermittently.

Faced with this conflict, we make a futile attempt to do both and, predictably, end up doing neither properly. Among the more idiotic tasks that we have attempted in the middle of the afternoon are servicing the engine, scrubbing the decks, polishing the stainless steel and varnishing the woodwork, the first and last of which are particularly ill-suited to being carried out in the middle of a blistering Mediterranean afternoon.

Servicing the engine involves contorting one's self into a confined engine bay and operating large tools in small places. Things are made worse by having had to run the engine so as to thin the oil so that it can be pumped out. This increases the temperature in the bay to the high fifties and, as a bonus, means that you have to lay in top of a hot cylinder head in order to reach the impeller housing and oil filters.

Varnishing is, as we soon found out, a notably ill-advised undertaking in high ambient temperatures and bright sunshine. The varnish goes off in nanoseconds, leaving the brush stuck fast to the woodwork before the end of the second stroke. You're no further ahead even when you manage to wrest the brush from the wheelhouse, leaving half the bristles stuck in the varnish like some sort of glossy processionary caterpillar, because in the interval the solvent has evaporated from the remaining varnish, leaving the tin full of what looks suspiciously like nut brittle.

We may be remarkably slow learners, but we get there eventually. By the end of the fourth season we had succumbed to the siren call of the siesta and left such tasks to cooler times and seasons. If jobs such as those absolutely *had* to be done in the middle of the summer, we would plan ahead and get up early to complete them before the sun got fully into its stride.

Must dash - got to check on the fridge.

Fethye also introduced us to our first serious experience of another hot-weather related phenomenon, the katabatic wind.

These are caused by hot air cooling, becoming denser and plummeting down a steep slope. For a good, hefty example you need a full set of very specific conditions.

Firstly, you need to get the topography right. Ideally you want a high mountain with a steep slope leading down to something expansive and relatively flat, such as a plain or the sea. If the steep slope has ridges and valleys running top to bottom, then so much the better. These will funnel and concentrate the gusts and so act as wind acceleration zones. Fethye has all these desiderata in spades.

Then you need a good stinking hot day followed by a nice clear sky at night; ten a penny in this area. All wound up and ready to go? Just sit back and wait. During the day the sun heats everything up, including the air at the top of the mountain, but it heats up the sea-level stuff more.

As the sun goes down, the rock and air at the top of the mountain radiate heat like a menopausal woman who's just put all her make-up on for a posh night out. The air cools, becomes denser and falls down the slope like a drunk on a staircase. It appears out of nowhere and can go from absolutely still to force eight or even higher in less than half an hour. It lasts until the temperature differential is eliminated and then stops just as suddenly.

We've experienced a few of these since we were in Fethye and we must have unconsciously picked up on the subtle cues that tell you when there's one on the way. On several occasions now I have become inexplicably nervous without knowing exactly why and we have then experienced a katabatic afterwards.

We had not yet acquired such skills at this time and went to bed relaxed and confident, fully expecting a good and refreshing night's sleep.

We were woken at three in the morning by the howling of the wind, the clattering of rigging, the lurching of the boat, the slapping of waves upon the hull, the rumble of powerful diesel engines and the clanking of anchor chains being lifted. It was blowing a force nine and throwing the boats around as if in a washing machine.

There is always a choice to be made in circumstances such as this, and it is frequently a difficult call. Usually, it comes down to either crossing your fingers and sitting it out or getting the Hell out of it. Effectively, you either stay where you are and take the risk of crunching up against the quay and neighbouring boats or you cast off and ride it out at sea, either underway or lying to your anchor. Both options have their pros and cons.

In the harbour you are very close to substantial collision opportunities such as quays, pontoons and other boats. If something nasty happens, such as losing a cleat or having a rope part, you have no time to react and significant damage is almost inevitable. On the plus side, quays and pontoons take a bit of pulling out of position and so usually tend to stay where they are. Usually, but not invariably.

Riding it out at sea has converse problems. You are, or at least you start off, much further from possible collisions, giving you more time to take avoiding action when disaster strikes. However, all you have to hold yourself in position is a piddling little anchor which may or may not be dug into something resistant or, failing that, your engine and/or storm sails. You also need to exercise pilotage and navigation in order to have a rough idea of where the Hell you are. The biggest risk is being driven on to rocks or overwhelmed by the rough sea.

We decided to sit it out in the harbour. This was partially inertia, reinforced by idleness and cowardice. If things went tits-up, we at least stood a chance of stepping off the boat and leaving her to it.

Another contributory factor in the decision was that we were on the inside of the quay, which protected us from the worst of the seas.

Not so the gulets, which were on the outside of the quay, lying to their anchors and held by lines ashore.

Gulets are now a prominent feature of the Turkish

coastal scene. They are traditional design two or three-masted wooden vessels, originally designed and used for fishing and sponge gathering. With the decline of these two industries, the gulets morphed into tourist cruise boats. They have proliferated. These boats are almost disposable. They range from 14 to 35 metres long and are frequently constructed of unseasoned wood. Their internal configuration is designed to maximise both the number of tourists they can carry, and the amount of food and booze said tourists can lay their hands on.

The local yards can knock out vessels like this unbelievably cheaply in rapid short order. After five to ten years the boat will have paid back its cost with interest and can be scrapped and replaced with a new one.

We have mixed feelings about gulets. On the one hand, the skippers and crew are almost invariably friendly and generous with both advice and with assistance. On several occasions gulet crew have come across to us in a RIB while we were in the middle of a difficult mooring procedure and proceeded to take lines ashore for us.

On the other hand, they are unbelievably noisy. This is hardly surprising considering that they are chocked to the gunwales with up to 50 bladdered holidaymakers all being bludgeoned into insensibility by a combination of cheap booze and even cheaper music, the latter being blasted out by speaker configurations the size of Jodrell Bank.

They also appear to have special dispensation from most laws and edicts. Remember the draconian anti-pollution regulations that caused us such worry on arrival in Turkey?

Don't apply to gulets.

Well, don't seem to. Gulets appear to dispose of their grey and black water at will and with impunity. I have first-hand experience of this. (Those of a sensitive disposition should look away now.)

I was scuba diving in a small bay, happily pottering along about 20 metres down when I heard the rumble of a big diesel and the thrumming of a large propeller, both of which were modulated by the muffled bass lines of Black

Lace's mindlessly vapid and ruthlessly catchy 1984 hit 'Agadoo'. I looked up to see a large gulet manoeuvring into position above us. They dropped a bloody great anchor which fortunately missed us, and they backed up to the shore. Obviously, code flag 'A' (diver down) meant nothing to them.

Once they had tied up, we ignored them and carried on with the dive. We discovered later that this gulet was stuffed to bursting with plastered Russians. All that booze, black pudding and borscht must have put a hell of a strain on the sanitary arrangements. Too much strain, in fact, as they pumped out their capacious holding tank.

A dark, grey-black cloud enveloped us, reducing visibility to about half a metre. We were very much aware that the seals between lips and mouthpiece and between mask and face were not completely watertight.

As it turned out, it wasn't my mouth or nose that should have been my primary concern. Within 24 hours I had a nice bilateral external ear canal infection of faecal staphylococcus. On its own, that would have been bad enough, but the little buggers tracked through the fascia into my upper and lower jaws down to the gums, where they had a good munch on the periodontal ligaments that hold the teeth in place. Despite throwing industrial quantities of antibiotics at the little sods I still managed to lose seven teeth.

Still, I was lucky in a way. If they'd chosen to turn right instead of left they'd have tracked through the mastoids and possibly into the meninges or the brain itself. In that case I probably wouldn't be here to inflict this torment on the unsuspecting reading public.

However, to return to the point, namely the gulets in Fethye being on the outside of the pontoon. They had little choice but to leave. They were pounding against the pontoon and were only held in place by their anchors. The skippers displayed superb seamanship but the honours must go to the boat boys, the youngest members of the crew.

Each of the gulets had three or four of these, all around 15 – 17 years old, unbelievably agile and either brave, congenitally fearless or severely lacking in imagination. Or perhaps, like most boys of that age, they just considered themselves immortal.

The gulets had their passarelles[10] lifted about two metres clear of the pontoon to stop them being pounded against it as the boats rocked and bucked from the wave action. The boat boys would get aboard by leaping up as the passarelle was at a low point and grabbing hold of the end with both hands. As the passarelle started to rise again they would hang on and wait until it got to its highest point, by now about four metres above the pontoon. As it began to descend again, they would let go with one hand, flick up their legs and execute a sort of Fosbury Flop to end up on the passarelle, supine on their hands and feet. They then flipped over and ran down the passarelle onto the boat. They all used the same technique, but I never did find out if it had evolved or been taught.

However, even these gymnastics paled into insignificance in comparison to their anchor weighing performance. Gulets are big boats, so they need correspondingly big anchors. The ones on the gulets opposite us were the traditional fisherman's type and looked to me as if they weighed about a hundred plus kilograms. They were lifted by a power windlass but were very difficult to stow. They needed to be manoeuvred into their stowage blocks by hand, otherwise they snagged on the martingale or the dolphin striker.

Perhaps it would help if I were to explain some of the terminology here. The martingale is the chain that runs from the bowsprit to the stem fitting. It serves to stop the bowsprit from bending upwards under the tension from the forestay when the foresails are full. The dolphin striker is a spar that runs from the stemhead to the martingale to redirect the tension downwards.

Does that clarify things? I thought not.

Actually, the whole subject of nautical terminology and its extensive influence on modern idiomatic English fascinates me, but I'm sure you will all be relieved to know that it will have to wait for book three. For our current purposes, it will suffice to say that the martingale is a chain or heavy rope that runs from the sharp end of the boat near the waterline to the far end of the stick poking out of the front of the boat at deck level.

Which puts it right in the way when you want to lift and stow the anchor.

This is where the boat boy comes in. Barefoot, he scrambles out on the pitching bowsprit. When he gets to the end, he squats down and swings his feet onto the martingale and walks down the wet, slippery chain, hanging on to the bowsprit lines above his head for balance.

As the anchor is lifted, he grabs hold of it and guides it deftly past the martingale and dolphin-striker until it is positioned in its mooring blocks, at which point he ties it off and secures it. All he has to do now is walk back up the martingale to the end of the bowsprit, swing himself up and scramble back to the relative safety of the deck.

All of this, remember, took place in the dark with horrendous seas throwing 80 tonnes of boat about like a cork and with not a lifejacket to be seen. Health and Safety would have had a blue fit.

The next leg involved a ten-hour slog to Kaş, and then on to Karaloz, a sheltered bay in Kekova island. We had been to these before on charter holidays and remembered them as beautiful, sparsely populated anchorages with good shelter and idyllic surroundings (ring any bells?). We set off with high expectations, and expectations are one of the characteristics by which the cruising tribe can be subdivided into distinct groups.

Most societies can be viewed as an overriding culture with certain core values and customs which can then be divided into subcultures. These subdivisions can be based on a number of factors, including class, religion, geographical distribution, income, skin colour, political affiliation, sexual orientation and favoured football team. The cruising fraternity is no exception.

At the bottom level it can be divided by nationality and mother tongue, but one level up from this is a division into a hierarchy of three categories. At the top are Proper Big Hairy Sailors. For the benefit of those tightwads still holding out on buying the first book, and in the interests of flagrantly padding out this one without having to go to the effort of actually writing something new, here are the descriptors lifted shamelessly from *An Idiot Aboard*:

Proper Big Hairy Sailors are men (and women) of rugged temperament. They relish the challenge of the elements and laugh scornfully in the face of anything the sea can throw at them. They will set sail into the teeth of a gale with a light heart and in joyful anticipation of spending 48 hours narrowly avoiding death or serious injury while leaning over at ridiculous angles, pounding up and down and getting bucketloads of freezing salt water thrown over them at regular intervals.

They are completely mad and impossible to reason with. It is futile to even try.

Proper Big Hairy Sailors spend inordinate amounts of time at sea, day and night. On the few occasions they are not at sea they usually anchor and only go into a marina when it is completely unavoidable, for example if they are down to their last egg-cup of fresh water and on the point of expiring from dehydration, or if the boat has hit a whale and is taking in water faster than their bilge pumps can handle, or when struck by Hurricane Katrina.

Below Proper Big Hairy Sailors are Yotties. To plagiarise the first book again:

Yotties go by a number of sobriquets, prime among them being wusses, big girls' blouses, soft southern gits and great bunch of Jessies. They head straight for the nearest marina when they get down to their penultimate packet of Jaffa cakes or if, through bad luck or (more likely) incompetence, a yottie actually experiences something mildly stressful.

It is, in reality, extremely difficult for a yottie to experience a truly stressful situation. It requires a combination of incompetence, lack of imagination, poor judgement and bad luck. It's not that rare though. It can't be – it has happened to us on several occasions.

These two categories, PBHSs and yotties, make up some 99% of liveaboard cruisers. At the bottom you've got us. Oh, and Jessie 'Blousy' McWetknickers of sailing vessel *Iwantmymum*. We make ordinary yotties look like the bastard offspring of Attila the Hun and Lucrezia Borgia on steroids.

There are many criteria by which cruisers can be assigned to the above categories. A good example being the maximum forecast wind strength in which they will venture out of the harbour. For yotties this ranges from a force three to an absolute maximum of force four for the hardier souls in the category. For the likes of us, a force two is pushing it. We have been known to venture out in a forecast force three, but only with the assistance of hefty doses of benzodiazepines.

Proper Big Hairy Sailors don't have a maximum. The Beaufort scale doesn't go high enough to put them off. They do have a minimum, though, due to the very real fear that, should they go out in anything under a force seven, they will be at a high risk of dying of boredom.

Of more relevance to the current point in the narrative, however, is the fact that the three groups demonstrate distinctly specific characteristics in their expectations. PBHSs have expectations totally in keeping with their circumstances and abilities. No matter what they go out in, they expect to come out the other end unscathed and triumphant, and they invariably do.

Yotties, on the other hand display two categories of unrealistic expectation. They expect every moment spent at sea to be a misery of abject purgatory whilst looking forward to anchorages and harbours that all, without fail, epitomise the paradises photoshopped up for the charter holiday brochures.

Meanwhile, we in the bottom one percent take the yottie outlook to an absurd extreme. We display totally unrealistic expectations that vary wildly between the utterly unreasonably optimistic and the sort of negativity that makes Schopenhauer look like Polly-bloody-anna by comparison. We expect every anchorage to be a prelapsarian idyll, whereas every second spent at sea is anticipated as one of the inner circles of Hell reserved for Ghengis Khan, Hitler, Stalin and Jeremy Beadle. Neither ever lives up to the fevered products of our overheated imaginations.

In keeping with the above, our ten hours along the extended lee shore of the Seven Capes was, far from the expected purgatory, merely tedious at worst. Kaş anchorage, however, was far from the nautical Eden of our imaginations.

Seventeen years earlier there had been an isolated, well protected bay, dotted with islands and anchorages. Many, if not most, of the areas could only be accessed by boat or, with extreme perseverance, on foot. Now, the shores and islands were lined with beach clubs, each of them and their associated beaches swarming with sunbathers. New roads had been cut out of the promontories, leaving deep scars along their whole length. The beaches had been transformed from almost empty crescents of pristine sand into regimented tourist-broilers. Each now sported ranks of sunbeds and umbrellas, all laid out in close formation. Every beach had at least two beach bars and most had a water sports centre leasing out pedalos and small motor boats. The lapping of the waves, the trill of birdsong and the evocative buzz of cicadas from seventeen years earlier were now overwhelmed by pounding europop. The whole area served as a vivid exemplar of the effects of expanding tourism.

And My God did Turkish tourism expand. OK, it went into free fall from 2015 onwards but up until then it had gone berserk. Tourist arrivals went from 1.3 million in 1983, through 7.2 million in 1992 to a staggering 40 million in 2014. This influx was concentrated on the Aegean south and south-west coasts of the country and it had profound implications for the Turks, culturally, socially, financially and politically.

Some of the effects are obvious, while others are more subtle, but have still had a dramatic and important impact. Perhaps the greatest effect has been to accelerate the polarisation of the population between the liberal, westernised, secular, usually middle-class Turks and the more devoutly Islamic, conservative, inward-looking, poorer elements of the population.

In general, the former are concentrated around the tourist coasts and in big cities such as Istanbul and Izmir. The latter tend to be found further east and further inland. There is probably more contrast between these two groups than there is between the average secular Turk and the average Dutchman, or between the average conservative Turk and the average Iraqi.

For a typical devout, conservative Turk from an Eastern Anatolian village, a visit to Marmaris in August would be akin to an ultra-orthodox Rabbi taking his family on a two-centre holiday to Sodom and Gomorrah. The main streets are lined with bars, out of which spill phalanxes of staggering, drunken tourists, shouting profanities at the tops of their voices. Alcohol, bacon and pork sausages are on open display in supermarkets. Tattooed women in microscopically skimpy bikinis teeter on high heels down busy streets in the middle of the day while swigging from plastic glasses of rum and coke. Meanwhile, their beer-gutted male counterparts waddle sweatily alongside them bellowing out obscene, usually football-related, tribal identification chants.[11]

It is easy to see why this Dante-esque vision would be met with outraged incomprehension by our hypothetical devout visitor. It is equally easy to see why secular Turks are minded to, if not approve of, then at least to tolerate these behaviours. For some it is from a genuine belief in the virtues of tolerance. For others the motivation is probably more mercenary.

The development of tourism has had other unforeseen, indeed probably unforeseeable effects.

We came across a good example of this phenomenon when we moored at Kale Koy. We got on well with Zeynep, the woman running one of the restaurants, and we ate there on several occasions. At the end of the meal she would frequently come and sit with us for a chat, aided by her daughter Aysun, who spoke excellent English.

At one point I commented that an unexpectedly large number of the tourist beach restaurants seemed to be run by women. At which they both burst out laughing. "*It's all to do with inheritance*" said Aysun.

Historically, Turkish society was very patriarchal, and sons were favoured over daughters. This extended to wills, where valuable good agricultural land was left to the sons and the almost worthless marginal land was left to daughters. Here's the clincher:

The marginal land was marginal because it was near the sea. Salt leachage and spray made it very poor for agriculture. Come the advent of tourism, though, the roles were reversed. The most valuable land was that nearest the tourists, and where the tourists wanted to go was near the shore. Within a decade the wealth disparity between the sexes had not just been eliminated, it had been reversed.

Zeynep put it down to Divine Justice. I favoured the Law of Unintended Consequences. I reckon the Law of Unintended Consequences is one of the fundamental laws of nature – almost, but not quite, as inviolable as the laws of thermodynamics. Theory has it that it covers three phenomena: unexpected benefit, unexpected drawback and perverse result.

Unexpected benefit is by far the rarest. It is otherwise known as serendipity or a windfall.

Unexpected drawback is where, for example, irrigation schemes benefit agriculture and food supplies but bring with them additional problems such as water-borne diseases like bilharzia which can devastate whole regions.

A perverse result is sometimes known as a backfire. It is where an intervention has the opposite effect to that intended. This is frequently encountered in politics and management. Such outcomes frequently fall into the category of 'It seemed like a good idea at the time' and are usually the result of implementing a quick, cheap, simplistic and populist solution to a time-consuming, expensive, complex and awkward problem.

From Kas we moved on to Karaloz, a deep, indented bay on Kekova island. This was a wild mooring, completely deserted with nothing ashore. It promised good shelter, peace, calm and splendid isolation. It did not deliver.

At first, things went according to plan. The entrance is

hard to see from offshore, but once you're in, it turns sharp left and opens up into a beautifully protected bay. On the chart it looks a bit like a chessboard knight. True to recollection, there was no sign of human habitation ashore. Note that I used the qualifier 'ashore'. Afloat, there were two yachts, three fishing boats, a couple of speedboats and five gulets. We circled round for about 20 minutes and eventually lined up a spot to take a line-ashore, only our second ever attempt ever at this procedure.

Mooring line-ashore is not a simple procedure like parking a car. It's more like trying to park an articulated lorry with dodgy brakes on an icy slope in a strong crosswind. *"Why do it then?"* is the obvious and understandable question, to which the obvious and understandable response is *"Because there's no bloody alternative"*.

A line-ashore is the technique employed by the reluctant yottie when he has run out of all other options. It is the fall-back he is left with when there are no solid quays or pontoons to tie up alongside; no lazy lines to secure your stern and hold you off the pontoon; no mooring buoys securely attached to gigantic concrete blocks on the seabed; no room to swing in 50 metre arcs around your anchor; or no decent holding so that your anchor pulls through the bottom like a spoon through Greek yoghourt.

Nope. In small, crowded, steep-to anchorages such as are common in Turkey, it's either line-ashore or nothing. The concept of the line-ashore is simplicity itself. You want your boat to end up at ninety degrees to the shore with the back end tied to something solid like a bloody great tree and with the whole thing held taut by the anchor off the bow.

Actually getting yourself into that position, though, is another matter entirely. First, you circle round looking for places on the shore that are unencumbered by other boats. Then you rule out half of those because they either have nothing you can tie on to or they are criss-crossed with reefs or rocks. You scrub half of the remaining 50 percent because when you check out the corresponding anchor positions you find it's either too deep, too shallow, crap holding or already occupied by someone else's anchor. This usually leaves you with a choice of two spots, one of which is between two fishing boats covered in rotting fish guts steaming gently in the afternoon sun, and the other is next to a gulet full of bladdered Russians doing impressions of the *Mannequin Pis* over the side. You choose the fish guts.

Having committed yourself, the fun starts. The first task is to try and guess where you want your anchor to be. Both distance and angles are difficult to judge on water. After you've thrown away the scraps of paper covered with scrawled sketches of half-remembered school geometry, you just make a wild guess and drop the anchor anyway. The next challenge is to make a vain and almost certainly futile attempt to manoeuvre the boat backwards into the minuscule gap between the two reservoirs of festering fish offal.

It's difficult enough trying to steer *Birvidik* backwards at the best of times. Being hobbled at the bow by a bloody great anchor and 40 metres of 10-millimetre chain is not the best of times. Usually we resort to my swimming ashore with the stern line clenched between my teeth like some manic pirate boarding an unsuspecting merchantman. In the unlikely event of this manoeuvre being successful, you're nearly home and dry. All that's needed is to tie off the stern line, swim back to the boat and adjust the stern line and anchor chain until the boat is in the right position and both line and chain are at the desired tension and angle.

Piece of piss.

This, of course, assumes that you have chosen your spot ashore wisely. Specifically, it assumes that you have arranged things so that it is flat calm and that such wind as there may be is blowing onshore, thus carrying the boat into your desired space.

Unusually for us, we had indeed arranged things so that this was the case. At least, it was the case until we dropped the anchor and started to manoeuvre astern, at which point the wind suddenly piped up.

Strongly.

Dead on the beam.

This put a completely different complexion on things. As I tried to swim ashore the wind blew *Birvidik* sideways, making it impossible to back her into the narrow gap between the two fishing boats. I flaked [12] out all 100 metres of sternline and valiantly swam it to shore, where I tied it round a convenient boulder and attempted to pull *Birvidik* into position against the still-increasing wind. Not a chance - couldn't do it, so I swam back to the boat, wrapped the rope round a winch and enlisted Liz's assistance. Even with double the grunt power and the eight times mechanical advantage of the winch it still took us nearly two hours in total to get her snugged in just the right position. By this time we were slippery, sweaty slicks. We had a quick dip, towelled ourselves down and relaxed.

At which point the wind direction shifted. This fractionally moved the position of the rope where it was tied round the boulder. Through the binoculars it became apparent that it was now rubbing against a rather sharp looking rock. Minor variations in the wind were now causing the rope to rub against the sharp rock in a sawing action. I swam back re-positioned the rope and buffered it with some rubber sheeting. Within minutes of my return to the boat the wind shifted again and rendered all my efforts futile. It took three more repositionings and the deployment of a chum[13] on the stern line to finally get *Birvidik* positioned to our satisfaction.

I finally made my way back to the boat, running the gauntlet of wasps that seemed to home in on anything doused in salt water. So it was that *Birvidik* joined the other boats in disciplined lines, reminiscent more of a multi-storey car park than an isolated, idyllic, relaxing anchorage.

No sooner had we settled in when half the boats left, thus freeing six mooring spaces, all of which were far more desirable than the one we were in. We decided to stay where we were, though. After all, we reasoned, we had gone through all the hassle of anchoring and tying up and were now securely moored.

Well, we were until the goats arrived. They were heralded by the mournful clanging of their bells. We looked on indulgently as they slowly grazed their way round the inlet. An air of bucolic calm enveloped *Birvidik* and we surrendered to the moment. This state of arcadian bliss lasted for all of five minutes until they arrived at our end of the inlet. Pickings must have been slim on the grazing front as they seemed to think that nylon mooring line was more nutritious fare than the scrub that they had been grazing on up until then.

Shouted threats failed to discourage them, nor did graphic descriptions of kebab-related scenarios that would follow if they failed to bugger off back to their normal diet and leave our mooring line alone. What did the trick eventually was my taking the dinghy ashore and shooing them off. A few thrown rocks convinced the last couple of die-hard stragglers.

As the anchorage returned to calm we settled back in the cockpit, but the atmosphere was gone. I was on tenterhooks all evening waiting for the bloody goats to come back and chew through our line ashore, leaving us to swing into neighbouring boats in the middle of the night. I spent most of the night laying in the cockpit, ears straining for the tell-tale tolling of the goat bells.

It never came, but the next morning we decided to cut our losses and continue our search for a winter home by way of Finike, Kemer and Antalya. Over the next few weeks we went to all three to check them out. They were quite contrasting options. Kemer was an upmarket holiday resort, Antalya marina was on the outskirts of a big city and Finike was a very Turkish market town for a large agricultural region.

This exercise involved a complex comparison process involving multifactorial analysis. Various factors were considered, weighted and compared before being entered on a spreadsheet and undergoing multiple factorial analysis and subsequently presented in graphical format and eventually listed in rank order.

Were they bollocks.

Such an approach, though admirably analytical, would be far too complicated and intellectually taxing for our poor aging brains. What we actually did was go to each marina and get a superficial impression of the following:

Shelter
Sanitary facilities
Services (water & electricity)
Opportunities for a social life.
Provisioning
Cultural opportunities
Technical support
General ambience
Cost

Only the last one was assessed objectively, mainly because it was the only one that could be assigned an exact number. All data except price was then summarily ignored and we went with a gut feeling of whether we liked the place or not. These gut feelings are developed on a subconscious level and are often remarkably accurate. OK, they can be way off the mark at times, but on balance they serve us well.[14]

Antalya was the first one to get the chop. OK, Antalya is a big city (one million and counting, but that's peanuts compared with Istanbul's 16 million at the last count). That means that you can get more or less anything you want there, but it has its drawbacks.

For a start, the marina is situated on a dusty, fly-blown estate fifteen kilometres from the city proper. Granted, it's flashily done out with posh restaurants and infinity pools and the like, but it's priced to match and anyway, we didn't think we'd fit in – we're a tad too plebeian we suspect.

As, we also suspect, are most yotties. Although the majority are not exactly scraping by in genteel poverty, it is considered bad form to appear to be anything other than down to your last sou. This is a yottie tribal norm.

Talking of tribal norms, it's pretty well documented that humans are a tribal species and yotties, contrary to popular opinion in some quarters, are humans. *Ergo*, yotties are tribal and can be expected to display most, if not all, of the defining characteristics of tribalism. Nowhere is this more apparent than in the field of dress codes.

Dress codes have flourished throughout history. Over the last half-century or so, we have seen Teddy Boys through Mods & Rockers, Hippies, Punks, New Romantics and Goths. Alongside these have been more establishment tribes such as the bowler-hatted city workers through investment bankers with their loud braces, irritating sense of entitlement and complete lack of morals, to the Boden-wearing Chipping Norton set, recently culminating in self-regarding Hipsters with their wafer-thin glasses, flat white coffees, absurdly over-the-top tattoos and ludicrously pretentious facial hair. In all these cases, dress codes affirm the identity of the tribe and signal membership and status. Tribal dress also serves to encode and reinforce the underlying values and beliefs of the tribe.

Yotties, as expected, have their identifying tribal dress too. On the street the trained eye can identify another yottie at 200 metres enabling, on closer approach, the exchange of secret signs and shibboleths so as to cement the tribal bond. These are so subtle that they make a freemasonry handshake appear about as quietly understated as a Las Vegas neon billboard with a voiceover by Brian Blessed.

Firstly, there is the identifying salute. This Approach Manoeuvre is executed at a range of ten metres and involves holding eye contact exactly 0.4 milliseconds longer than normal and executing an almost imperceptible 3mm nod of the head in the direction of the other yottie. This action is invisible to anyone untrained in its arcane intricacies.

The Approach Manoeuvre is then followed by the Weather Referral. This comprises a brief glance at the sky, immediately followed by a minuscule raising of the right eyebrow, a slightly rueful expression and a further two rapid 3mm nods of the head in quick succession.

Following the successful completion of the introductory ritual, conversation can be initiated to determine relative status. Convention dictates that this is, at least in the beginning, conducted in English. Which is handy.

There is a rigid and strictly enforced hierarchy in

cruising and the Introductory Coded Exchange, as alluded to in the introduction, serves to establish the relative positions of the two yotties within this hierarchy. Although there are many subtle sub-distinctions within it, the outline pecking order is as follows:

1. Full time cruisers who have been living aboard since before the advent of GPS and have at least one complete circumnavigation under their belts.

2. Other full time, liveaboard cruisers.

3. Those who own their own boat and live on board for at least 5 months of the year.

4. Dilettante owners who flit between their boat and one of their numerous properties spread across the globe.

5. Charterers.

6. Flotilla holidaymakers.

7. Holiday speedboat hirers.

8. Vermin including, but not limited to, rats and cockroaches.

9. Jet skiers.

You will note that singlehanders are not included in this bestiary. This is because they belong in a separate category of their own, being, as they are, just too weird to be included in normal social discourse. A discussion of the single handed yottie will have to wait for the next book, which will have a section devoted solely to him (it's almost invariably a him).

However, to drag ourselves reluctantly back to the point which, in case you've forgotten, was dress codes. What follows lets you, gentle reader, into the secret world of the

Yottie. Having read this you will be able to identify one at 200 metres and bluff your way into yottie society, although why any sane person would actually want to do such a thing is beyond me.

Let us start with the top and work our way down, so to speak.

The hat:

Any self respecting yottie must wear a hat. It must be wide-brimmed to shade the face and neck from the sun and to enable a mysterious, penetrating gaze to shine out from its shade. The exact material is not important, it can be linen, straw or anything, as long as its style and colour are restrained, preferably grey or beige. What is important is that it must be dishevelled. Shevellment in any shape or form is absolutely *verboten*.

The glasses:

This covers sun, prescription and reading glasses or any permutation thereof. Like the hat they must on no account be shevelled. Ideally, they should be held together with surgical sticking plaster. For prescription spectacles, clip-on, flip-up sunglasses are a useful and stylish way to accessorise. In all cases they must be attached to a worn and faded retaining cord that loops casually under the ears and round the back of the neck. When out of use they should be left dangling on the chest. Older yotties may have up to four pairs hanging here. Attempting to perch them all on the head produces a look like an overgrown wolf spider.

The beard:

For male yotties this is *de rigueur*. For the ladies it is optional. On a gentleman the beard should be wild and unrestrained as nature intended. Should a lady wish to sport a beard then artistic trimming in the style of a Brazilian is permitted, if not actively encouraged,

It is true that there are a few clean-shaven male yotties, but these are looked upon with suspicion and discomfort. They are generally regarded as being lacking in moral fibre and probably homosexual. Designer stubble is beyond the pale.

The T shirt:

This is where the yottie can really let his creativity run riot. Nothing is forbidden (except, of course, shevellment). The reason for this lack of constraint is that T shirts are not so much bought as accumulated. They are picked up from community rooms, boat jumbles, rubbish skips and rag piles. *In extremis*, should Mrs yottie be so unbearably mortified with embarrassment that she can't bear to be seen out with him, she may have to resort to buying new T shirts of dubious and inappropriately youthful design from Lidls.

As with the entire ensemble, dishevelment is the *sine qua non* of the T shirt in the yottie wardrobe . Battery acid holes are good; tears, rips and areas worn to gossamer thinness are better. Paint splashes add an air of piratical charm and an overwhelming and eye-blistering fragrance of white spirit and old engine oil completes the effect.

The shorts:

These follow the same rules as the T shirt but have a few additional requirements of their own. Firstly, they must be of the right length. Certainly not over knee length as that is too fashionable and possibly refined. Furthermore they must on no account be very short, constricting the thighs and displaying nauseating amounts of lower buttock curve. Such abominations immediately result in the same sorts of suspicions as are aroused by being clean shaven, only more so. The ideal length is one hand's span above the knee which makes the wearer look like the sort of middle-aged perv who goes to school-dinners parties in seedy night clubs.

The shoes:

These are the only seasonal part of the yottie wardrobe. In the summer they should be sandals, preferably sporting loose soles and exhausted Velcro straps, both of which slap irritatingly with every step. In the winter, wellies are the apparel of choice. For maximum effect these should be expensive but abused beyond redemption. Hunters liberally splattered with antifoul and a selection of gloss paints give the right impression.

And finally, the accessories:

These are many and varied and irretrievably beyond

the scope of this brief treatment. They most commonly include the watch, the tape measure, and, most importantly, the shopping trolley.

The watch should be cheap, easy to read and waterproof. The strap should be on its last legs and the glass crazed and scratched, thus negating the easy to read specification. The tape measure, worn at the hip like a cowboy's Colt 45, signals to all that here is a man above mere fashion and appearances. Here is a man at one with himself and the sea, a self-sufficient mariner, relying on no-one and no-thing other than himself and his skills. Here is a man who can hold his head up high and proclaim loudly and proudly to the assembled multitudes *"I have a shopping trolley!"*

Ah yes - the shopping trolley. This is the signature accessory but few other than true yotties can carry it off with the necessary panache as it requires the sort of total lack of embarrassment which results from having no grasp whatsoever of just how much of an absolute dick you look. From such shortcomings comes greatness and with it the recognition of the scattered tribe of true yotties.

Look upon my works, ye mighty, and despair.

Kemer fell by the wayside next, mainly on a combination of price and sub-standard sanitary facilities so Finike won by default. This was a fortuitous result as it turned out to be an excellent wintering hole. Another advantage to Finike in comparison to the other two was that it wasn't over-run with Russians.

This last statement is obviously not very PC and flies in the face of my professed lefty-liberal, diversity-celebrating, stereotype-abhorring, Guardianista credentials. Such an accurate accusation is also reinforced by my previous less than complimentary reference to the Russians.

I blame evolution.

It's a ball-achingly slow process and it hasn't caught up with the considerable technical, social and cultural developments of the last 20,000 years or so separating us from our hunter-gatherer ancestors.

We spent millennia as hunter-gathers, living in small

tribes of about 150 people. In those millennia we evolved behaviours and ways of thought that helped us to survive and reproduce in those particular circumstances. Most important of the factors that promoted survival and reproduction was the support of the tribe. Humans are pretty puny specimens who find it rather difficult to survive on their own. Trying to reproduce on your own is even more problematic, but that doesn't seem to stop a lot of people trying with remarkable frequency.

Some basic psychological characteristics evolved to reinforce this, and these became embedded as cultural values:

Tribe = good

Not-tribe = threat

Protect Tribe

Distrust not-tribe.

Help Tribe

Screw not-tribe

In addition to these basic values, humans developed the mechanisms necessary to make effective decisions based on limited evidence. These are characterised by heuristic thinking (the use of rules of thumb). Decisions made like this aren't always right but by 'eck they're quick and if you need to decide whether a sudden movement was caused by potential prey or a potential predator then quick is good. Bloody quick is better.

These characteristics persist to this day, but they're not very useful in a modern environment. Even the most soft-hearted liberal such as me will retain the tribal values and heuristic thought patterns on the border between the conscious and the subconscious. I make automatic judgements based on very limited evidence on a daily basis. So do you. So, unfortunately, does Donald Trump[15].

Thus it is with my feelings on Russians. I make judgements based on a relatively small and almost certainly unrepresentative sample.

By way of comparison, consider the drunken Brits

aggressively staggering, vomiting, swearing and fornicating their way down the streets of Kavos, Magaluf, Riga and the like. I know we're not all like that. You know we're not all like that. That's because we've both seen lots of other Brits who aren't like that. But to the locals and other holidaymakers we *are* all like that, because that's all they've seen.

Equally, the vast majority of Russians we've seen while cruising have been from a very limited demographic. The reasons for this are fiendishly complicated and impossible to explain succinctly. This task is made even more difficult by the fact that I know diddley-squat about it.

But that's never stopped me before.

So here goes.

Once upon a time (well, December 1991 to be precise) a big, big country broke up into one not quite so big country and fourteen little ones. (Actually, a lot of the little ones were big by European standards). The not quite so big country kept all the bombs and stuff but let some of the little ones keep the radioactive waste and toxic dumps and stuff.

The men who used to run the big, big country were very nasty and wouldn't let the people buy turnips or go on holiday to Benidorm, so the people sat in the snow being miserable and drank lots of vodka. After the big, big country broke up, the people were very happy, so they all bought lots of turnips and celebrated by drinking even more vodka.

Luckily, the big, big country had lots of useful stuff like oil and gas and mines and factories. (and turnips). When the very nasty men were in charge of the big big country, all this useful stuff was owned by The People.

Apparently.

At least, that's what the nasty men said.

After the break up, the not quite so big country was run by people who still drank a lot of vodka but weren't quite so nasty. They did have lots of quite nasty friends though. The quite nasty friends got their chum Anatoly to take the not quite so nasty men who now ran the country to one side and say "*Look – about all this useful stuff that's owned by The People. We think it would be better all-round if it was owned by not quite so many people. Say, you, me, Boris, Mikhail and Vladimir here."*

The not quite so nasty men agreed and the price of oil, gas and turnips quadrupled overnight. Now the people had the right to buy all the turnips they could afford. Which turned out to be none. Same thing went for coal, gas, electricity and holidays to Benidorm.

Some people got very cross with this and asked for help from the judges and policemen and stuff. Unfortunately, some other people came to see the judges and policemen and stuff and gave them some health advice. These people definitely weren't working for Boris, Mikhail and Vladimir. Oh No Siree. Absolutely not. It just happened that the judges and policemen and stuff decided that everything was hunky-dorey just the way it was.

This meant that everyone had the absolute right to go away on holiday as many times as they could afford.

Which was none.

Unless you happened to be a close friend or business associate of Boris, Mikhail or Vladimir. My, what friendly people Boris, Mikhail and Vladimir turned out to be. They had thousands of really good friends and colleagues who could all go on holiday as many times as they liked. But they didn't want to go to Benidorm. Oh No. Too many drunken Brits. No they went to Turkey, especially Kemer and Antalya.

Which simplistic analysis explains my lapse into Farage mode. The vast majority of the Russians we encountered were what many other Russians would describe as *nekulturny*. The literal translation of this is 'uncultured', but it has implications beyond that. It acts as synonym for 'uneducated', 'coarse', or 'ill-bred'. It implies a person or action that is ill-mannered and inconsiderate.

They lived up to this sobriquet almost without exception. Those under about fifty walked with the arrogant swagger of the small-time thug that is found in almost every culture. The older ones were more frightening, tending as they did to the quietly threatening air of the stereotypical Mafia Don. Most were grossly overweight but nevertheless persisted in wearing the briefest of speedos which were almost completely obscured by the huge pot bellies cantilevered over their generally far from impressive genitalia. They didn't seem to have heard of the old rock-star trick of the sock down the front of the pants.

To complement this visual feast, they were all blinged up to the eyebrows. Heavy gold chains clanked on forearms and gaudy medallions nestled between sweaty man-boobs. All fingers were encrusted with ornate rings the size of unshelled walnuts. Well, either that or they'd forgotten to take off their knuckledusters.

Those losing their hair, which was most of them, either grew it long and slicked it back into an oiled salt and pepper pony tail. (not a good look) or sported appallingly obvious wigs (ditto).

And my God, did they drink. A bunch of these guys on a Monday afternoon make Saturday night at the Bigg Market in Newcastle look like a Quaker temperance meeting

All in all, their self-presentation could hardly be described as the epitome of restrained good taste. The same accusation could be levelled at their choice of boats. If, as was mentioned earlier, the yottie plays down such wealth and status as he may have, then the converse is true of the stereotypical Russian on the Turkish Riviera. There are no charming little wooden sailing boats here. In fact, there are virtually no sailing boats of any description.

They're all bloody great gin-palaces. Even the little boats are bloody great gin-palaces. We, of course, were never invited on board one, but you can easily see inside from the quay. I'm sure that this is deliberate policy and that the design spec has as one of its prime criteria 'Must be able to flaunt it to the plebs' although I suspect that we plebs are far from the real targets of these conspicuous displays of wealth and consumption. The real target audience is their near peers. There is no point in trying to impress those too far below or above you on the ladder. What you are really trying to do is to climb up over the shoulders of the ones immediately above you while simultaneously stopping those immediately below from doing the same to you.

This seems to be a universal human characteristic. Unless they're specifically out on the pull, women don't dress to impress men; they dress to impress other women. Men do not primarily, pose, preen, swagger and strut to impress women[16], they do it to assert their position *vis-à-vis* other men. In the unlikely event of their actually impressing an attractive woman, then her attentions become another tool with which to impress other men.

The interiors of the boats continue this tradition. They are a blingtastic extravaganza of conspicuous consumption. Gold plate vies for supremacy with glistening crystal, white leather upholstery and highly glossed expensive hardwoods, all raucously lit with high intensity halogen spotlights. Any areas unaccountably left unsullied by the above are immediately colonised by an unco-ordinated miscellany of cluttered, naff knick-knacks. Wall paintings and statuary pay homage to the 'soft porn masquerading as art' school of interior design.

All this excess echoes the personal adornment of the owners, merely writ large. Their personal bling blends seamlessly with that of the boat to the extent that it acts as a form of camouflage. When an owner is on board it is difficult to discern exactly where he ends and the boat interior begins.

All of these, of course, are status symbols, designed, as we saw, to impress others with their owners' wealth, power and influence. The ultimate status symbols, however, they carry on one, or both, of their arms. These are usually made in the Czech Republic and are in most cases blonde, slim and about 19 – 20 years old. They are usually clad, if that's the word, in what purport to be bikinis but are, in fact, little more than expensive fabric sticking plasters whose sole purpose is to draw attention to that which they most signally fail to quite cover; a task they carry out most effectively.

Our *nekulturnies* make a point of completely ignoring their nubile companions, who fulfil their part of the deal by gliding elegantly along beside their employers, which can't be easy in those ludicrously high–heeled hooker shoes. They complete the performance by simpering inanely, throwing pouting poses for the camera and giving a passable impersonation of being a ditzy air-head in the throes of a passionate, breathless infatuation. Maybe it's my imagination, but I swear that sometimes I could see the hollow emptiness in their eyes as they teetered up the gangplank for part II of the job description. I hope they're paid a lot; they earn it. And I bet there's no job security or pension plan.

I know what you're thinking, and I agree with you. I may be a self-professed lefty-liberal, diversity-celebrating, stereotype-abhorring, Guardianista, but I'm also an appalling snob. Nothing beats that nice, warm inner glow that comes from feeling superior to someone, especially someone much richer and more powerful[17].

I blame evolution.

The First Turkish Winter – Finike

October 19th 2009 - May 5th 2010.

And so it came to pass that we settled in to Finike for the winter. Finike is a bijou little town of 11,200 inhabitants, nestling on the seaward edge of a semi-circular alluvial flood plain surrounded by snow-capped mountains. Most of the flood plain is dedicated to citrus fruit and growing vegetables under polythene. The Finike area exports oranges all over Europe. Here endeth the geography lesson.

I mentioned, did I not, that one of the most important criteria in choosing a wintering hole is having plenty of opportunities for socialising? On the surface, Finike didn't seem over endowed in this department. The marina management had made a portacabin-like building available for liveaboards to use, but when we looked inside in the middle of the summer it had about as much atmosphere as an underfunded village youth club on a wet Wednesday. It went under the apparently misleadingly nautical name of 'The Porthole'

It is people though, not buildings, that make for a social scene and Finike came up trumps in that department.

There were a large number of winter liveaboards who were almost without exception enthusiastic joiners-in. These were supported and encouraged by a core of liveaboards and shore-based expats who knew the area intimately.

In fact, about one in every 140 people in the area was an overwintering yottie. That's not bad odds if mid-19th century China's anything to go by. All we'd need are a couple of gunboats, a few heavily one-sided trading agreements and an unscrupulous disregard for the Turks' open friendliness and hospitality and we could take the place over and force them to buy our opium.

If you speak to most liveaboard yotties, one of the main reasons they give for choosing the lifestyle is a desire to get away from the regimentation and rat-race of their previous existence. Why is it then that, once settled in a marina for the winter, they instantly set up a regime of such fearsome regimentation that it would bring tears of envy to the eyes of a French Foreign Legion commandant?

The outline timetable for The Porthole detailed 35 different activity sessions over the course of each week, ranging from Pilates to music night by way of craft evenings, quiz night, badminton, topic night and line dancing. This was just the standing agenda. On top of this were the extraordinary events which were shoehorned into any minute space inadvertently and inexplicably left vacant.

In addition to these opportunities, there were the fortnightly excursions to the Concert Hall in Antalya, organised by a tireless Dutch liveaboard called Ewoud.

A sod of a long time ago, before we embarked on this lifestyle, we had, in our minds' eyes, a totally unrealistic vision of a life of adventure melded with cultural and social exploration leading to an in-depth understanding of different cultures and societies. A major component of this absurdly naïve fantasy was experiencing the music and art of different societies in their natural habitat; the Celtic musical influences of Brittany and Galicia; the Fado of Portugal; flamenco in Andalucía; Grand Opera in the open air in Italy and rebetika in Greece; belly dancers undulating sinuously in Turkey followed by Dervishes spinning themselves into a vertigo-defying state of beatitude.

And what did we get?

In most cases nothing. *Zilch. Nada. Rien.* The reason for our failure in this area was our immaculately appalling timing. Whenever we arrived somewhere new, our first expedition was usually a trip to the local tourist office or town hall to find out what was on. In most cases, the answer was 'nothing'. Apologetic officials would grimace from behind their desk and wring their hands whilst saying how sorry they were and how we should have been here last week when the month-long festival of music and culture had come to its shuddering climax.

This was all rectified in Finike, thanks to Ewoud's sterling efforts.

Over the winter we went to about ten concerts. Among them were works by Beethoven and Mozart, and a performance of *Die Fledermaus.* The last-mentioned was not an unqualified success, performed as it was in Turkish. This led to a lot of disappointed German-speakers in the audience.

We went along under the naïve impression that an operetta was a little opera. Oh no it's not. It's as long as or longer than a normal opera (nearly three hours in this case) but with less singing and lots more talking. In Turkish. We had great difficulty in following the plot, but what we did manage to work out suggested it was, in essence, a Whitehall farce in 3/4 time. There was much opening and closing of doors, mistaken identity and rushing in and out of windows. No dropped trousers though.

However, Liz, our resident aesthete and opera critic passed judgement that "*The hall was nice and warm and the seats were very comfy*". Can't argue with that for an in-depth cultural analysis.

This was followed by an evening of Russian composers performed by the Antalya State Orchestra, not one of whom bothered to immerse themselves in the role by coming on stage accompanied by a 19 year old Czech in killer heels and a skimpy bikini.

Mussorgsky was excellent (A night on bald mountain)

and the Tchaikovsky was rousing stuff too, but I discovered that the intervening 45 years have failed to dispel my childhood aversion to Prokofiev. His violin concerto was no doubt a technical *tour de force*, but it still sounded to me like a rather poor school orchestra tuning up.

In addition to things musical, the frenzied pitch continued unabated with other activities. I went to the Turkish lessons, which did not prove up to explaining the intricacies of 19th Century Viennese farces, and to the music club. Unfortunately, this was populated in its entirety by guitarists, most of them extreme beginners. They could only play in the key of C. This would have been fine for me, were the tenor sax not a transposing instrument. This would have meant my having to transpose into two sharps. This was (and still is) beyond my competence. My request that they transposed into two flats was met with either baffled stares or open hostility, so I settled for bawling out 'The wild rover' and 'dirty old town', more with gusto than musical sensitivity.

Liz ventured to the local *hammam*, or Turkish bath along with a group of other female yotties. The hammam is open to women on Tuesdays and to men on all the other days. Possibly the men are much filthier than the women (quite feasible) or Tuesday night is nookie night.

On entering the baths Liz was presented with a supposedly modesty-preserving towel the size of a large serviette (or 'table napkin' if you're posh) and waved over to the changing rooms. From there she was directed to the main room which was octagonal in shape and constructed entirely of marble. Each face accommodated an alcove containing seating and a supply of hot water.

After a few minutes of refined chat, they were called one by one to the sacrificial slab. A vigorous scrubbing, twisting, bending and dousing with water (hot and cold) left her feeling clean, refreshed and as if one nipple had been scoured off.

I didn't meet the entry criteria for ladies night at the hammam on several points, but I was very excited by the prospect of the weekly quiz night. I'm a bit of a cocky bugger when it comes to quizzes. My mind is a badly-indexed storehouse of utterly useless information from which I manage to dredge up such pointless gems as the fact that the little plastic cylinders on the end of shoelaces are called aglets, the collective noun for owls is a *parliament* and Ján Ludvík Hyman Binyamin Hoch was better known as Robert Maxwell. I scuttled down there like a dog with two tails, clutching my magic lucky pencil[18].

Disaster.

I met my nemesis in the form of Sheila who managed to whup my ass on every quiz that we both entered. Eventually, I decided to get my own back by devising and presenting a quiz of my own that was so fiendishly difficult that even she wouldn't be able to win it. (*Fundamental flaw in logic here somewhere - ed*)

Quiz nights are an interesting phenomenon to observe, for in these there do not seem to be any standard yottie behaviour patterns. All human life is there, along with several examples that don't really fit in that category.

It seems to me that any quiz team member can be described by his or her position on three scales:

-   Competitive versus co-operative

-   Knowledgeable versus pig-ignorant

-   Aggressively cantankerous versus easy-going

If you have a suitable program and a desktop with the computing power of the International Space Station you can produce a spherical hologram with these axes intersecting in three dimensions. Any individual can then have his or her characteristics plotted so that they can be defined by exactly one point in the hologram. The absolutely average individual will be positioned in the dead centre of the sphere where all three axes intersect. These are boring to study. The really interesting stuff comes from those on the extremes and how they interact.

This model allows for eight extremes, but the two most interesting outliers are the Hawks and the Doves.

Hawks are highly aggressively cantankerous, extremely

competitive and absolutely pig-ignorant; so pig-ignorant in fact that they're too stupid to appreciate just how stupid they are[19].

Doves on the other hand are highly co-operative, extremely knowledgeable and so easy-going that they make Louis Theroux sound like Paul Dacre (or Rush Limbaugh, if you're listening across The Pond).

On the surface, one would expect the co-operative, knowledgeable doves to wipe the floor with the cantankerous, pig-ignorant hawks, but this is not always the case. Hawks frequently win by sheer force of will. They will argue with the quizmaster even when they know full well that they are manifestly wrong. When they mark another team's paper, they do so with a strictness that would put a professional dominatrix to shame. Marks are deducted for minor spelling errors such as the obviously accidental transposition of letters, or for reasons as indefensible as failure to use a capital letter for a proper noun. When their papers are marked, however, they splutter with righteous indignation when not given a mark for such glaring solecisms as writing 'Watling Street' when asked for the name of the Roman Road linking Rome to Brindisi, along which 6000 members of Spartacus's army were crucified.[20]

This is a genuine example. The team in question argued, vociferously, that Watling Street was a Roman road and therefore their answer was near enough. If all this bluster fails to work, they resort to feigning a weak bladder at three-minute intervals and sneak off to the toilets for a quick surreptitious google.

The doves, on the other hand, respond to these challenges and provocations with an airy 'Yeah – Whatever' and carry on getting drunk and having a good time. It would appear likely, then, that a quiz between hawks and doves would be guaranteed to lead to rancour and possibly even fisticuffs. Not so. In such a case both sides get what is most important to them. The hawks win and the doves have a good time. Everybody wins. Unless the hawks keel over from a coronary mid-bluster, in which case the doves win by default.

Concerts were not the only string to Ewoud's versatile bow. He managed to blag a couple of girls from the marina office to act as guides and interpreters and organised a trip to Demre to watch the annual camel wrestling festival. *"Ooh"* we thought. *"That sounds good - experience a bit of local colour. We'll have some of that."* The festival takes place in the middle of the winter when both sexes come into heat. From March to November they're not interested and would rather settle down with a good book and a nice cup of tea.

The flyers that Ewoud had distributed were obviously designed with Western European sensitivities in mind. They proclaimed to the assembled yotties that the camels were 'not damaged or hurt' in the event, which was 'More like arm wrestling'. They seemed to think that it was important. They've obviously not met any Spanish.

At first sight the venue was not exactly enticing. As our minibus approached, we gazed out over a desolate, windy, cold plateau. Areas still in shadow from the low, watery February sun retained a covering of snow, and the scrub that struggled through it sported the crystalline veil of hoar frost. A few small, tired-looking concrete houses were scattered around the bleak tundra, but it was mostly barren wasteland. Why, we wondered, would anyone want to live in, or even visit, such an empty, godforsaken place?

As we ventured nearer to the centre of activity, the strains of music began to fight their way through the howl of the icy wind.

Well, I say 'music'.

I appreciate that musical appreciation is a cultural construct. I understand, at least on an intellectual level, that an individual's liking for any particular style of music is enhanced by increasing exposure, preferably at an early age. I accept that if I take this argument to its logical conclusion, I should consider the possibility that all forms of music could be looked upon as of equivalent value.

But I can't. I am a prime example of the adage that at the age of around 35 something awful invariably happens to music.

God, I hate Rap.

And modern jazz(zzzz).

Punk's not much better.

Rap makes no effort at melody, personifying, as it does, the absolute rout of anything approaching a tune by an unholy trinity of beat, rhythm and profanity. Punk also dispenses with melody, effectively replacing it with shouting. This is mainly, I suspect, a vain attempt to disguise the fact that the overwhelming majority of its practitioners have no discernible musical talent or skill whatsoever and are therefore unable to render even so much as a recognisable 'Three Blind Mice' on a xylophone.

Modern jazz also dispenses with melody, but for diametrically opposite reasons. It has been aptly described as *"Always sounding as if it's about to break into a tune but never quite managing to."* This is not, however, driven by a lack of musical ability; very much the converse. Melody constrains what you can play, thus severely limiting the musicians' opportunities to show off just how technically bloody marvellous they are. Modern jazz musicians do not play to bring bliss and enjoyment to their audience. They play to show off to other modern jazz musicians[21].

Hearing any of the three aforementioned genres induces headaches and overwhelming waves of irrational irritation in me. Middle eastern music does the same, despite my best efforts at cross cultural respect and understanding. It just sounds like a gratingly dissonant, thin, tinny, jumbled, tuneless cacophony.

One reason may be that my ear is trained to the western even-tempered scale, in which the octave is divided into twelve semitones. This is actually a bit of a bodge job, as you can't fit twelve even semitones exactly into an octave. A bit of compromise is required. As a result, there is always a slight degree of dissonance in any music using the western scale. We, however, don't notice this as we are used to it, having been immersed in it from nursery rhymes and lullabies at bed-time onwards. There is even some evidence that we start to pick it up in the womb.

What our ears are not trained to are the non-duodecimal scales used in many other parts of the world.

Instead of the division into twelve scale steps familiar to western ears, Middle Eastern scales divide the octave into up to 53 steps and if you think that's excessive, keep away from Southern India, where they split it into 72. It is the use of these intervals that gives music from such areas their characteristic cadence. Despite my knowing this, it still sounds bloody awful to me[22].

Things were not helped by the instruments used in the various bands that were milling around the site. The most prominent was the zurna, which looks like the mouthpiece has snapped off a hookah and sounds like a kazoo being played by a duck with a sore throat. It is also incredibly loud; so loud, in fact, that it effectively drowns out all the other instruments in the vicinity. This, in itself, is actually no bad thing, seeing as those other instruments include the cura, which is the bastard offspring of a bouzouki and a ukulele, and whose thin, reedy tones make a harpsichord sound like a Steinway concert grand in full flow. These are complemented, if that's the word, by kavals, which are the runt of the litter in the woodwind family; penny-whistle wannabees which produce a faint, high-pitched asthmatic wheeze reminiscent of a vole with emphysema. Think primary school recorder playing, only ten times worse. At least there weren't any bloody fey South American pan pipes

Braving the increasing volume of the Zurnas, we made our way to the centre of the site, where the ring was being prepared. A large area of scrub was cleared and flattened by a JCB, which then paraded triumphantly around the newly formed arena. I reckoned that if it came down to a contest between a 200 kg camel and a JCB, then my money was on the JCB.

Once the digger had made its triumphant exit from the ring, the perimeter was sealed. Well, O.K., not so much 'sealed' as 'vaguely marked'. Bits of old reinforcing rod were haphazardly stuck into the ground and pathetic strips of red and white boundary tape were strung loosely between them. This posed no impediment to the crowds getting through for a closer look, but the patrolling Jandarma, with their sub machine guns and ugly-looking 1 ½ metre night sticks, acted as a fairly effective backup.

Around the ring were flat bed lorries with tiers of seating, all of which were packed to bursting. Most were furnished with hard wooden benches, but the toffs' lorry also had cushioned bench tables and paper tablecloths. Women and female children were segregated into their own couple of lorries, (no cushions, natch) but there seemed to be no antipathy to females from our party mixing it with the boys, not even our very westernised (and attractive) Turkish female guides from the marina.

Interspersed among the trucks, buildings and camel stations were numerous doner kebab stalls. The doner was invented in Turkey and has become a global fast food phenomenon, almost on a par with pizza and knocking fish and chips into a poor third place. In the UK it's particularly popular as a late-night edible sponge to soak up the twelve pints of Fosters sloshing around in the belly. Most doners are made from what is alleged to be lamb, although purported beef and supposed chicken can also be found. All three were represented at this gathering, although it was the chicken variety that grabbed the attention. Even by the unappealing visual and olfactory standards of the more familiar lamb versions, the chicken kebabs were a shock & awe assault on the senses.

They were composed of layers of spatchcocked chickens that were covered in an odious semi-congealed mixture of grease and virulently lurid swirls of red, yellow and green. Feet and wingtips protruded at odd angles. The whole thing dripped fat and gave off a pungent odour of slightly rancid yak lard.

How could a culture that has produced such an exquisite and refined culinary tradition as Turkey has done also manage to come up with an abomination like the doner kebab?

Even before I went veggie I looked askance at doners. To me they seem to be a bacteriological version of Russian roulette. It was the meat that worried me, on several counts. Doners are made by packing slices of meat, gradually increasing in diameter, onto a spike, resulting in an inverted cone of what can vary from prime steak to a dubious mix of connective tissue, sinew and gristle, all padded out with the odd sprinkling of ground lung and occasional bits of eyeball. The resulting flesh shillelagh is then deep frozen to try and stop it going off quite so quickly. When the time comes to inflict it on the unsuspecting general public it is removed from the freezer and stuck on a rotating mechanism in front of a fierce grill. The outside then proceeds to burn to a crisp while the interior remains frozen. This is the bit that worries me as it sets up a temperature gradient between about -20 and +200 degrees C. Somewhere between the two, there has to be a Goldilocks zone for bacteria of around 35 degrees. This, I reckoned, would turn into a prolific breeding ground for a host of pathogens, from salmonella and campylobacter, through E. Coli and listeria to staphylococcus and clostridium. One bite and your entire digestive tract turns into a reasonable facsimile of a high-pressure hose and you'd be pebble-dashing the toilet walls from both ends. This belief enables me to enter self-righteous, self-satisfied mode and to adopt an air of smug superiority.

To help me on my way to this oh-so-tempting state I did some research. As is usual in my case, research consisted of selectively looking for evidence that supported my existing beliefs and reinforced my prejudices, while studiously ignoring any findings that cast doubt on my preconceptions. I am then in a position to use this balanced and unbiased investigation to confirm and proclaim my perspicacity and exquisite judgement. Unfortunately, I failed.

Well, sort of failed. Studies did suggest that around one in twenty kebabs sold in the UK are, indeed, contaminated with potential pathogens. Unfortunately for me and other complacent veggies, the primary source of contamination wasn't the meat, but the salad and then the sauces. Chilli sauce presented the biggest hazard among the sauces, but topping the lot was the cucumber in the salad. Apparently, its shape means that it is handled more than all the others in the preparation phase. I also suspect that its shape also means that it falls on the floor more often and is then picked up, given a peremptory sluice under the tap and slung back in the bowl.

Never mind though. If the bacteria don't get you then the astronomical levels of calories, salt and saturated fat should ensure an early demise from a stroke, heart attack or complications from type II diabetes.

As we waited in the cold, stamping our feet and rubbing our hands together, a caravan of camels made its way slowly down the valley. As they arrived, they were paraded around the ring before being revved up for the forthcoming contest.

The system works by subverting the camels' mating behaviour, whereby males compete for females. They square up to each other and cross their necks. Each then tries to wrest the other to the ground and press him into submission – very much like arm wrestling, in fact.

First, however, the trainers must get their charges in the mood, which they do in an echo of the ritual cross-provocation that is seen at the weigh-in to a heavyweight boxing match. To do this, the handlers take a leaf out of the WBO handbook and employ ring girls. They set up a honey trap of an in-season female who is led, prancing coquettishly, in front of the assembled males. Well, when I say 'coquettishly' I mean coquettishly for a camel, which can best be described as a sack full of spanners wrapped up in a matted, moth-eaten fur coat having a major epileptic seizure.

It seems to work on the males though as they secrete large amounts of slobber from their mouths which foams up and drools and dribbles all over them. Every time they shake their heads, which is often, great spirals of spume fly in all directions, ending up in hair, faces and all over clothes. In fact, the only noticeable difference from human males in a similar circumstance is that the camels are also able to inflate their tongues, which hang out of the side of their mouths like great, glistening, crimson, vibrating, slather-covered bladders. Human males would probably do the same if they could. There you go ladies – that, at least, is one thing to be grateful for.

Despite many attempts at explanation, the rules remained a mystery. They seemed to be similar to the 'two falls, two submissions or a knockout' of human wrestling, but without the overwrought histrionics. Everyone around us seemed very involved and knowledgeable, but we didn't have the vaguest idea what was going on. Sudden roars of approval erupted for no discernible reason, as did vociferous complaints about the ref's eyesight, cheating opponents or interference by opposing owners or trainers. It was a bit like plonking a group of Amazonian hunter-gatherers in front of an international cricket match and expecting them to work out the rules.

We spent the best part of three hours racking our collective brains trying to decipher the arcane intricacies of the spectacle but had to admit defeat. We retired hurt to the minibus and left the locals still at it, enthusiastically egging on their favourites and hurling abuse at their opponents. They were loving it. Apparently, this festival is keenly anticipated over the course of the whole year.

I'm all for going back to basics and enjoying the homely pleasures and fundamental virtues of the simple life, but if the high point of the year on the social calendar is standing around in the freezing cold listening to some discordant wall of white noise while simultaneously contracting dysentery and watching a couple of threadbare fleabags fighting over a twin-humped Vicky Pollard[23] then I'm glad to stick to the modern world, even if it does come bundled with rap, modern jazz, public relations companies and reality television.

Some of you may be wondering about the title of this book, possibly beginning to come to the conclusion that it was produced by a computer algorithm that generates random English phrases for printing on Japanese T shirts. Worry yourself no longer – all is about to be revealed. It was in Finike that a life-changing event unfurled. It all started just before Christmas, when Liz went for a shower.

Finike marina, like most port areas in the Mediterranean, is home to a large population of feral cats. These cats, as is their wont, breed prolifically and between them they produce scores of kittens every year, most of which don't see their first birthday.

Those kittens that haven't yet succumbed to disease,

injury, dogs or motor cars tend to hang out around the marina shower block, begging for scraps. It acts as a sort of feline shopping mall or coffee bar.

And adoption centre.

When we set off on our cruising, we handed over our elderly cat to our friend Karen and swore not to take on any more animals. This was despite our always having been animal people. We had always had cats and/or dogs. Our record simultaneous total comprised a hamster, an English setter, a Pyrenean mountain dog and a three-legged cat.

We had held out valiantly. We callously spurned the pitiful advances of wretched, skeletal, kittens. We heartlessly refused the desperate appeals of wide-eyed pleading puppies. We listened stoically to the blandishments and emotional blackmail of the animal charities[24] and summarily dismissed their requests to 'just foster' a dog or cat until a permanent home could be found. We know where that tactic leads, thank you very much. Give the manipulative little four-legged sods an opportunity to inveigle themselves into your affections and you'll be stuck with the buggers for life.

We had, however, reckoned without the Machiavellian wiles of the tiny, scrawny ginger and white bundle of fluff laying in ambush by the shower block.

All the other kittens were very people-shy. Although they would approach when driven by desperation, they did so very gingerly, grabbing a proffered scrap and promptly scuttling off. Not so the ginger and white one. She would come up to you and rub herself round your ankles, purring. If not immediately rejected she would climb up your legs and trunk and nestle under your chin with her face stuck in your armpit while the purring rose to a crescendo. When she was finally peeled off and returned to the floor she would mewl piteously and attempt to climb back up. She gave a convincing (and, as we later discovered, totally erroneous) impression of craving attention and comfort far more than food.

Still we held firm, so she moved up a gear and employed plan B.

This was a high-risk strategy, but she was playing for a

huge payoff. Essentially, it involved risking life and limb in an attempt to demonstrate a total inability to survive in the wild, thus inducing irresistible sensations of pity, sympathy and guilt in the unsuspecting yotties.

Step one was to meander innocently down the pontoon, adopting an air of cute innocence while cynically feigning ignorance of the large dog further down. She stopped and nonchalantly sniffed around the water and electricity pods as the dog came slowly closer, curious as to what this cocky little bugger was up to. She continued to pretend she hadn't seen it. In fact, she turned her back on it. You've got to admire her chutzpah. This was the equivalent of a matador turning his back on a raging bull and making a pass with his cloak. The assembled yotties held their collective breaths.

Her timing was immaculate. Just as the moment of truth approached and an untimely end seemed inevitable, she turned round, lifted up her front paws in faux astonishment and executed a perfect backflip into the water. This came as a surprise to the dog, but it came as even more of a surprise to her. She obviously hadn't thought this through completely as it became obvious that she had never been swimming before.

It's a commonly held fallacy that cats can't swim. They can, instinctively. That doesn't mean that they'd do it out of choice though. She scrabbled around in the water in a blue funk, ignoring the attempts by the assembled yotties to get hold of her and haul her out. Eventually, she managed to scrabble on the stern platform of one of the boats and Linda from *Vino Tinto* grabbed a towel and scooped her up. We saw our chance and sloped off, leaving her to it.

The kitten vanished from the scene after that, probably sulking and licking her wounded pride. It was during this period that Liz made that one little, but critical, error. She and Linda were laughing over the cat's impromptu swimarathon and Liz said that she was tempted to take her on as she obviously didn't have the nous to survive in the wild. Liz felt safe in making this statement as the cat had disappeared.

Two hours later there was a knock on the hull and there stood Linda with the ginger kitten cradled in her arms. Our bluff had been called; we were lumbered. We took the kitten on board and gave her some of the biscuits that Linda had brought along in case we tried to use that as an excuse.

We were now a cat boat.

All we had to do now was get her chipped, tested and checked over by a vet. Oh – and jabbed, de-wormed, de-flea-ed,[25] de-fungussed and documented. And named, of course. Shouldn't take long – a couple of weeks maybe?

It took three months in all. The biggest hassle was getting her rabies jab verified so that we could get her issued with a pet passport. Rabies is still endemic in Turkey, in both wild and domestic animals. It has been almost completely eradicated in Greece, so it is unsurprising that the Greek authorities look askance at any attempt to import an animal without demonstrable proof that it's not going to start foaming at the mouth and single-handedly initiating an epidemic of agonising deaths.

Legitimising the cat's status for entry to the EU required following a strict bureaucratic, veterinary and scientific protocol. Firstly, she had to be fitted with a microchip. Once this had been inserted between her shoulder blades using a needle of a bore that made your eyes water just thinking about it, she was ready for her rabies jab. Then you had to wait for more than 30 but less than 90 days, before returning to the vet and having another legful of blood drawn off. This was then sent by private courier to a special, Government-approved laboratory in Antalya for a blood titre to confirm she was protected against rabies.

By the end of this we had had the cat a whisker under three months and we were already well over budget. It didn't seem to bother her though.

Nor did her newly acquired name. We were originally going to follow tradition and call her Charlie. All our previous cats had been called Charlie. This latest addition, though, didn't fit the pattern. All our previous Charlies had been agile, smart, wily, street-wise ambush killers in the peak of physical condition and mental acuity. This one was the antithesis of all her predecessors. She warranted a name that encapsulated her many qualities; a name that combined klutz with couch potato; a name that conveyed the intellectual capabilities of a concussed woodlouse; a name that encapsulated the concept of the physical perfection of a professional darts player combined with the reactions and co-ordination of a slime mould.

Of course, there wasn't one that could do justice to such an abundance of shortcomings, so we decided to fall back on irony and called her 'Einstein'[26].

The cat may have come to the conclusion that she had struck lucky and now had a cushy little number for life, but she was soon to be disabused of this notion. She may well have been labouring under the same delusion as us, namely that Finike marina was bomb-proof as far as the weather was concerned. She was wrong. As were we.

And so it was that on the tenth day to Christmas, the Met sent Finike:

10 Metre waves

Nine Tree trunks floating

Eighty three knot gusts

Seven Shredded foresails

Sixty three knot winds

Five tons of hail

Four sea wall breaches

Three tattered sprayhoods

Two opened deck joints

And a scared cat behind the PC

It wasn't a bad forecast - Southerly 17 to 20 knots with some rain. And we were snugly tied up in a marina. Feeling smug and blasé I had a quick turn around the deck, gave the lines and fittings a cursory once over and proclaimed everything satisfactory and secure before retiring for the night.

Hah!

We were woken at about four in the morning by the wind getting up and it deteriorated steadily from then on.

The wind was from the South, blowing over our stern and pulling on the single, bar-tight sternline that was the only thing that was holding *Birvidik* off the concrete quay. The sky darkened further and the wind increased, howling through the rigging and throwing the boats about in all directions.

The bow was getting worrisomely close to the quay, a situation further complicated by the fact that the wooden buffers attached to it had rotted away, leaving a large, rusty steel bolt protruding 30 cm in the direction of *Birvidik*'s hull. I crawled heroically onto the foredeck with the large bow fender, blew it up, positioned it between the bow and the quay and scuttled back into the cockpit.

The rain fell in torrents and the wind continued to increase. By daybreak it was blowing at about 45 knots (Force nine). The Southerly wind had a long fetch and had built up ten-metre-high waves pounding straight onto the shore and the marina breakwater. The boats were now rolling so much that the fenders between them were being rolled out, leaving the hulls to bang and grate against each other. Just to exacerbate things we had a large, rusty steel boat next to us which was threatening to give us a good hiding. We had to go out and reposition the fenders about every ten minutes

The wind continued to increase, now accompanied by thunder and lightning, which grew steadily closer. Suddenly the wind fell to nothing and the sky changed to a clear blue - we were obviously in the eye of the storm, still surrounded by threatening black and purple clouds.

While we were standing in the cockpit, savouring the unnatural calm, there was a loud bang, just like a rifle shot and the boat rang with vibration. Completely disorientated we looked round, trying to identify the source. Then there was another, closely followed by a staccato of more, which steadily increased to a torrent as hailstones the size of hens' eggs clattered down. The kinetic energy in these hailstones was immense and the noise was deafening. We couldn't hear each other even if we shouted at close range. The decibel level was so high that we had to cover our ears or it hurt. We stood there helpless, hoping the Perspex and toughened glass in the wheelhouse and hatches was strong enough to withstand the battering they were receiving. The decks and pontoons were 20 centimetres deep in hail. Our newly acquired cat completely freaked and skedaddled below to hide in the space behind the computer at the nav station.

Looking around the marina afterwards we could see the damage wrought by the hailstones. External instrument sensors had been shattered, the plastic windows in sprayhoods were shredded. A large polycarbonate roof onshore ended up looking like a pepper pot. We got off fairly lightly, with just our lifebuoys and man overboard recovery gear pitted and with chunks missing. Street lamps were shattered and the orange crops devastated. God knows what the hailstones' terminal velocity was, but I suspect they could have inflicted serious damage on an unprotected head[27].

Then the wind, thunder and lightning returned with a vengeance. It climbed to 50 knots (force ten) and then to 63 knots. At sustained 64 knots and above it is rated hurricane force 12. Huge waves were now bearing down on the shore and marina breakwater. They thundered into the breakwater and crashed over it, and water swept across the quays and poured into the marina, which by now had considerable waves of its own, although these paled into insignificance compared with the monsters sweeping past the entrance on their way to taking large chunks out of the town sea wall and promenade.

The electrical activity eased slightly, and just as we were thinking that it was starting to moderate, the sky turned an evil dark yellow-green and all Hell was let loose. The thunder and lightning were right on top of us, with nasty similarities to The Unpleasantness at Mourtos, as described in the first book. The wind climbed even further, screaming through the rigging and throwing boats about like lottery balls. Several boats lost their foresails, which were torn unfurled by the wind and flapped to shreds within minutes.

There were a series of gusts which were measured at between 70 and 80 knots before the *pièce de résistance*, a gust which screamed in over the starboard quarter. Our inclinometer shows us the amount of lean up to 35 degrees from the vertical. It went right past the stops and still the boat continued to lean more and more, we were knocked almost flat on our side, unable to do anything other than hold on and hope we didn't get caught under the hull of the next door boat or end up with our masts entangled. This did, in fact happen to one of the boats, a 45 foot Bavaria, which caught its capping rail on the next door boat. When the two boats righted, the shear force lifted the Bavaria's deck away from its hull, leaving the deck semi-detached like an old boot whose sole had torn away from the toecap.

Slowly, the gusts eased, *Birvidik* returned nearer to the vertical and we could resume moving about and panicking. Over the next two hours things slowly returned to some semblance of normality and the cat tentatively tip-toed out from behind the computer and began to reconsider the wisdom of her current choice of lifestyle.

The heavy rain and hail brought large amounts of flotsam down rivers and roads into the sea, including the marina. The water was thick with mud and covered in a deep layer of tree trunks, twigs and vegetation, which confused the local dogs, who jumped blithely onto it thinking it was just an extension of the devastated land around. Yotties spent many a happy hour pulling confused and disorientated mutts out of the water before the marina staff finished the laborious task of pulling all the flotsam out by hand using garden forks.

This was, as I mentioned, just before Christmas. This was the first Christmas we had spent in a country that was not, at least nominally, Christian. We wondered how this was going to pan out. Christmas can hold untold horrors for the unwary yottie, especially if (s)he falls into the insidious clutches of a *Manager*.

Back in what is laughingly referred to as normal life, Christmas has a reputation as an emotional hot-house of intra-familial strife, characterised by frayed tempers, the unexpected violent eruption of long-suppressed grievances and an overall air of pervasive sullen ill-will, all exacerbated by a lethal combination of boredom, claustrophobia, dyspepsia and alcohol. One could be forgiven, therefore, for thinking that upon joining the diaspora of liveaboard yotties such unpleasantness would become a thing of the past. After all, one is dealt one's family, but one may choose one's friends.

Think again.

We humans are a social species and have evolved a need for rituals to reinforce group identity and loyalty. Other than rites of passage, Christmas remains one of the biggest of these rituals in nominally Christian cultures. Try as we might, it has a hold on us. We were born with an instinctive need for ritual and this was given form and specific meaning throughout our impressionable years. The Jesuits worked that out over 450 years ago: *"Give me a child until he is seven and I will show you the man"*.

As most of the yotties in the Med come from nominally Christian cultures it's no surprise that most of them try to celebrate Christmas in some form or other. What does come as a surprise (to me, anyway) is that there always seems to be a ready supply of hardcore masochists willing to take on the thankless task of organizing the group meals on Christmas Day and New Year's Eve. This reservoir of potential volunteers is handy, as very few individuals are naïve enough or mentally resilient enough to do it a second time.

As a public service, therefore, I incorporate into this book a free bonus feature, namely the *'Yottie Christmas Organising Guide for Dummies ©'*.

This valuable little pamphlet gives the reader access to the accumulated knowledge and insights garnered from the experience of nine winters afloat, but its core secret can be summed up in one sentence:

'Don't be an organiser; be a manager.'

Organisers do the work. Managers get other people to do the work. Managers can be any nationality but are usually British or German and more often than not called Gabby. If you get to be a manager then you've won. Someone else does all the work and takes all the flak, the complaints and the whinging behind the back. You take the credit.

One of the key life-skills for a yottie is to know when

you are being stalked by a manager. The approach usually employs a mixture of flattery, faux bonhomie, subterfuge and, occasionally, moral blackmail. Actual, or even threatened, physical violence is rare and somewhat frowned upon, even amongst managers.

For a novice, identifying a manager is not easy. Like all predators they are well camouflaged. The novice can improve his chances of survival by taking advantage of the wisdom of crowds. Watch the rest of the herd and note their reactions. Be on the lookout for the defence response of attention deflection and flocking. This usually manifests itself in downward looks, the avoidance of eye contact and a shuffling motion resulting in the herd bunching together and leaving obvious open space around the approaching manager. This behaviour is frequently accompanied by an alarm call of a low murmur, interspersed with the occasional grunt. This sometimes even appears to take on the characteristics of speech, almost sounding like "Oh-oh", "Watch out" and "Here comes ...". Some managers may be more skilful and cunning than others, but their reputation frequently precedes them.

The manager's predatory instincts are aroused whenever someone displays any form of talent or enthusiasm, however slight. On no account should you demonstrate proficiency at any task that the manager may be able to put to profitable use. Neither should you make any exclamation of interest in, or liking for, any activity whatsoever.

Anywhere.

Ever.

Especially in their favoured hunting ground, which is the bar.

Should you be so unwise as to pique a manager's interest, however, you will be in the unenviable position of observing at close quarters the characteristic behaviour of an ambush predator. This starts off with a subtle, tangential, circling approach, feigning disinterest and trying to put you at your ease. Direct eye contact is not made at this stage.

As the range lessens the manager brings flattery and

bonhomie into play. "*What an accomplished display of musicianship!*" she will purr when all you have demonstrated is that even a tone deaf arrhythmic philistine with acute hiccups can play the bloody kazoo. "*Public speaking is such a rare talent - what mastery and accomplishment! Are you by any chance RADA trained?*" is the standard managerial response to your yelling at everyone to shut the fuck up as no-one can hear the bloody kazoo player. Most lethal of all is to make any statement whatsoever along the lines of "*Oh I love a good party / barbeque / quiz / mud wrestling competition - the social scene is such an important part of the cruising life, don't you think?*" Before you can say *coup de grâce* she will strike and you will find yourself appointed social secretary and general dogsbody in perpetuity. The rest of the herd will snort, shiver with relief then relax and carry on grazing the buffet, content in the knowledge that your sacrifice has ensured that they are safe from attack.

For the time being.

For you, however, the Hell is only just beginning. Having failed in the necessary avoidance tactics, you find yourself in the default position of Christmas organiser and must resign yourself to around six weeks of purgatory. Here is what lies ahead for you (those of a nervous disposition should look away now).

Firstly, you must attempt to gauge demand. Given the fluid nature of a winter liveaboard community this is an impossible task. Yotties are capricious beasts. They will fly, drive, sail, bus or scrounge a lift to anywhere on the globe without so much as a by-your-leave or a moment's notice. They themselves don't know where they are likely to be after breakfast tomorrow, let alone in a month's time. Measuring participation in events more than a couple of days ahead is subject to a social form of Heisenberg's Uncertainty Principle, whereby it is impossible to know both the number of people and where they will be. Either one on its own is just about possible, but not both simultaneously.

You can make announcements on the VHF net, stick sign-up notices in the social centre, flood Facebook with increasingly desperate, pleading missives and even hide in the shower block in order to ambush people at their most vulnerable. All will be to no avail. Eventually you are reduced to the degrading resort of traipsing forlornly up and down every pontoon armed only with a clipboard and a rictus smile. You spend the best part of a week knocking on each boat in turn and asking them directly whether they are interested.

Despite asking a direct question, you will receive very few direct answers. About two boats will whole-heartedly commit themselves to both events. These people are almost invariably lying, being too soft hearted and embarrassed to hurt your feelings. Come the 25th they will either have decamped to Ulan Bator or will be hiding in a shuttered boat claiming to be quarantined with Ebola. At the other end of the scale, two boats will curtly reply something along the lines of *"I'd rather stick needles in my eyes"*. These people are sociopaths, but they display a disarming honesty.

After all this effort you will be left with 247 responses of varying degrees of 'maybe'. You therefore, on no rational or evidential basis whatsoever, guess that about 80 will turn up. All you need to do now is find a restaurant that is both able and willing to cater for nearly a hundred bladdered yotties on Christmas day. Before you do this, though, you bump into Pierre and Antoinette from *Mépris Raffiné*, who tell you that *Les Français* don't have their celebratory meal on Christmas day, but on Christmas Eve. As, they pointedly explain, does virtually every European country except the UK and Greece.

Do not, under any circumstances, incur the wrath of the British contingent by suggesting that we accommodate to our continental cousins and celebrate on the evening of the 24th. You run the serious risk of drowning in a deluge of apoplectic righteously indignant splutter or being beaten to a pulp under a frenzied hail of tightly rolled Daily Mails wielded by a mob of incandescent, puce-complexioned ex-commodores. Come what may, you must force the British tradition on the event. For you, this is a matter of self-preservation. If there are more Brits than all the others combined, you can plead democratic principles and impose the dictatorship of the majority. If this is not the case mutter some pathetic drivel about positive discrimination and obligations to minority groups and then unilaterally plump for the 25th.

This stratagem has its advantages in that most of the non-Brits will withdraw, muttering under their breath about Perfidious Bloody Albion. This leaves you with the much easier task of organizing a meal for about 40 people. (ish). A sigh of relief at this point is premature, however. The worst is yet to come.

So, to sum up:

After three weeks constant slog you have no hard information as to the number coming and you have alienated 60% of your fellow liveaboards, most of whom now refuse to speak to you and will cross busy main roads awash with maniac local drivers just to avoid passing within ten feet of you. On top of that, your sleep patterns are disturbed, you have started sniping at your partner and you appear to have descended into a catatonic state of learned helplessness in spite of the antidepressants. Oh - and you're now back on 50 a day after 25 years of fag-free abstinence. Yup - that's about par for the course.

Now you must square the circle and sort out the venue and the menu. To do this you have to extract a consensus from 50 or so of the most congenitally unco-operative, egotistic and egoistic[28] curmudgeons on the planet. Believe me, this lot make Joe Stalin look like the Dalai Llama by comparison.

The first thing you need to do is canvas views of likely restaurants. But you can't do that because the choice of restaurants affects the menu options. OK, you think, we'll work out the menu and then look at the restaurants.

Optimistic fool.

Although you have standardised your sample of yotties by the simple expedient of driving off all the non-Brits except for a couple of inexplicably anglophile Dutch, you are far from dealing with a homogenized group. They all want what they personally are used to in a Christmas. This is a psychological comfort blanket to them and if thwarted in their desires they react with all the sophistication and self-control of a two year old.

Firstly, you have the problem of timing. Most British Christmas blow-outs are scheduled to begin about 3 p.m. despite this being rarely, if ever, achieved in practice. This target time is far from unanimous, though. Some will have been brought up to start eating at 12:30 on the dot whereas others are unlikely to be back from the pub until it finally kicks them out so that the staff can get to their own festivities. Appeals to reason and fair play are pointless here. You will just have to bite the bullet, plump for 3 p.m. and resign yourself to alienating another six of the few people who are still talking to you. On the plus side it reduces your seating plan to an even more manageable thirty-odd.

Having successfully navigated the preliminary negotiations you must now embark upon the real challenge, namely the menu. On the one hand you have The Buffet and on the other you have The Traditional Christmas Dinner With All The Trimmings Especially Sprouts. (TTCDWATTES, or TWATS in the interests of brevity). In between you have the á la carte option which manages to combine the disadvantages of both options with the advantages of neither. Discard this out of hand.

The Restaurateur will argue strongly for the buffet on practical grounds. It is a logistical nightmare trying to dish up three (or worse, more) courses to large numbers of drunken yotties, most of whom have forgotten what they ordered in the first place. Invariably someone has his dessert slapped down in front of him while his wife, still waiting for the arrival of her amuse-bouche, is on the verge of fainting from hypoglycaemia. The buffet option is also favoured by vegetarians and pescatarians, along with attention-seeking saddos who purport to be either allergic to or intolerant of virtually every known food group. Most other assorted weirdoes will favour this option.

If confronted with someone who claims special treatment because of a serious food allergy, ask to see his epi-pen. Anyone seriously at risk of anaphylaxis will always carry one and will know exactly where it is at all times. If all you get is some feeble excuse such as "*Oh - I must have left it in my other jacket*" or "*I accidentally sat on it last Thursday.*" just snort derisively and shove a peanut up his left nostril[29].

In view of the above you may be leaning to the view that The Buffet is probably the least hysteria-inducing option. Don't be fooled. Such thinking seriously underestimates the blinkered tenacity and petulant bloody-mindedness of the TWATS aficionado. He (it's usually a he) has had a TWATS every Christmas day of his life. His mental equanimity (such as it is) depends on it. His mummy always ensured he had one, and when she finally put her foot down and withdrew TWATS privileges, his wife (AKA mummy II) continued the tradition.

You have to make a delicate, nuanced judgment at this stage. Practicalities lean toward The Buffet whereas the perils of tantrums and untrammelled petulance suggest taking the coward's option and conceding to the TWATS. Whichever way you go, your guest list will shrink by about 50% and you will be subjected to unprecedented levels of virulent personal abuse. If it's too finely balanced to call, go for the buffet.

Now you're on the home straight. All you have to do is get a consensus on the venue and prise the deposits out of their hermetically sealed wallets. The former should be easy for you by now as you have honed the necessary skills to a fine art. Just impose the solution that is most convenient to you and tell the resulting whiners that if they don't bloody like it then they can bloody well organise it themselves. That usually shuts them up.

Getting actual money out of the buggers, though, is an intellectual and ethical challenge of the highest order. Various techniques have been advocated, but I would suggest constant harassment combined with public embarrassment and humiliation followed up as a last resort by the firm application of a pair of pliers to the inside of the thigh. In particularly obstinate cases a counter clockwise rotation of the pliers usually has the desired effect.

Just as you think you've cracked it, fortune's smile turns into a snarl. You've plumped for The Buffet, booked the restaurant, got all of the deposits by fair means or foul and drawn up the seating plan. You tune in to the VHF net on the morning of the 21st to announce the final arrangements. To your horror and dismay a spluttering TWAT comes on the air to inform you that he and his good lady wife arrived back from Blighty the night before and were HORRIFIED to discover that not only had he not been posted a handwritten invitation in best copperplate but that, without his having been personally consulted (at international telephone rates) it will be a BUFFET.

His outrage knows no bounds. Arguments that the decision was made by the majority of yotties are dismissed peremptorily. He has, he informs you in a tone that suggests his finger has just gone through the toilet paper, consulted with others of like mind. He calculates that the arrival of his party and the Nice-But-Dims on m/v *Easily Persuaded* means that the TWATS now outnumber The Buffet supporters by three (or three and a quarter if you count the Jack Russell). He therefore reckons that four days is ample time to cancel the restaurant booking, negotiate with an establishment that has the wherewithal to provide a proper Christmas dinner and notify everyone of the change. He DEMANDS that this be effected without further delay or argument.

You reply in language that would make an RSM blush and in doing so successfully reduce the number of people willing to publicly acknowledge you to single figures. But it was worth it - you haven't felt so alive in months. And the vision of him trying to contort himself into the position you so graphically suggested on an open channel will keep many people amused for the coming year.

So, Christmas day dawns and, against all the odds, you pull it off. Apart from the usual couple of tiffs, raised voices, dramatic flouncing exits and muttered complaints about the gravy, everything goes well, and people seem to enjoy themselves.

At the end, The Manager rises serenely and taps her

glass with her spoon while looking indulgently at her assembled brood. She thanks everyone for coming to what has turned out to be the epitome of a successful liveaboard Christmas and hopes that all the efforts that went into it (by which she implies her efforts) were worthwhile.

As an aside, she mentions that people should show their appreciation for your modest contribution to the sum of human happiness and unilaterally asserts that she is sure that you would be more than happy to take on the challenge again next year.

At this point, should you not have had the foresight to have locked away all sharp objects or blunt instruments, I can only suggest that you study the defence of justifiable homicide as it applies in the country in which you happen to be.

Luckily, Christmas in Finike did not require the abovementioned skills. This happy, and rare, state of affairs was due to three factors: Christmas Day is a normal working day in Turkey; the liveaboard contingent were an unusually co-operative bunch and there was an inexplicable absence of Managers. We made the most of it – it was the only Christmas in eleven years that was totally without discord.

It being a normal working day meant that there was no shortage of restaurants available and that none of them had to charge exorbitant prices to cover the staff costs and inconvenience of opening on Christmas day. The unusually co-operative nature of the assembled overwintering yotties meant that everyone was happy to go along with whichever was the easiest option, and the absence of a manager facilitated the emergence of true volunteers to organise the meal.

Step forward Miggy and Neal. Take a bow.

They achieved the seemingly impossible, a TCDWATTES for 41 people of 14 different nationalities, all in a country that had no tradition of Christmas Dinner, no history of roasting turkeys and no idea what to do with a sprout.

Their first problem, therefore, was to find a restaurant

that could deliver a TCDWATTES for 41 people. This was not an easy task, so they decided to do what all yotties do when faced with a little local difficulty, they asked the marina staff, who did what they always did when asked a question. They said '*Ask Faik*'.

Faik was the local Mister Fixit. He was also a prime example of the amazing Turkish work ethic, a phenomenon that will be addressed in more detail in the section on the following Turkish winter, in Marmaris. Any yottie in Finike came across Faik sooner or later – usually sooner. He was a one-man service industry. He ran the chandlers in the marina and operated the local car hire business whilst simultaneously supervising his yacht maintenance and repair business. In his copious spare time he acted as the co-ordinator for the local taxis and side-lined as a travel agent and tour operator. He interspersed all these with bouts as the local tourist information wallah. He also spoke English, German and French (after a fashion). If you wanted to know anything about anything in Finike, then Faik was your man.

So Neal and Miggie approached Faik and asked him if he knew of a restaurant nearby that might be willing to give this challenging task a go. "*Sure*" he replied. "*We'll give it a go in my family restaurant.*"

Faik's family restaurant? This was news to all of us yotties. Where in God's name did he find the time to run a restaurant? And how come we'd never come across it? Never mind, we'd found ourselves a restaurant for Christmas dinner.

It turned out that there were a couple of potential snags with using Faik's restaurant. The first was that it was a good league hence[30], situated on a picturesque river crossing. This was easily and quickly overcome with the use of the fleet of minibuses that Faik conjured out of thin air.

The second was a little bit more of a challenge. Turkish cuisine can be amongst the most exquisite on the planet; a fusion of Asian, Ottoman, and Levantine traditions characterised by the subtle and imaginative use of a multitude of herbs and spices. Turkish chefs have a battery of tricks, techniques and skills up their sleeves, but preparing a TCDWATTES is not among them.

They may have invented dolmades and taken the kebab to new culinary heights; they may have created the pide, which would knock the best of pizzas into a cocked hat; they may have given the world the borek, compared to which Chinese spring rolls are a soggy and revolting insult to the taste buds, but virtually none of them have ever roasted a turkey, despite its name[31].

They use a wide range of vegetables, from spinach, leek, cauliflower, globe artichoke and cabbage through, celery, aubergine, green and red peppers and string beans to Jerusalem artichokes, but they've never cooked a carrot and most have never even seen a brussel sprout.

Neal and Miggy rose to the challenge magnificently. They organised a dry run, in the course of which they fed a full Christmas dinner to Faik and sixteen of his extended family. The turkeys were roasted whole in the large brick-lined ovens and were eaten with gusto and enthusiasm. The sprouts were nibbled at with polite appreciation and then hidden.

On the 25th they played a blinder and served up a perfect TCDWATTES to 41 carnivorous yotties and four awkward vegetarians, without so much as a cross word or a single complaint - probably a unique occurrence in the whole of yottiedom.

It was not long after this that we had our first experience of the Turkish health system. The two events are not linked, I hasten to add.

One of the disadvantages of the internet age is that one can drive oneself into a frenzy of panic-ridden hypochondria by googling suitably obscure, hideous and invariably fatal diseases. If you think that's bad, try being medically trained. Doctors and nurses are the worst ones out for reading terminal prognoses into seemingly innocent symptoms. It's psychology again. They see a lot of examples of illnesses, so they perceive them as being much more prevalent than they actually are. It's called availability bias.

Liz's speciality in theatre was ear, nose and throat. She

has seen a lot of very nasty oral and throat tumours and the ones that come to theatre are usually the worst among them. As a result, every sore throat, every slight hoarseness, every minor lump, scratch or difficulty swallowing, sends her rushing for the pharyngeal mirror and re-writing her will. This usually goes away when the symptoms do.

In addition, despite, or perhaps because of, her being a nurse she displays a distinct reluctance to go and see a doctor. She only resorts to this *in extremis*. By the time she'd had a sore throat for four weeks it had reached that point. With her extensive experience and knowledge of ear, nose and throat pathology she had immediately thought the worst and made the diagnosis of throat cancer and imminent demise. I stuck a torch down her throat and said it looked more like a generalised inflammation of the soft palate to me, but she's the expert.

We had noted from our perusing of the Jersey Evening Post website that Islanders were in fits of apoplectic self-righteous indignation about so-called 'health tourism' where bloody foreigners were purportedly flooding into the island with suppurating exotic diseases and conditions and subsequently conning the hardworking Jersey tax evaders (Sorry - tax *payers*) into supplying them with medical services.

They could learn a lot from the Turks.

We enquired of the marina office and they said to go to the local hospital and make an appointment with the ENT department. So we did.

It was like a scene out of MASH. Finike is mainly an agricultural town. Very dangerous occupation, agriculture. The place was mobbed with people milling around with bandaged limbs, horrendous burns, patched up heads and blood everywhere, as if they'd just escaped from a war zone. Or I suppose it could have been St. Helier on a Saturday night.

Few people in Turkey, outside of the holiday hotspots, speak English, and Finike is a small little market town, well off the tourist trail, so it wasn't surprising that the reception staff spoke little or no English. They did, however, have a sheet of paper with the various departments listed in English and Turkish, so we pointed at ENT (KBB, since you ask) and made approving noises. The receptionist banged a few keys and waggled the mouse a couple of times and turned the screen to us, showing a large red rectangle containing the words KBB *Dolu!* (full). This was hardly surprising, given the heaving mass of suffering humanity around us, so we tried to indicate that we would like to make an appointment for a future and, one hoped, less crowded time.

At this point the combined efforts of phrase book, dictionary and sign language fell down. Despite the mob of people trying to get his attention, the receptionist kept smiling, indicated that we should wait to one side and made a phone call.

Soon after, a guy in blue scrubs appeared and asked us in English how he could help. We explained, and he said to wait a moment and waded his way through the walking wounded in the corridor. About five minutes later he returned and told us to follow him back whence he'd come. We followed him through the milling casualties, trying not to exacerbate any injuries, until we came to the KBB department, outside of which was a crowd of around 40 people all waiting for their name to come up on the screens above the door, which showed the lucky five at the top of the list.

He ushered us past the assembled throng and straight into the consulting rooms. We thought we were going to get lynched.

Once inside the *'Uzmani'* (translates as 'specialist' - probably equivalent to consultant or registrar) examined Liz, who was pleased make the professional observation that he had 'all the proper gear'. He diagnosed chronic pharyngitis, thus putting Liz's mind at rest apart from the guilt about queue jumping which now went into overdrive.

We went back to reception and paid the standard charge that a Turk would pay - 15 Turkish Lira, about 6 quid.

We were not just treated as well as the locals, we were treated better. As we were escorted out by our friend in scrubs, I asked him about our jumping the queue of almost certainly more deserving patients. "*You are guests in our country*" he replied. "*It is our duty to be hospitable*".

Sometimes even seasoned cynics like me are humbled by events.

Mind you, I don't know if the poor buggers in the queue would agree with my sentiments.

An advantage of our newly-acquired feline crew member was the increased peace of mind that she gave us in respect to vermin infestations. Getting a mouse, or even worse a rat, on board is a constant source of nagging worry for the cruising yottie. This is one of the few occurrences which do pose both health and safety issues. On the health side, rats are vectors for a wide range of nasties, among them the hantavirus, Leishmaniasis, Weill's disease and bubonic plague. This list is by no means exhaustive.

On the safety side there are two main risks, both of them linked to both rats and mice being members of the order *rodentia*, which comes, appropriately, from the Latin *Roderer*, meaning 'to gnaw'.

It's bad enough that the little bastards gnaw their way through your Tupperware containers and demolish your last three Jaffa cakes. It's worse when they reduce your magnum opus manuscript to hamster bedding, but it's downright dangerous when they make a start on your electric wiring and/or your sea-cock hoses. The latter sinks your boat while the former sets fire to it. At least if they do both at the same time the sinking will put the fire out.

Yotties go to great lengths to avoid this, all of them to little or no avail. Rat guards can be put on shore lines, but their effectiveness is suspect, especially as rats have been known to swim out to anchored boats and scrabble up their anchor chains. If you're moored to a pontoon or a quay you're defenceless.

We had been lucky in that we had thus far escaped rodent invasion, but it had always been a nagging worry at the back of the mind. Now with Einstein aboard we could rest more easily. Just the smell of a cat was supposed to be enough to deter all but the most intrepid rodent invader and even if an anosmic rat were to scuttle on board then we fully expected Einstein to rapidly disembowel it and dispose of the carcass. So far it seems to have worked and we've had no signs of rats or mice.

The same, unfortunately, cannot be said for cockroaches.

Just before we were due to leave Finike, Liz spotted something scuttling behind the heater in the forward heads. 'Probably just a beetle' we optimistically declared. It wasn't - it was a cockroach[32]. An hour later another was spotted in the forepeak and then one in the main saloon. It's surprising, actually that it took this long for the little buggers to get their feet in the door. We had tried all the usual precautions such as not bringing cardboard on board and checking fruit etc, but these are only ever delaying tactics. They hide in books, under the labels of cans, in toothpaste cartons. They crawl up mooring ropes and anyway the little sods can fly.

All our ecological ethics shot out of the window in a desperate attempt to eradicate the tenacious little bastards. Apparently, cockroaches are one of the very few species that will have no problem surviving climate change and even a nuclear holocaust.

We went to a local specialist poison shop (they have them here - makes you wonder). I strode confidently in, brandishing my Turkish – English dictionary. The man behind the counter asked me what I wanted to kill. I was tempted to say 'The entire Galatasaray front line', just to see the look on his face[33], but I chickened out and settled for *hamamböceği*, which I hoped was the Turkish for 'cockroach' and not 'local Imam'.

I explained the problem and we discussed possible strategies and weaponry. In addition to 'cockroach' I now know the Turkish for 'kill', 'exterminate', 'without mercy', 'poison', 'Sod the environment', 'CBW suit', 'chemical warfare,' 'nerve gas', 'boric acid', 'dioxin' and 'alpha-cypermethrin'.

The boat was dismantled, and I sprayed every toxin known to science (and several that weren't) into every nook and cranny. Areas of the boat were sealed off and the cat exiled to the aft deck. Chemical smoke bombs were let off and allowed to permeate the interior. As the survivors came staggering and coughing out of the cracks and channels into other areas of the boat they were swatted, sprayed and trapped in glue. Having presided over this mass extermination we scattered baited traps throughout the boat and decided to stay put for a few days, just to check.

No luck. They were down, but not out. They were outbreeding our war of attrition. You've got to admire the little bastards. Admire, but not sympathise.

Further research led us to a home-made solution. This called for pure boric acid[34] and condensed milk. Strangely enough it was the condensed milk that proved difficult to get hold of. Well, when I say 'difficult' I actually mean 'impossible'. The boric acid was readily available from our friendly Chemical & Biological Warfare shop down the road.

Liz showed the ingenuity for which she is justly famed by knocking up some ersatz condensed milk. She achieved this miraculous transformation by boiling up a 50 – 50 mixture of milk and sugar until it turned to goo. She then stirred the boric acid in and let it cool, whereupon it congealed into a mass with the consistency and adhesiveness of discarded chewing gum. We rolled this up into pellets which we secreted in inaccessible parts of the boat that looked attractive to cockroaches, yet where the cat would have trouble finding it and wolfing it down. We also put down some sticky roach traps. We reckoned that if they stayed empty for about three days we'd have cracked the problem.

Stay empty for three days they did, the bucket chemistry seemed to have done the trick. We remained cockroach free.

Well, until we got to Albania, but that's another story.

Three days later, cockroach-free, we set off back West.

The Aegean Coast – Finike to Lesbos.

(and most of the way back)

May 5th 2010 – October 17th 2010.

The 5th of May 2010 marked Einstein's first time out of the relative calm of the harbour. It also marked the day we first discovered that we had taken on a seasickness-prone cat. We also learned that motion-sickness medication doesn't work on cats.[35]

We had set off into a one metre head sea, which caused *Birvidik* to pitch up and down like a manic rocking horse. We decided to shut Einstein in the forepeak, where it would be warm dark and comforting for her. At least, that's what we thought. The pitiful howling and scratching emanating from the forepeak soon convinced us that this was far from the case.

Liz went to let her out and comfort her. Upon opening the door, she was confronted with a scene of devastation comparable to the aftermath of an outbreak of cholera in a student flat. Cushions and bedding were scattered throughout the cabin and all were liberally coated in an aromatic mix of saliva, urine, vomit and catshit. Liz took Einstein out and nursed her in her arms, trying to comfort her. This merely resulted in liz's clothes being coated in the same fragrant mixture.

We came, with practice, to identify distinct stages in Einstein's reaction to rough weather, or in fact to any stress source at all. These we have named the DEFCON scale and it runs from DEFCON 0 to DEFCON 4.

Just as one judges the windstrength on the Beaufort scale by observing its effects on the sea state, so one can judge the effect of the boat's motion on the cat's DEFCON level by observing its consequences on her digestive tract:

DEFCON 0: No effect. Eats normally (i.e. almost incessantly). Uses litter tray normally and covers up the evidence scrupulously.

DEFCON 1: Minimal effect. Eats occasionally. Sleeps. Uses litter tray normally. Intermittent light salivation.

DEFCON 2: Noticeable effect. Does not eat. Sleeps sporadically. Uses litter tray frequently. Makes no attempt to bury evidence. Salivates heavily.

DEFCON 3: Severe effect. Does not eat or sleep. Yowls reproachfully. Makes half-hearted attempts to use litter tray but misses frequently. Salivates constantly.

DEFCON 4: Very severe effect. Yowls pathetically. Lurches from one part of the boat to another at two-minute intervals. Makes no attempt to use litter tray. Leaves ejecta from both ends of digestive tract wherever she happens to be at the time. This has, in the past, included the bed. Drools strings of saliva wherever she goes.

This was definitely a DEFCON 4. Fortunately, she recovers very quickly. Within five minutes of dropping the anchor in Gokkaya she was contentedly stuffing her face and wrinkling her nose up accusingly at the state of the upholstery.

Our proposed route involved our retracing our steps via Fethye, Kas and Marmaris and then on to Bodrum before turning the corner and heading North towards the Bosphorus and Istanbul. The whole of the Turkish coast in this area is surrounded by islands. Almost without exception, and much to the chagrin of the Turks, these islands are Greek.

Greece and Turkey have been at each others' throats for most of the last 200 years. We can give such an exact time span for the simple reason that prior to 1831, Greece as a nation state did not exist. In fact, until the late 1700's, nation states as such did not really exist. Neither did passports. Borders were a somewhat fuzzy concept, compared with the modern idea of hard national frontiers with their walls, watch-towers, razor wire and customs posts. Individuals and populations drifted from one sphere of influence to another without once being asked for a passport, or any other form of identification for that matter.

People did not identify themselves by nationality, because nationalities as such did not exist. They still had ethnic, linguistic, religious and cultural identities but these did not necessarily have any correlation with the political entity that ruled where they lived. The major political units of the time were either small city states or expansive, tribute-demanding empires. The latter generally had local representatives in place to ensure the tribute kept flowing, but apart from that the locals were left to their own devices and allowed, indeed expected, to sort out their own social organisation and get on with things.

They identified with their family, their tribe, their village, their religion or their dialect. They could tell you who sent the tax-collectors round, but if you asked them what their nationality was, you'd just get a blank look. In 1800 France stretched as far north as Friesland, now in the north of The Netherlands. At the time of the French Revolution, eleven years earlier, half of its population did not speak French. When Italy emerged as an independent nation in 1860 only one in forty of its residents spoke fluent Italian. Its leaders conversed in French. Indeed, Massimo d'Azeglio, one of the founders of Italian independence is quoted as saying *"We have made Italy, now we must make Italians"*.

In the case of ethnic Greeks, most of them lived in lands under the control of the Ottoman Empire, which really came into its own in 1453 when the Hellenised Byzantine capital of Constantinople fell to the Ottoman Turks. The Ottoman empire expanded rapidly and in less than 30 years it incorporated virtually all of what is now modern Greece and Serbia along with a fair-sized chunk of the middle east. It hung on to these for nearly 300 years. During this time ordinary Turks and Greeks seemed to rub along OK, frequently living reasonably harmoniously as close neighbours. This state of affairs continued, albeit with the odd rumble, until the Greek war of independence which ran from 1821 to 1830.

After Greece achieved independence in 1831, things continued to blow hot and cold. There were a few decades of reconciliation before they were at it hammer and tongs again, facing each other in four major wars between 1897 and 1922. That's about a war every six years.

There followed a period of more normalised relations after the two countries exchanged their ethnic populations in 1923. I say 'ethnic', but the exchange was actually based on religious affiliation rather than ethnicity. Nearly half a million Muslim Greek citizens were forcibly relocated to what is now modern Turkey. Going the other way, over 1.2 million Greek Orthodox Turks were rounded up and packed off to Greece whether they fancied the idea or not.

The state of more civilised co-existence continued through the 1930s and 1950s, with both countries joining NATO in 1952 and NATO members are definitely *not* allowed to go to war with each other. If they do it completely buggers up the whole alliance business. Just as things were starting to look all hunky-dory, Cyprus raised its ugly head and things went tits-up again, made worse by the Istanbul pogrom of 1955 and the expulsion of the Istanbul Greeks in the 1960s. The Greek-led Cyprus coup *d'état* and the subsequent Turkish invasion of Cyprus in 1974 really put the tin hat on things.

Despite intermittent thaws, relations between Greece and Turkey remain characterised by suspicion and distrust. Indeed, Greek animosity about the Cyprus issue effectively put the kybosh on Turkish efforts to become part of the EU.

This mutual rancour presents certain bureaucratic hurdles for the yottie. Prime amongst them is the fact that yotties must obtain a visa upon entry to Turkey. This a fairly simple procedure, apparently derived from the postal service. Upon arrival in the country you hand over ten quid and are presented with a pretty little adhesive stamp which they lick and then stick in your passport. You then take the passport to the immigration police who stamp it with the date of entry, a bit like a postmark. You are then free to wander about the country at will for 90 days.

As long as you don't mention the Armenians.

Or the Kurds.

Or the Alevis.

Or the mob attacks on the aforementioned.

Oh, and the attack on the art gallery reception in Istanbul which had the effrontery to serve wine to those attending - better not mention that either.

If you stay more than 90 days they whack you with a sodding great fine on exit and bar you from re-entering the country for a period that correlates with the amount of time by which you have overstayed your visa. Fair enough. If you were a Turk trying to get into the UK then after 90 days you'd probably still be face down on the floor of Heathrow immigration suite in an armlock, unless you were lucky enough to be banged up in Yarl's Wood for the duration. If you were in Singapore and overstayed your visa you'd be chucked in the slammer for three months, given a good thrashing on the bare buttocks with a rattan cane and then deported and told never to show your face (or buttocks for that matter) again.

Turkey, though, has a different but equally stringent regime. The authorities ruthlessly insist that before your visa expires you must, irrespective of the personal, emotional or financial cost, stiffen the sinews, summon up the blood

And...

(I can barely bring myself to write this)

Ready?

Deep breath...

OK – here we go...

Take a day trip to Greece.

I know, heartless isn't it.

On your return you are forced to buy another pretty little stamp which gives you another 90 days. You can repeat this process as many times as you like. Eat your hearts out, UK Borders Agency. That's what I call strict immigration control.

Yotties on the SW coast of Turkey get around this minor administrative problem by organising little jaunts called 'visa trips'. These involve a bus trip to Kas, Marmaris or Bodrum and then a day's boat excursion to Kastellorizon, Rhodes or Kos respectively. To add to the misery of this bureaucratic burden, they are then forced to return loaded with such un-Islamic delights as cheap booze, bacon, black pudding and pigs' trotters.

An email from friends of ours, Stuart and Steph on *Matador*, told us that this imaginative and creative organisational solution (or 'scam' as it is technically known) had been stymied. Apparently, the Turkish authorities had decided to introduce a degree of what they termed 'reciprocity' into their visa arrangements - basically, let's make things almost as awkward for you as you make it for us. Well, not really. What they said was that on entry you would get a 180-day, multiple entry visa, but that once you'd done 180 days you'd have to stay out for another 180 days or... fill in a form and get a residency permit.

Well, OK, fill in a form and pay £200 and get a residency permit.

This news spread through the cruising community like wildfire, leaving apoplexy, panic and pandemonium in its wake. For permanent liveaboards such as us the new regulations did pose a bit of a problem. It would have been rather expensive to leave the boat in Turkey and go and stay in a hotel in Greece or Bulgaria for six months. That's aside from finding something to do with the cat.[36] Our options were limited to paying for a residency permit each or looking for a winter berth in Greece. On investigation it became apparent that there weren't any marinas on this side of Greece that met our stringent requirements and so we resigned ourselves to paying up and making the best of it.

Not so some of our fellow cruisers. The internet forum for liveaboards, mainly Brits, went incandescent. 85 posts were knocked up in a few days.

So here is the stereotypical British Yottie as constructed from internet fora postings[37]:

Sex: Almost invariably male.

Chronological age: Rarely below 60

Emotional age: Pre school

Politics: Somewhat to the right of Ghengis Khan.

Reading matter: Daily Mail. The Telegraph if he's feeling particularly liberal and mellow (Unlikely if he's recently read the Daily Mail).

Hobbies: Xenophobia; writing letters to the editor bemoaning the state of almost everything; living in constant fear of being ripped off; bemoaning modern education and then writing posts containing 'seperate', 'priviledge' and 'their' for 'they're'.

Likes: Boats; long, rambling discussions on obscure aspects of the collision regulations; whiskey; Golf Clubs (not too keen on the game itself); gin & tonic; the saloon bars of waterside pubs; USING CAPITAL LETTERS ON INTERNET POSTS; the days when people knew their place; The Ladies, God Bless 'em (as long as they don't get ideas above their station); proper comedy (i.e. Bernard Manning).

Dislikes: Foreigners; taxes; unions; benefits scroungers; bogus asylum seekers (which is all of them); taxes again; political correctness gone mad; The EU; students; public sector workers; public sector workers' pensions; more foreigners; 'Elf n Safety; Dungaree-wearing bra-burning feminists; the BBC (except Strictly Come Dancing); Blacks; Asians; Gypsies; Eastern Europeans and most of the Irish. He's not sure about Jews.

A couple still stood out, even from this lot. They were so incoherently apoplectic that they even provoked a reaction from their fellow posters. It was just possible to discern from their solipsistic ramblings that they were long term liveaboards in Turkey and had been for some years. What wasn't possible to discern, given their swivel-eyed, spittle-spraying dislike of all things Turkish, was why. It led to one beautiful post asking, in a spirit of sympathetic concern, if they had actually made a wise lifestyle choice and gently suggesting that they might have a quieter, calmer and altogether much less stressful time if they opted for a nice little bungalow in Surbiton.

Just as things were reaching fever pitch on the forum, news came through that the Turkish authorities had decided that the whole thing would perhaps benefit from a little more studied approach prior to implementation and had cancelled the entire business and gone back to the *status quo ante*. This was good news for everyone concerned except our internet posters who now had to find something else to whinge about.

Everyone else heaved a sigh of relief and reverted to plan A, except those efficient buggers who had managed, in the space of a few days, to book and pay the deposit on a winter berth in some desolate, dusty, fly-blown, God-forsaken boatyard on a virtually uninhabited Aegean Greek island.

Please God, let those two raving tossers from the internet forum be amongst them.

Our visas were close to expiry, so we decided to make our way to Bodrum and take a visa run across to Kos. Bodrum was one of the first resorts in Turkey to be developed for mass tourism and it seems to specialise in a particular demographic.

Quiet, it ain't.

Kumbahce is the easternmost of the two bays, separated by a promontory capped by a fortress, that make up Bodrum's seafront. It's a picturesque little spot from the sea, but the Turkish Waters Pilot describes it as "a churning decibel Hell". Closer examination through binoculars gave a hint as to why. Along the bay are ranks of bars and restaurants, including the exquisite culinary delights of a Burger King and a McDonald's.

At either end of the bay were expansive open-air discos sporting speaker stacks capable of liquefying the kidneys at a range of several hundred metres. On the eastern end was 'Halicarnassus', which recently boasted itself as being the loudest open-air disco in the Mediterranean. On the Western end were several other establishments that seemed determined to wrest the title from it.

Among these was a huge catamaran of the type used as high-speed ferries between islands. The roof had been removed with a tin opener and gantries erected bearing laser lights and yet more giant speakers. At the front were two searchlights of the type used to target B52s on a high-altitude bombing run. This thing, apparently, set off at one in the morning loaded to the gunwales with already well-plastered holidaymakers and wandered round the bays blasting them even further into insensibility with a mixture of lager, vodka and club/garage/shed/shithouse classics at 140 dB. It returned, so the notices said, at five in the morning at which point all those revellers that had inexplicably failed to fall overboard were unceremoniously disgorged in a dishevelled heap on the quay

As darkness fell myriad coloured lights and signs lit up and reflected attractively, if somewhat gaudily, on the water. Then the music started, firstly from the bars and restaurants whose pathetic sound systems were able to do little more than make our ears bleed. About midnight the big guns from either end of the bay kicked in. We were anchored a fair distance from all of these and so were able to converse in the cockpit after a fashion by leaning close and shouting in each other's ears. Unfortunately, we were situated roughly equidistant from all of them and so received an equal mix of all of their auditory offerings, which presented itself as a wall of white noise with nothing else distinguishable other than the underlying 120 bpm thud that seemed common to every track in every establishment.

Still, thank God it was too early in the season for the catamaran to be running.

We were still there a week later when the bad weather hit. We weren't supposed to be in Bodrum. We weren't even supposed to be in Turkey - we had been trying to get into Kos for the last week. We wanted to do the paperwork to check into Greece, fill up with 1000 litres of diesel (£250 cheaper than doing it in Turkey), replace two new domestic batteries and convert Einstein's Turkish passport to an EU one while there was still an EU to do it in.

Kos is reckoned to be one of the best (and cheapest) marinas in Greece and the town has all the facilities we would need. Unfortunately, too many people seem to know about this and no matter which dates we tried to book a berth for, they always came back with 'Sorry - full up'. We decided to sit tight and give it another go when the weather had blown through.

"*We are currently holed up at anchor, waiting out a blow*" I put on the blog entry for that time. That implied a degree of security and cosiness, didn't it? Not so. The stress drove even the cat to drink.

The anchorage at Bodrum was crowded with moored gulets and anchored yachts all, like us, hiding from the forecast winds. The etiquette when anchoring is that when you arrive you have to keep clear of all those that arrived before you. Any that arrive after you, well that's their problem. They should have got up earlier. We were the last to arrive. The anchorage was so crowded that there was only really one place we could drop our anchor while still being able to veer enough chain without bumping into one of the other boats or straying onto rocks/shallow water/concrete jetties etc as the wind direction varied.

We dropped the anchor at the chosen spot, dug it in and waited for the blow. It did not disappoint. The wind climbed to 30 knots with some seriously nasty, much stronger, gusts suddenly hacking in from different directions. When a gust hit, the bow would swing off downwind until brought to a sudden halt when the anchor chain snatched bar-tight. Then the wind would force the stern downwind until the boat was pointing into wind and the stress on the anchor chain lessened a little. Things would settle down a little until another gust hacked in from a different direction and set the whole process off again.

I dived on the anchor. When it is really dug in it almost disappears below the sea bed, with only the chain and a little bit of roll bar showing. Not in this case. The anchor point was buried, but the rest was laying on its side, barely penetrating the seabed. Waggling it bout by hand didn't seem to do much good and we didn't have the sea room to go astern and try to dig it in more. I came up not overflowing with confidence.

It did hold, however, until early evening, when an extremely nasty gust pulled it out and we started drifting at a rather alarming rate.

It's not always easy to spot when you drag anchor. There's no loud bang followed by the boat suddenly lurching about. It may be followed by a series of loud bangs as you bagatelle off the other boats downwind, ripping chunks out of each other (mostly out of you if they're bloody great gulets). If you're lucky you spot more subtle signs before this happens, such as the fact that the relative positions of landmarks and other boats change rapidly, and the aspect of your boat to the wind remains constant instead of swinging about. A dead give-away, of course, is the anchor drag alarm screaming like a banshee. This was no use in this case as we had so little room around us that we would have been made aware of our plight by a moored tripper boat taking a chunk out of our topsides before the alarm had had time to go off.

We started the engine in record time and motored into wind, lifted the anchor, went further ahead than was really wise and dropped and reset it again. I dived on it again - same thing: In, but not enough to fill me with confidence and brio.

There was little else we could do but sit it out and keep a close eye on things. We sat down to a rather subdued and tee-total dinner. I elected to stay on anchor watch. Just after darkness fell, we dragged again. We blundered about in the darkness, trying to find a possible anchoring spot whilst simultaneously doing our best to avoid the other anchored boats. Some of these were not lit and it was difficult to pick out those anchor lights that there were from the background lights on the shore. We managed it and reset the anchor. Twice. We did three-hour spells on anchor watch during the hours of darkness. When the sun came up, Liz made a decision.

Perhaps we should clarify the command structure on *Birvidik*.

I am Captain - Master and Commander under God. My power is despotically absolute, and my word is law. I am responsible for all decisions on matters of seamanship and navigation. I determine, without let, hindrance or question, all actions on the boat and all tactics and boathandling.

This is where we come to trying to define the rather

fuzzy line between tactics and strategy, because Liz is Admiral and therefore responsible for all strategy. In effect, this means that I issue whatever orders Liz tells me to issue. It's a dandy system - works just fine and everyone's happy.

Liz's strategy was along the lines of 'Soddit, I've had enough of this - we'll go and pick up a buoy'.

On arrival we had noticed about 14 large mooring buoys just off the peninsula between the bays. They were obviously new and substantial, but there was no indication anywhere as to their ownership or purpose. There were no boats moored to them and no names or information on them. I had considered mooring up to one at the time, but had decided against it, not wanting to be turfed off by the rightful owner in the middle of the night and then having to find an anchoring spot in strong winds and darkness.

We went and picked up a buoy.

Having done so, I dived on the mooring. You can't be too careful with these. We have known bloody great buoys that look suitable for ocean going freighters to be attached to a weight you couldn't drown a cat with (sorry Einstein). Conversely, we've seen similar buoys attached to concrete blocks the size of Hertfordshire with what looks like a length of frayed knicker elastic. Neither in this case. The moorings were substantial enough to take an inter-island ferry. This is what worried me. I had visions of said leviathan returning at three in the morning and demanding its mooring back.

No-one bothered us. The security RIB from the marina came along after a couple of hours, circled us a couple of times, muttered something into his radio, listened to the squawked reply and then shot off again. We had, however, set a trend. By the evening loads of other yachts had come along, seen us moored to a buoy and thought 'That's a good idea'. The place was like a marine car-park in 24 hours.

We had two days on the buoy, during which we took the ferry trip to Kos in order to renew our Turkish visas. While we were there, we visited the marina in person to try to book in. Still no luck. So we decided to just turn up to try and force their hand.

Those of you who are paying attention may be

wondering why we bothered to renew our Turkish visas, given that we intended to be back in the EU in a couple of days.

The answer to this conundrum lies in a combination of geopolitical factors, navigational requirements, pointless bureaucratic obstinacy and personal idleness.

The first two combine to produce a situation where the best, safest and most enjoyable routes through the area involve jumping from island to mainland and back again in a series of zigzags. This, however, would require travelling from Turkey to Greece and back again every few days. This can be done, but if you did it properly you'd be spending most of your waking hours standing in a queue, groaning under the weight of great wads of paperwork. The rest of your waking hours would be spent watching the money pour out of your bank account as you paid all the associated costs.

Every time you enter Turkey from Greece you are supposed to go through the procedure detailed at the end of *An Idiot Aboard*. This includes buying a Turkish cruising log, which entitles you to cruise Turkish waters. The cruising log costs $40 and lasts for one year, which is very reasonable.

Unless you leave Turkey early that is, in which case you must check out and surrender your cruising log. If you come back into Turkey, you have buy a new one. This starts to add up if you're doing it every couple of days.

Things are no easier or cheaper on the Greek side. In fact, if anything the bureaucratic tedium is longer and more intense. However, as the Italian proverb goes, *Venire la legge, arriva il mezzo di evasione* (As comes the law, so comes the means of getting round it)[38]. The way round it, in this case, needs a combination of brass neck, bare-faced lies and, preferably, a boat with a very weak radar echo. It relies on the fact that bureaucrats the world over are very narrow minded and generally unimaginative. They are focussed on correct procedure to the exclusion of almost everything else and don't even recognise the existence of anything or anyone not specifically mentioned in their policy and instruction manuals.

In both countries, they have five prime interests:

Who are you?

Where have you come from?

Where are you going?

Do you owe us any money?

and (most importantly)

Are all your papers in order?

These interests, however, only apply to their own spheres of influence. As far as the Greeks are concerned, only Greek paperwork is important. Their ears prick up if they hear that you have come from Turkey as that affects *their* paperwork. It never even occurs to them to check your Turkish paperwork to see if you've checked out there. The same regime and attitudes prevail on the Turkish side. The basic rule is get yourself properly checked in and don't, whatever you do, check out.

You now have two mutually incompatible sets of paperwork. Do not get these confused. Keep them well away from each other. Opposite ends of the boat is good. Waving Greek paperwork at a Turkish official, or *vice versa*, causes consternation and confusion

Officials don't like anomalies or anything out of the ordinary. It unsettles them and makes them suspicious and that rarely leads to harmony and delight

All you have to do now is lie through your teeth on switching countries. Interestingly, they're only interested in where you've just come from, not where you came from before that. A little preparation here goes a long way. Before arriving at a Greek port from Turkey, for example, have a look at the chart and find a little Greek anchorage or small harbour, preferably uninhabited but certainly not big enough to warrant harbour officials or Port Police. Don't worry if it's poor holding or dangerously open to the weather – you're not going there. You're just going to *say* that you went there.

Memorise this name so that when asked where your last port of call was, call it out with bright confidence and without hesitation. This is usually enough to convince the most punctilious harbour official. The only time it is known to fail is when the area you named has, since the chart was printed, been converted to a huge naval base and declared off limits to all non-military vessels. That can lead to a degree of awkwardness.

When asked for your next port of call, casually name any Greek port in a 120 nautical mile radius. They're not interested, and they only ask it because the rule book says they have to. They never pass this information on and there's never a dejected-looking port official sitting on the quay forlornly waiting for the yacht that never came.

Firstly, though, we had to check back into Greece, so we cast off from the buoy and headed for Kos.

Kos, remember, has a reputation as the marina to which all other Greek marinas should aspire. It reputedly has helpful staff, good facilities, pleasant surroundings and low prices. Possibly for those reasons it appeared to be extremely popular. We had been trying to get in there over a period of three weeks. We particularly wanted Kos for several reasons, including the fact that it was a port of entry so we could do the paperwork, it had good chandlers so we could get some spares we needed, and it had a number of English speaking vets so we could organise Einstein's paperwork.

Our first approach, by email, elicited the response that they were full up, but try again in a few days. We tried again in a few days - still full up. This went on at intervals until they stopped replying to our emails. When we went over on the ferry and tried in person we still had no luck. We decided to just turn up and see what happened, and so we set off from Bodrum after The Unpleasantness and arrived off the marina. I called them on the radio. No reply. After the third unsuccessful call we just motored blithely into the marina, only to be met by a chappie in a RIB who told us they were full and would we kindly clear off and stop cluttering up his nice marina. He directed us to the old harbour about half a mile away, which the pilot says is usually full and advises that boats should go to the marina instead.

There was, however, plenty of room in the harbour and we dropped our stern anchor and moored bows to the quay. I set off to do the paperwork required for re-entering Greece from outside the EU. This involved first presenting our passports to immigration control, and then finding a port policewoman to accompany us back to the boat. She looked at our passports, looked at us, looked back at our passports, looked at the boat, looked at her watch and then filled in a two page form and crew list, stamped it several times, and told us we had to then take it back to immigration control. They stamped it several more times and laboriously hand copied the contents onto another, apparently identical form. Then they photocopied our form three times, their copy once, and sent us next door to customs.

Customs looked at all our forms, stamped them with a variety of different stamps and charged us 30 euros for a form (lovingly hand stamped) stating that we didn't owe them any money. They then sent us next door to Health, who repeated the process before issuing us with another form stating that we were fine healthy specimens and fit to be let into the EU. They did this without asking us any questions, let alone giving either of us even the most cursory of medical examinations. In fact, the whole procedure was carried out without so much a word from them and without Liz even being there. We could have been going down with virulent cases of swine flu, bubonic plague and Ebola virus simultaneously for all they knew.

The final hurdle was to clear through the Port Police, who were over the other side of the harbour. They won't even let you through the door there until the guy on the door has given you the third degree and you've waved all the aforementioned forms in his face. When he finally realises that you've done all the required paperwork and that he can't find a single reason to tell you to go away, he, rather disappointedly, presses a button and lets you in to the main building. Once in, you go down the corridor and wait patiently at the counter of the main office. This office had four people in it. One looked up from his desk as I walked in and immediately went out into what turned out to be the kitchen. Two others were going through a large pile of forms minutely scrutinising each one before stuffing them all in a large file and sticking it in a cupboard. They then opened another cupboard full of files and started on another pile.

Neither of them looked up.

The fourth member of the team had a bit of a problem here as she was sitting at the counter and I caught her off guard as I came in. She recovered magnificently though and promptly knocked a pile of files onto the floor which she then had to pick up. I suspect that she had a panic button under the desk for just such an eventuality because her phone then rang and she had to spend ten minutes on a long conversation.

She finally realised that I wasn't going to go away and took all my nice new forms, along with the boat's registration papers, the Greek cruising log, the insurance certificate, the crew list and our passports. She then wanted to know our fathers' forenames and our mothers' names, including maiden names along with their dates and places of birth. I just made up the last two.

The process culminated in a crescendo of stamping and signing. She had a range of stamps, ranging from elaborate neo-gothics at least 10 cm across, all scrolls and filigree, to several nifty little spring-loaded ones which sprang out of a cylinder the size of a fountain pen. She was particularly proud of these and made sure I saw the way they unfolded with a flourish at a flick of the wrist. I looked suitably impressed, smiled and made appreciative noises. I thought this wisest as she also had a bloody great gun and one of those spring-loaded batons. Well it was either that or one hell of a stamp. I paid the 15 euro fee for this entertainment and left. We were officially back in Greece. All that was left now was Einstein's paperwork.

Dreading the Kafkaesque nightmare that we anticipated, we found the vet. At first we thought our fears were well founded. "*Oooh no - bringing a cat in from Turkey - many problems. Hide all the Turkish documents, don't let anyone see them.*" She then said that we needed to start the whole process over again in Greece, new rabies jabs, new everything, wait a month, get blood serum tested, take out Turkish chip, put in new EU chip, put her in quarantine, burn all the evidence etc. When she mentioned quarantine it slowly dawned on us that she thought we wanted to take the cat back into Britain from Greece. When we said that this wasn't the case everything changed. Apparently it was only the UK that required all this. Everywhere else in the EU was perfectly happy with the documentation we already had.

Relieved, we left the vet's and decided to take a stroll to the see the jam-packed marina. When we got there, in the early evening, there were 40 unoccupied berths, over 10% of the total available. Each unoccupied berth cost the marina owners the berthing fee and potentially loses custom for all the businesses within and around the marina - bars, restaurants, shops, chandlers, laundries

I don't know what scam they're running there, but it's losing quite a number of people quite a bit of money. However, we had got done what we had wanted to get done and set off.

From Kos it was a quick hop North via Kalymnos, Leros and Lipsos before cutting back to Turkey at Kuşadası so that we could visit Ephesus, one of the major classical sites, up there with Delphi. It is so popular, in fact, that there can be up to eight bloody great cruise ships moored in Kuşadası harbour at any one time, all ready to disgorge over a thousand people each into fleets of coaches to ferry them to Ephesus. Add to that the coaches from all the other tourist sites in the near (and not so near) vicinity and you can see that it can get just a teensy bit crowded.

Kuşadası is a good example of the way that cruise ships distort the local economy; a point we will return to when we get to Olympia in Greece.

Given the popularity of the site, it was strange then that there appeared to be only one set of toilets in the whole 3km x 2 km area. To be fair, there was a communal Roman era toilet in front of the library, but the sewer wasn't connected and anyway, they'd run out of sponges on sticks for the post-defecatory ablutions.

Public transport to the site was also fairly sparse, consisting of buses or dolmuses[39] that dropped you off on the main road at the turning for Ephesus. It was a pleasant enough stroll the two kilometres or so through the countryside to the site entrance, although if you'd believed the taxi drivers that swarmed round you when you got off the dolmus, you'd have thought it was the equivalent of crossing the Sahara on foot.

Ephesus was a major port in Roman times, and it shows in the grandeur and scale of the place. We took a hint from Stuart and Steph and timed our visit to coincide with the extended lunches provided for all the tour groups. It was packed when we arrived at about 11:30, but by one o'clock it was virtually deserted and remained so.

The signs and notices all around had great screeds on them in Turkish and what purported to be English. It wasn't the sort of cod-English and appalling translations that returning travellers recount at dinner parties with an air of smug, patronising superiority. You know, things like

Please do not empty your dog here

Tree worrying is an offence. Sheep caught will be shot.

Please SING your bill before chucking out

Take notice of safe – the slippery are very crafty.

Or finally, my favourite, which is so surreal I can't even start to work out what it's trying to say:

Please present your octopus on entry

No, these signs were in very erudite English - so erudite, in fact, that we couldn't understand it. They either used very obscure technical English or they had just Anglicised technical Turkish or Greek words. To give you a flavour: *"In front of the apse stood an altar, which eventually yielded to a semicircular synthronos. The substructure of the ambos is bounded by the templon. The chapel-like pastopheries show apsidal characteristics and have a narrow narthex added."* Well, all I can say is that had to sit on my *synthronos* and ponder the mysteries of the *narthex* before seeing if I could find anything to eat in the *pastopheries*.

Much play is made of St. Paul's visit to Ephesus. As a kid I'd had to suffer interminable, droning sermons reading out his epistles to the Ephesians, but I'd no idea who or what they were and cared even less. Here it was brought to life.

Ephesus was a centre for the worship of the Goddess Artemis and made a substantial amount of money out of this, thank you very much.

Craftsmen such as stonemasons and silversmiths made a tidy living flogging effigies of Artemis and similar tat to the pilgrims and devotees that visited in their thousands. I think their descendants are keeping up the family tradition in the innumerable stalls lining both approaches to the site.

When they heard that Paul was preaching One God and that idols made by man could not be Gods and should not be worshipped, they saw a bit of a cloud on the business horizon. I mean - Statues and stuff, that's real craftsmanship. Any old tinpot stone-chipper can knock out a cross.

A silversmith called Demetrious turned out to be a Roman forerunner of the President of the Chamber of Commerce. When Paul was due to preach in the large amphitheatre, Demetrious rounded up all the artisans, who descended on the place in their thousands (I told you it was big business). They drowned Paul out with chants of *"Artemis is Great! Artemis is Great!"* and proceeded to wrap things up with a good riot. All of this, we feel, gives support and credence to those of us bemoaning the inexorable decline in the quality of philosophical discourse today. The Classical Era truly was a golden age

The artisans won, and Paul was told to sling his hook by the city authorities and went away to irritate the Macedonians. Life, and business, went on as normal for the Ephesians and the trinket shops continued doing a roaring trade. Now you wouldn't get that sort of exploitation of the gullible and the credulous from a monotheistic religion, would you?

Talking of monotheistic religions, we overheard a couple of tour guides talking to each other. Apparently, guide A was describing to guide B how she had been showing round a group of Americans from a cruise ship and had got as far as the amphitheatre. She began the story of Paul's preaching there, as outlined above, and was thrown off her stride somewhat when one of her charges emitted a strangled cry and fell to his knees crying *"Lord, Brother*

Paul, I feel your presence here!" This set off about twenty others, some of whom started writhing on the floor and speaking in tongues (or 'gibberish' as we ex-scientists call it). The cruise company hadn't told her that the group were mainly evangelists from the American bible belt. This, of course, provoked the interest of the rest of the tourists much more than a bunch of old ruins did and she and her charges soon became hemmed in on all sides by rubber-neckers. She didn't know where to put herself and just whistled nonchalantly and pretended she'd never seen these strange people before in her life.

I just wish we'd been there at the time. We could have started all the onlookers up chanting *"Artemis is Great! Artemis is Great!"* and drowned the evangelists out.

We got our come-uppance for our heretical frivolity the next day when a thunderstorm hit the marina. We weren't unduly worried as we were secured to a concrete quay at the bow and had a strong line out the stern, pulled tight to the marina's heavy mooring blocks. The rain fell in torrents so that it was impossible to see one end of the boat from the other and the wind built up to an impressive strength. We took all the cushions from the cockpit and retired below to snug it out. Smug turned to *'ooh - that doesn't look right'* when I looked out of the window during a particularly evil gust and saw that we were alongside a boat that was originally about eight metres away and were moving forwards relative to it. As I dived for the hatch there was a resounding bang and a crunch from the bow as it ploughed into the concrete quay, taking a chunk out of it (the bow, not the quay).

We ran on deck, started the engine and went astern to pull us off the quay. Then we plonked fenders in the most needed spots and attended to the stern line. It had gone completely slack. I pulled on it, expecting to find a loose end, but it gradually pulled up tight and, with aid of our biggest winch, we pulled in about six metres of line and dragged ourselves back into the right position. We have no idea exactly what happened there. We suspect that the lines had been crossed at some point and that a loop had been trapped somewhere and had pulled through with the massive load on it. Luckily, Aegean thunderstorms only hang around for an hour or two. Shouldn't take me long to patch up the bow.

Our confidence in the shelter and security of the marina somewhat undermined, we set off into the Aegean the next day for a few anchorages before going back into Greece.

The Aegean? Don't talk to me about the bloody Aegean. Wine-dark sea my arse; wind-tossed sea more like. The predominant wind in the summer is the meltemi, which gets its name from the Turkish for 'bad tempered'. Calling this bastard 'bad tempered' is on a par with saying that Victor Meldrew is somewhat less than charitable in his assessment of his fellow man.

After the quay-ramming debacle in Kuşadası we set of for Kirkdilim, a secluded little anchorage about 40 nautical miles to the North West. The forecast was for a West to South-westerly force 3. A nice gentle sail. Hah!

The sea was quite lumpy as we pulled out of the marina, but nothing serious. We put it down to a hangover from the storm of the day before. Einstein was in DEFCON 1, which we thought was good for these conditions. She must have been getting used to things.

The wind (and waves) steadily increased and veered round to end up dead on the nose. It blew up to about 25 - 30 knots and produced one of those nasty short steep seas that the Aegean seems so fond of throwing at us. It got the wavelength exactly right at just over half the length of the boat. At this length the waves and boat head straight at each other in a game of chicken. The boat climbs the approaching wave and, as it reaches the crest, the bow projects past the crest into thin air, counterbalanced by the greater weight of the remainder of the boat aft of the fulcrum. As they continue past each other the bow rises higher above the water surface until the crest of the wave passes under the centre of gravity of the boat. At this point the forward half of the boat finds itself unsupported some two metres up in the air. Gravity takes over and 16 tonnes of boat dives down into the trough, just in time for the next approaching wave to dump on top of it. The buoyancy of the bow, now about half a metre under water, forces it to rise and sends a wall of green water back along the deck and the whole process starts off again. This continued at about 12 second intervals for 6 hours until we got into the lee of the anchorage. Einstein, meanwhile, moved rapidly from DEFCON 1 through to DEFCON 3.

Kirkdilim, like many of the anchorages mentioned in the pilot, is described as 'Good shelter from the Meltemi'. Whenever I read that phrase, my mind's eye conjures up a comforting little picture of a calm, quiet, idyllic oasis, protected from the wind and the waves wreaking havoc outside on the open sea. In this oasis, *Birvidik* would sit calmly at anchor, snugly protected while we lay on deck and took refreshing swims in the cosily sheltered waters.

Wrong.

'Good shelter from the Meltemi' means that the really big, nasty waves it knocks up can't get in and give you a good kicking. The wind itself almost invariably can, and does. If it can't gust through a gap in the mountains and get you, it will work its way round them or, if all else fails, just climb up over the top of them, whistle down the other side like a schoolboy on a banister and dump on you with the added assistance of gravity. Just to make things even more interesting it does this in gusts of wildly varying strength and direction, slewing the bow from one side to the other *á la* Bodrum. It puts enough of a strain on the anchor to make you wary of leaving the boat unattended and taking a look ashore. Just to make sure you stay marooned on the boat it also kicks up enough of a chop in the limited fetch of the anchorage to ensure that any dinghy ride to shore is certain to get you seriously wet.

The Aegean took its eye off the ball for the next couple of days and we had a calm and pleasant trip up to the tiny Greek island of Inoussa before going on to Lesbos.

Inoussa is a paradoxical little island. It is only seven kilometres by two kilometres and has a population of under 800. It is sleepy almost to the point of comatose. We walked from one end to the other and didn't see a soul. Not a solitary vehicle passed us. There is only one shop on the whole island, a baker. All shopping other than for bread involves a 20-kilometre ferry trip across the Khios straits to Khios town.

It is also the mother-island to five of the most successful ship owning families in Greece and as a result is one of the wealthiest islands in the country. Most of its richer alumni live elsewhere most of the year but they maintain their links and have palatial and well-appointed houses on the island.

They also earn the gratitude and acceptance of their fellow Oinoussans by sponsoring public works and community facilities. Public buildings are immaculately maintained, and the island boasts a sports and social centre that would not be out of place in a town the size and wealth of Sevenoaks.

The Oinoussans' attitude to money seems to be that there is so much of it sloshing around that it is treated as a sort of disposable resource. This worked to our advantage.

The harbour is well sheltered and equipped with strong moorings along with water and electricity points. I enquired at the only other occupied boat as to how I went about paying for mooring fees, water and electricity. *"You don't"*, he replied. *"Just plug in and take what you like – it's all free."* I expressed gratitude and surprise at this unparalleled generosity. He replied that the facilities were installed and maintained by wealthy expatriate Oinoussans and the local municipality thought it was more effort than it was worth to go to the bother of collecting payments from passing yotties.

The only stipulation, he continued, was that you all had to clear out of it in August. That was when the expatriate cash dispensers returned to their home island for the annual visit and homage paying. They did this in their flash gin palaces, which completely filled the small harbour and enabled their owners to strut up and down the harbour playing *"Look! Haven't I done well - mine's bigger/more expensive/flashier than yours."*

It struck me as a parallel with old school reunions. People don't attend them to rekindle old friendships. They do it to measure up what they've achieved in life with the pathetic efforts of their erstwhile school contemporaries. Who's got the flashest car, who's best kept their figure (and hair), who's gone on to fame and fortune. That's why only the flashest, best looking, most successful bastards with the most stunning trophy spouses ever bother turning up. Saddos like me keep well out of it and send apologetic notes saying we'd love to attend but it clashes with the James Bond audition and anyway that Nobel Prize acceptance speech isn't going to write itself.

We took grateful advantage of the island's largesse and stayed three days before heading off North to Mytilini on Lesbos.

Once we got there, however, the Aegean got back into its stride. The forecast was for 25 - 30 knots from the North. The reality was 35 knots gusting 45. This continued for two weeks solid. We remained in Mytilini with our heads down. Others, either less fortunate or more foolhardy, limped in over the duration in varying states of disrepair - blown out foresails, various bits broken or missing.

Wusses 1, big hairy sailors nil.

On our arrival in Mytilini, we were surprised to see that the town quay was almost deserted, and those few boats that were in residence were moored alongside. This was virtually unheard of. Greek town quays are usually packed to the gunwales in high summer and you have to moor bows or stern-to. We eventually discovered that this unusual state of affairs was the result of a prime example of one of the defining traits of the yottie, namely a level of parsimony that would put Scrooge to shame. Our archetypal yottie is a cheapskate *par excellence.*

Yotties may look like a bunch of down and outs living a semi-feral existence on the fraying edges of society, but don't be fooled by appearances. Most of us are reasonably comfortably off. OK, we're not up there with the Warren Buffets, the Roman Abramoviches and the Jeff Bezos of this world, but the vast majority of us are far from skint. Most of us certainly have considerably more wealth and income than do most of those living in the countries we visit.

This, however, fails to stop Mr Yottie from displaying an extreme degree of financial paranoia.[40] He lives in a state of constant anxiety, convinced that he is about to be ripped off at every turn by swarthy Johnny Foreigner. His prime objective is to get as much as he feasibly can for as close to nothing as is humanly possible.

He eschews those picturesque waterside bars with their crisp white linen tablecloths and their bougainvillea-shaded comfortable seats. He patronises (in both senses of the word) some seedy, grubby, care-worn, dusty shack with a view over the main road to the local sewage works, all because it saves him 20 cents on a beer. He reckons that the fact that the beer is warm and flat and that the glass is chipped and smeared with fingerprints and a smudge of lipstick is a small price to pay for such a saving.

He also argues that roughing it like this brings him closer to the real people of the country and gives him a truer and more real experience of the culture.

No it bloody doesn't.

His drinking companions would be down at those waterside bars in a flash if they weren't undocumented immigrants hired on a daily basis and paid three euros a fortnight for 12-hour days in the blistering sun picking prickly pears with their bare hands.

Our yottie's eating out is primarily based on gyros or doners, which are congealed rancid fat-burgers stuffed into a stale pita. If not those, then his staple foodstuffs are *soi-disant* casseroles constructed primarily of the minced viscera of thankfully unidentifiable roadkill. OK – it's furring up his arteries like a kebab shop's drains but look how much it's saving him. Should Mrs. Yottie actually manage to cajole him into a halfway decent restaurant (say for a significant birthday or wedding anniversary) he finally capitulates with extremely bad grace and expects eternal abject gratitude and daily marital privileges in perpetuity. He is invariably disappointed. On both counts.

Spending on clothes in any form is obviously anathema. He makes an exception for tools, which he classifies as 'essentials' and looks upon as 'investment' rather than 'expenditure'. This classification holds even when it becomes glaringly apparent that the tool in question is only ever going to be used once and will then be consigned to obscurity under a pile of frayed bits of rope in the bottom of the most inaccessible locker on the boat.

The most important target for his frugality is expenditure on mooring charges. He will forego water, electricity, easy access to shore and even secure shelter unless driven to it. He avoids marinas except in absolute emergencies.

Unless, of course, it happens to be free.

This is not as rare as the non-yottie might on the surface expect, especially in Greece. Up until the bubble burst in 2008, EU Regional Development and Infrastructure grants led to construction being started on a rash of marinas throughout the country.

In the EU's mind the plan was simple and virtually foolproof. They would give the Greek municipality a low or no interest loan, which would be used to finance the construction of the basic infrastructure of the marina or harbour – breakwaters, pontoons, moorings, water, electricity supplies and the like. Once all this had been done, the local municipality would take over, start renting out spaces in the harbour or marina, and repay the loan out of the proceeds. Wonderful system; the region gets its harbour or marina and a steady income stream, and the EU gets its money back to fund someone else's development. Everybody wins.

The EU, however, didn't have the measure of the Greeks. They should have known better, especially as even a cursory glance at the amateurishly doctored national accounts the Greek government brazenly put forward to it[41] should have set alarm bells ringing loud enough to wake up even a Brussels techno-bureaucrat after a heavy lunch. I don't know about bewaring Greeks bearing gifts. The EU would have been better served bewaring Greeks receiving gifts, for there was a glaring hole in the EU's logic which, to the Byzantine Greek mind, stood out like a Rasta at Glyndebourne. All they had to do was not finish it. Almost finish it, but not quite. If it's not finished, then they can't rent out spaces. If they can't rent out spaces, then they have no income stream.

Not looking so good a plan so far, is it. Stick with me.

If it's not finished and they have no income stream, then they don't have to repay the loan.

But...

They have a perfectly useable harbour which local boat owners, fishermen and ferries can use to their heart's content, and all absolutely free. In addition, the free mooring attracts hordes of yotties who spend in the local businesses. OK, most of them are so tight they squeak when they walk and could be outspent by a hermit on an economy drive, but no plan's perfect.

It was just such a phenomenon that explained the great availability of mooring space on Mytilini town quay. Just across the bay was an almost, but not quite, finished marina. It was complete with moorings, sanitary block, utility pods and lifting bay. We had a look and reckoned the only things they hadn't done were plant flowers in the display pots and get the swinging barrier on the road entrance operational.

It was chocker – jam packed with ferries, yotties and local fishing and pleasure boats, all plugged into the mains and hosing their boats down liberally. Admittedly it was far less conveniently situated than the town quay and had an atmosphere of isolated desolation, but by God it was free and so were water and electricity. Our assembled yotties were in hog heaven.

Their ecstatic bliss, however, was short-lived. The local municipality had failed to keep up to speed with Greek/EU procedures and had rashly finished the marina. The first we heard of this was on the Saturday, when the Port Police knocked on the hull and informed us that we could no longer lay alongside but would have to pull off and moor bows-to. *"Why is this necessary all of a sudden?"* I asked.

"Because as from Monday" she replied *"we are expecting a lot of boats. On Monday the marina starts charging."* She was right. The marina started charging at midday. By eight in the morning they were pouring out in

hordes. By nine thirty the bay resembled a re-enactment of Dunkirk and by eleven o'clock the boats on the town quay were so tightly packed you couldn't slide a rizla in between them.

Things eased somewhat the next morning when most of the yotties discovered that they still had to pay some trifling amount for electricity, water and mooring. A good 80 percent of them buggered off to sit it out at some god-forsaken, swell-ridden, wind-blasted anchorage.

"*Sod that!*" we thought. We paid up and stayed put.

If you ask him (in truth, even if you don't), the average yottie will happily blether on interminably about the many noble reasons why he chose the cruising lifestyle. These will be numerous, varied and often internally inconsistent. We have, for example, been solemnly informed on more than one occasion that the speaker had left England for foreign shores because the country was being over-run with bloody foreigners. Other reasons will frequently include '*experiencing different cultures*' and '*meeting like-minded people*' (possibly just a tad contradictory), but they will almost invariably mention a burning desire to be free of the overweening bureaucracy and petty restrictions that characterize modern life.

These noble sentiments are, of course, a load of old tosh. In reality, they are a psychological re-write to act as justification for a far baser motive, namely the state of his wallet. A desire to remain below the bureaucratic radar has more to do with avoiding taxes than with reveling in the heady freedoms of self-reliance.

Imagine the reaction, then, when the Greeks, having been lectured by all and sundry (including most of the cruising community) on the virtues of fiscal responsibility, paying their taxes and living within their means, announced that they intended to introduce a tax on all boats using Greek waters. Cue apoplectic outbursts of spluttering rage from the assembled yotties. It became the prime subject of bar-room debating clubs and yottie internet fora throughout the Mediterranean.

This, of course, should come as no surprise to anyone

with even a modicum of understanding of the human psyche. I suspect that cognitive dissonance, or the ability to hold two contradictory beliefs in the head simultaneously, is the default position for the human mind. It is for mine anyway.

Considerable psychological research has shown that not just Bono but the majority of people would, if given a referendum on such matters, vote for reduced taxes *and* increased public spending. If it is gently pointed out to them that increased public spending inevitably requires increased taxation then they go down one of two routes: either they suggest that public spending is increased where it would benefit them and decreased where it wouldn't or they employ a similar tactic on taxation whereby it should be decreased if it applies to them and increased on some other demographic. The really clever ones conflate the two approaches and completely muddy the waters. These people usually enter politics or own/edit newspapers.

You can instantly gauge the target demographic of a newspaper by the type of tax it demonises and the areas of public spending it advocates. Thus the tax *bêtes noir* of the Torygraph are the top rate of income tax, corporation tax, any form of tax on unearned income and inheritance tax. Especially inheritance tax. In the realm of public spending it argues for cuts in benefits and in favour of taxpayer bailouts of failed banks. The Grauniad, by contrast, bleats on about the bedroom tax, offshore avoidance schemes, universal credit shortcomings and why gay cyclists, especially female or transgender ones, should be entitled to tax breaks. The Daily Wail, meanwhile, concentrates on such lofty topics as speed cameras, parking fines, unrepaired potholes and anything that affects the price of gin and tonics.

So, how does our yottie deal with this new taxation, this loss of a fundamental foundation of his equanimity? The Kübler-Ross model in psychological theory predicts he should go through the classic five stages of bereavement – denial, anger, bargaining, depression and acceptance[42]. Many yotties, however, seem to get stuck before they even hit the halfway mark.

Denial is easy – Fingers in the ears and shout *'la la la*

la' very loudly. Many yotties, therefore, claim that the whole business is just a rumour put about by trolls trying to frighten honest cruisers off so that said trolls have a better choice of mooring spots. This belief becomes more difficult to maintain as evidence builds up to the point of official communications from Greek government departments confirming the tax. These usually lead to a change of tactic whereby the yotties accept that the tax is there, but argue that the Greeks will never get organised enough to actually implement it. The history of Greek bureaucracy lends some credence to this belief even, or perhaps especially, amongst many Greeks.

Anger - ah yes. Yotties can be very good at that. Unfortunately for most of them, especially the green ink brigade that tend to lurk in the darker recesses of internet fora, this is as far as they get. Raising the subject simultaneously raises blood pressure, indignation and myocardial infarction rates dramatically. These are frequently accompanied by stereotype-riddled, xenophobic outbursts of which even Greece's Golden Dawn thugs would be proud; except that in the yotties' diatribes the vitriol is aimed at the Greeks themselves rather than the Roma, Albanians, Arabs, Pakistanis and all nationalities of sub-saharan Africa as is the case with Golden Dawn.

The arguments proffered by our yotties against their having to pay this tax are a simmering mélange of special pleading, reasoning from false premises, straw men. *ad hominem* attacks, dark threats of fiscal ruin for the Greek holiday industry and shooting the messenger. Bar-room lawyers bring out outrageously unsubstantiated interpretations of half invented provisions of international maritime law relating to the right of innocent passage. The Cruising Association and the RYA are slandered and pilloried for failing to use their supposed mighty international influence to compel a sovereign government to follow their instructions regarding matters of internal taxation. How on earth do these rabid lunatics expect them to do that - they're yachting organisations for God's sake, not the bloody European Commission or Rupert Murdoch.

In essence though, their reaction boils down to the following beautifully structured line of reasoning: *"It's not fair! Don't wanna pay it. Why do I have to pay it? Other countries' yotties don't have to pay it. Someone make them stop making me pay it. I'm gonna take my boat and go home. So there!"*

We though, in common with about six other yotties in the whole of Greece, have worked our way through all five stages to acceptance. *If* they finally work out how to collect it, *and* they find us, *and* they make the effort to ask us, then we'll pay it. In our case this works out at 120 euros a month, or 70 euros a month if paid a year in advance.

We can live with that.

Just.[43]

All of this reflects and exemplifies a common facet of the yottie lifestyle. Whenever yotties are faced with more taxation, or additional costs in any form, there is the usual furore in cheap bars and on internet fora. During these full and frank discussions, the view is often proposed that the authorities have shot themselves in the foot with these unjust and rapacious demands. Liveaboard yotties, they confidently assert, make a significant year-round contribution to the local economy; a contribution that will be lost when armadas of indignant yotties vote with their keels and bugger off to fairer, more amenable and financially compliant jurisdictions who know how to balance a budget.

This, of course, is absolute balls.

Fairness and morality don't come into it. It's all about maximising income. The authorities know how the financial land lies. The liveaboard yottie is hoist by his own frugal petard. The average flotilla holidaymaker spends more on a couple of lunches than our yottie does in total over half the year. Our flotilla skipper isn't bothered in the slightest by a 1500 euro a year cruising tax on his boat that will add about 20 quid a head to the cost of the holiday; they'll spend that on breakfast without blinking an eye.

When the wind eventually dropped to the merely vile, we decided we'd had enough of the Aegean, scrapped the idea of going up to the Bosphorus and turned and ran South. Two long and lumpy (but at least downwind) runs brought us to Posidionion on Samos where we spent a welcome, uncharacteristic and unexpected three days at anchor, snugly protected while we lay on deck and took refreshing swims in the cosily sheltered waters etc. The met showed NE force fours so we thought it would be an exhilarating downhill run to the tiny island of Agathonisi.

It's amazing how quickly you forget, isn't it? What we got were 25 knots on the nose and those nasty short seas again. Einstein to DEFCON 3. The main anchorage in Agathonisi was crowded and plagued by ferries so we anchored with a line ashore in a smaller bay which promised better shelter from the rapidly increasing wind.

The advantage of anchoring with a line to the shore, as I've mentioned before, is that one end of the boat is attached to a bloody great rock or tree which, generally, tends to stay in roughly the same place. The disadvantage is that the other end of the boat is held in place by your anchor. This isn't too too bad (deliberate repetition, Jersey dialect) as long as the wind comes from behind, when the tree takes the strain, or dead ahead, when the anchor is pulled in a straight line, the way it's designed to be loaded, and where the boat presents the minimum surface area to the wind. What you don't want, which of course is what we got, is for the wind to blow directly beam on. In this situation the boat presents the maximum surface area to the wind and the pull on the anchor is sideways, which it doesn't like too much. The only situation less secure than this is when the wind switches through 180 degrees and then blows beam on from the other side, thus giving the anchor a nice little waggle as well. Well, obviously, we got that too.

Winds generally die down a bit at night, but not this time. We took turns on anchor watch throughout the night. The big worry is that if the anchor drags, the stern of the boat is still attached to the land by about 50 metres of 12-millimetre rope. The boat would then describe a graceful arc, pivoting about the tree or rock and nestle sideways onto the rocky shore and bump up and down vigorously. As trying to manoeuvre your way out of this while tied to a tree is somewhat problematic, we tied a knife next to the rope so that when disaster struck we could cut it and run. As a precaution we'd taken a compass bearing which should have got us out of the bay and into the open sea.

The anchor held, though, and at first light we heaved a sigh of relief, cast off and hi-tailed it back to Turkey, where you tend to be on the edges of the Meltemi rather than slap bang in the middle of it.

Once back in Turkey, we turned right and gently pottered our way South. The nice little cottage in the Cotswolds, which had been beginning to seem very desirable, slowly started to lose its appeal. I suppose cruising is a bit like childbirth - if you could actually remember it in all its gruesome detail, you'd only do it the once.

You can never completely relax in the cruising life, though. The Aegean hadn't finished with us yet. Before we escaped its clutches by rounding Turkey's south-western corner we had to suffer *The Gust from Hell*.

Gulluk Korfezi is a large bay indented into the Turkish coast, scattered with what promised to be sheltered anchorages and harbours. We made our way along the north coast of the bay, *via* a couple of anchorages that seemed, at first, to live up to expectations. Until the night that is. The winds around here are supposed to have a thermal component and to peak in mid-afternoon and die off at night. Well, they peaked at mid-afternoon alright, but resolutely refused to die off at night, gusting strongly until about six in the morning when they took a break to gather their strength for the next day's onslaught.

The winds are hot; it feels as if someone has just opened the door on a gigantic fan-assisted oven. This, combined with the fierce sun, managed to produce ambient daytime temperatures in the mid 40s. Such a combination has a desiccating effect. Despite drinking around seven litres of water each per day we were still dehydrated, producing tiny amounts of dark, mahogany-coloured urine. You didn't really want that much detail, did you. We had visions of a local fisherman coming across *Birvidik* drifting aimlessly like the *Marie Celeste*, its spectral, mummified crew sitting round the cockpit table staring sightlessly at an empty water bottle; their shrivelled, wrinkled skins tanned like old leather armchairs.

We ventured further into the gulf, searching for that elusive shelter, meeting force seven winds off several of the capes, and eventually motored into Asin Limani at the head of the bay. This is a picturesque little harbour, protected by Byzantine breakwaters and towers, overlooked by the ruins of ancient Iassos. It also had the added attraction of water taps on the quay. We were by now down to our 20 litre emergency backup jerry can. We dropped the stern anchor and moored bows to.

The wind, characteristically, blew strongly on the beam and slewed *Birvidik* over, bring her bow perilously close to the concrete quay. We pulled in on the stern anchor and put out lines from both sides to stop her moving sideways. This seemed to do the trick and we entered smug mode and sat in the cockpit surveying our handiwork. Poseidon obviously took umbrage at this hubris and conjured a large swell out of nowhere which proceeded to make the boat pitch up and down, putting extra strain on the stern anchor and pounding the bow perilously close to the quay (again). We slacked off the bow lines and pulled up on the stern line to take us further off. This had the desired effect, but you now needed to be an Olympic long jump contender to get on or off the boat.

Never mind, it seemed to do the trick and the wind and swell even died off early evening and, as a bonus, remained absent the next morning. We took advantage of this to do shopping and ruin visiting. We returned to the boat, planning to go out for a well-deserved meal that evening. Liz went off for an extended swim and I relaxed in the cockpit with some penny-dreadful novel. This relaxation lasted for all of an hour and a half.

There was no wind at all, and no swell. Flat calm. I laid the book down, closed my eyes and savoured the moment; the soft lapping of the water, the calls of the kingfishers as they swooped over the harbour edge and the gentle rocking of the boat. In less than five seconds my idyll was rudely shattered. *The Gust From Hell* appeared out of nowhere. It hit the boat on the beam at about 35 - 40 knots, rolling the boat over by about 45 degrees and tipping me onto the cockpit floor. The wind generator screamed and the sunshades cracked like whips. The contents of shelves threw themselves on the floor and lay higgledy-piggledy all over the saloon and aft cabin. After about 15 seconds of this the stern anchor gave up the unequal struggle and the boat lurched forwards and crunched sickeningly into the rough concrete quay. Why does this always happen on rough concrete quays and never on nice rubber-fendered pontoons?

I leapt to my feet, uttered several seamanlike incantations ("*What the F...?*"), started the engine and put the boat astern against the bow lines to take her off the quay. Just as I did this, the wind disappeared as suddenly and as unexpectedly as it had arrived. The least it could have done was to have said goodbye. The whole episode has lasted less than a minute. I, however, was still in a state of jittery, swivel-eyed nervous expectation when Liz got back to the boat. The gust must have been incredibly localised as she had not felt anything, and she was just on the other side of the small harbour.

We pulled up on the stern anchor, but no longer had any faith in it. That put the block on the evening meal out. We cast off and got the Hell out of there. Just as well as it turned out. When we lifted the stern anchor it was apparent that the harbour floor was very soft, runny mud. As the anchor came up the mud just ran off it. Any decent blow would have pulled it through, and we'd have head-butted the quay again. We left the harbour and anchored around the corner, in a large bay with plenty of swinging and dragging room. Hardly had we dropped the anchor and checked it by reversing against it at 1000 revs when the wind came up again, gusting to 30 - odd knots from different directions.

Sod this, we decided, we're off to a marina for a couple of days. Yalikavak looked tempting.

The wind picked up as we approached Yalikavak marina, which made mooring an interesting experience, but

Liz was getting pretty good at the technicalities of boat handling; namely wiggling the wheel, waggling the throttle and woggling the bow thrusters. After The Unpleasantness at Kuşadası, we gave the lazy line a good testing with the engine, just to be on the safe side. We then relaxed into the luxuries of marina life - secure mooring, no worries about dragging anchors, easy access to shore, plentiful and convenient supplies and unlimited water and electricity. There was, however, the slight drawback of 55 euros a day, but we just put our fingers in our ears and shouted 'La la la la'. We washed the boat and ourselves with copious quantities of water, strolled into town for a pizza, wandered round the lively and colourful town, came back to the boat, crashed out early and slept like logs.

The next morning we got up, let Einstein out, and settled in the cockpit with tea and coffee to enjoy the early morning. Einstein, of course, was thrilled to find boats either side and set off to have a good sniff and explore. She had developed a habit of doing this whenever the opportunity arises and usually came back demanding food after about half an hour.

After about an hour and a half, Liz thought she really ought to go and see what Einstein was up to - we didn't want someone casting off and sailing halfway across the Aegean before finding a ginger stowaway throwing up on their bedding. There was no sign of her on the adjoining boat, or any of the boats nearby. Neither was she on the pontoon. Liz got out the sure-fire 'retrieve the cat' tools of the birdie whistle and the box of treats. Blowing the whistle and rattling the box usually brings her running from even the furthest reaches of a marina. No luck.

Liz started walking up and down the pontoons, blowing the birdie whistle and rattling the treats box. This elicited no cat, although she was the recipient of a considerable number of askance looks.

(*"Mummy - why is that strange lady walking up and down the pontoon, doing a really rather realistic impersonation of a nightingale whilst rattling a box, and shouting out the name of a well-known, but deceased physicist?"*

"Shh dear. Just ignore her and with any luck she won't come over and try to engage us in conversation.")

As an aside, this has echoes of when our English Setter, 'Bones', escaped one night and I garnered some very dubious looks wandering through the nearby churchyard at midnight shouting *"Bones! Bones! Come here Bones!"* They can be very superstitious in Jersey. When I realised how my actions might have been interpreted, I half expected a procession of retarded, disfigured, in-bred, flaming torch carrying peasants to march up to the house and burn it to the ground. All it needed was a thunderstorm.

However, to return to the subject. Liz did, eventually, hear a faint cry of distress. Casting off shame and self-consciousness, she continued up and down the pontoon which appeared to be the source of the cries until she homed in on one spot. Underneath the pontoon was Einstein; standing on a wooden cross tree up to her neck in water and shivering uncontrollably. Liz lay on the pontoon, reached under and hauled her out by the harness. How the cat managed to fall off a metre and a half wide pontoon while the sea was flat calm is beyond us. But obviously not beyond her.

Back on board we towel-dried the bedraggled, shivering, complaining mess and then put antiseptic and tape on all the claw marks covering our arms and upper torsos.

That cat is bloody useless. She has the grace and co-ordination of Ted Bundy when they threw the switch on Old Sparky and the delicate, feline sure-footedness of Boris Karloff's Frankenstein.

She does, however, have one unexpected talent that belies her air of general incompetence. She's a genius at computing. She loves computers. It's the heat, I suspect. We would go to inordinate lengths to provide her with nice comfy bedding, only to find her slumped uncomfortably and inelegantly on a hard laptop.

"Nice, cosy box, complete with furry rug madame?"
"Nah! Where's that Acer Aspire E15?"

"How about a cushioned cat bed, ergonomically designed for maximum pussy comfort?"

"Haven't you got a Lenovo Thinkpad E580, preferably with a UHD graphics 620 and a nice hard titanium case?"

If there's one thing she likes more than a nice, warm, comfy closed laptop, it's a nice, warm, comfy open laptop, with a nice, warm, comfy, knobbly keyboard to sit on. This is bliss in Einstein world, especially when the hard drive kicks in.[44] The only thing that could possibly improve on this ecstatic state of affairs is my trying to do some work on it at the time. This provokes her interest and she decides to join in by dabbing her paws at random letters and sitting on great swathes of the function keys. The gravity and solemnity of letters of complaint to the bank are undermined by the sudden appearance of random strings of letters. Book manuscripts are suddenly interrupted by gibberish such as AsldvksvklvsW'E'wffFVdvddk\z**/, which leads the reader to assume that I've either suffered a stroke or have unaccountably chosen to complete the book in Klingon.

Should I leave the computer unattended, say to make a cup of tea or take a leak, I am met on my return by a self-satisfied cat and 127 pages of the letter k interspersed with the odd forward slash. I have tried to counter this by closing the computer down, but she has circumvented this ploy by learning to step on the power button. She also seems to have discovered that sitting on the mouse has some interesting effects.

I'm sure she does this deliberately, taking a perverse pleasure in outwitting a mere human. The pinnacle of her achievements in this field came halfway through the writing of this book, when she demonstrated her deep and comprehensive knowledge of windows 10. I came back from the galley (kitchen) to find a smug cat sitting on the keyboard, and my elegant, erudite prose replaced by gobbledygook.

I turfed the cat off the keyboard and set about recovering my document, only to discover that, not only had she managed to turn on the computer, load my file and scramble it, but she had also managed to turn the image on the screen upside down.

This was a new one on me. I didn't know that it was even possible to do that, let alone how to do it. Why do they incorporate features like this? What possible use could they be to anyone? They're about as much use as a pole bearing a notice saying, *"Beware of this pole when reversing"*, or a sign saying *"Do not throw stones at this notice"*.

The obvious response to finding oneself in a situation such as this is to enlist the help of Mister Google. To do that, however, I had to use the computer.

Have you ever tried to read a computer screen upside down? It's difficulty enough if you're an adolescent with the visual acuity of a peregrine falcon. If, like me, you're the proud possessor of a range of different strength spectacles then you're on a hiding to nothing. For wrinklies such as me, reading from a screen is mostly guesswork at the best of times and leaning on a chair getting a crick in your neck is not the best of times. I could contort myself so that I could read the screen, or I could operate the keyboard and mouse, but I couldn't do both at the same time.

I tried propping the computer up on its side and cranking my neck over at 90 degrees. That just made the neckache worse. I put the computer on a chair behind me and bent over to look at it through my legs. All that achieved was a throbbing sinus headache. Trying to flip the image over with a magnifying glass merely gave me eyestrain.

In the end I found the secret. You have to hold down the ALT, CTRL and up arrow keys simultaneously. Using different arrow keys turns the screen in different ways. There are around 100 keys on a standard extended keyboard. To press the correct three keys at random would only occur once in about every 6 followed by 170 noughts attempts. It is very tempting to see this as driven by something other than chance.[45]

Einstein's I.T. skills, admirable and probability-defying though they may be, have little survival value for a cat.

So the score so far is six lives down, three to go.

She'd never have survived in the wild.

It's a miracle she made it this far.

Talking of making it so far, we had almost made it out of the malign influence of the Meltemi. All we had to do was get round the cape at Turgutreis and we would be into the gulf of Gökova. We decided to head for Gümüşlük which promised a beautiful enclosed bay with plenty of good holding and excellent shelter as well as good shoreside facilities.

It had all of those. It also had a multitude of anchored boats and a pandemonium of swimmers, snorkelers, and floundering children lolling about on li-los and inflatable animals of all shapes, sizes and descriptions. This became apparent once we had turned into the bay and found ourselves coasting into the middle of the mêlée. Obviously, everyone else in Western Turkey had the same opinion of the Aegean as we did and had shot off to the first available spot that wasn't in it.

It would have been difficult enough to manoeuvre in that confined space had it just been all the boats there. With wall-to-wall bodies in the sea as well it was impossible to manoeuvre safely. Our momentum continued to carry us into the seething mass of boats and humanity - once a boat is moving it keeps on moving. Remember Newton? That's his first law.

Whilst on the subject of Newton's laws, Non-scientists frequently misunderstand the scientific terms *law, theory* and *hypothesis,* especially theory. This enables evolution deniers and other assorted flat-earthers to dismiss all the evidence with an airy *"After all, evolution is only a theory."*

This shows either profound ignorance or deliberate disingenuity. A scientific theory is not a half-baked, unsupported fairy tale that some bloke thought up in a pub last Friday. It is a well substantiated explanation, acquired by the scientific method, and repeatedly tested by observation and experimentation. It has had to have withstood rigorous attempts to invalidate it by other scientists.

However, to return to Newton, the only way you can get 16 tonnes of boat to slow down or change direction is to apply huge amounts of force to it, preferably not by ramming it into something.

Boats don't have brakes. The only way you can slow one down or stop it is to go astern. This requires spinning a sodding great propeller at about 500 revs, which has a tendency to turn the surrounding water into a red, sludgy consistency if the boat is hemmed in on all sides by children floundering around in flotation aids.

The same problem presents itself if you try to change direction, say to stop yourself ploughing into a moored gulet for example, or in a vain attempt to halve the number of happy holidaymakers you inadvertently purée. In most cases this is achieved by getting a flow of water over the rudder, which requires the previously mentioned rapidly rotating people-chopper. You could, if you were lucky enough to have one, use the bowthruster but all does is replace one spinning propeller with two slightly smaller ones.

The hordes in the water showed not the slightest indication of being aware of the danger they were in, splashing and frolicking within arm's length of *Birvidik* and the one other boat frantically trying to manoeuvre its way out of the chaotic mayhem without incurring multiple manslaughter charges. We finally extricated ourselves by having me on the aft deck, waving people away from the propeller with Liz operating it in short bursts when I indicated that it was relatively clear. Once clear, we heaved a sigh of relief and headed south and east to the Gulf of Gökova.

And so we entered potter mode – short hops in sheltered gulfs, frequently revisiting favourite places. After the trials of the Aegean, this was a welcome relief, so much so that we revised our plans. Instead of making our way back to Finike for the winter, we decided to winter in Marmaris, thus giving ourselves a head start next year to get the Hell across the Aegean before the Meltemi kicked in. A welcome additional benefit this accrued was that we were now free to spend the rest of the current season in potter mode, which we did with relish.

We spent our time criss-crossing the gulfs of Gökova and Hisarönü. Some our favourite places we revisited several times. Our greatest favourite was Keçi Bükü, near the village of Orhaniye. This was only 11 kilometres from Marmaris as the crow flies. It was only 14 kilometres by road. Such was the convoluted geography of the area, though, that to get Marmaris by sea would have involved a trip of just under 200 kilometres.

We came back to Keçi Bükü six times in total and finally left from there at the end of the summer, heading for Marmaris. We decided to break the journey with a visit to the Greek island of Symi. We were still ostensibly checked in to Greece, so we had to check out before hunkering down in Marmaris for the winter. It would also allow us to assess its suitability as a first stop on the next season's cruising so that we could then check back into Greece and the EU on our way to the Saronic and then Crete.

There are two possible moorings: the harbour of the capital, Symi town and the isolated anchorage of Panormitis on the other end of the island. We chose Symi as it was nearer all the action, and the Port Police and other dens of officialdom were all situated there. This was not one of our more astute decisions.

Symi town is definitely an extremely picturesque spot. The harbour is at the end of an inlet on the north east of the island. All around it the vertiginous slopes are covered in whitewashed houses, enlivened with splashes of yellow and blue paint. The bougainvillea that cascades down the faces of the houses adds a riotous counterpoint of reds, whites and yellows. The clusters of dwellings are dissected by steep, narrow, winding streets, with the centre sections stepped to assist the donkey carts for which they were originally intended. The whole town is more suitable for donkeys than motor cars and vans. That doesn't stop them though.

The houses contrast strikingly with the dark ultramarine blue of the water. There's a reason it's dark blue: it's bloody deep.

A rule of thumb for a yottie trying to guess the underwater topography of a potential anchorage or mooring is to look at the topography above the water. The odds are that what you see above the water will carry on below the water. All around the harbour, the hills rose precipitously from the water's edge. Judging by what we could see, we expected the sea bed to fall steeply away from the quays. We prepared for such an eventuality. I set up stern ropes to attach to the bollards on the quay and set up the chain locker so that we could easily and quickly deploy our full length of chain over the bow – all 100 metres of it.

We decided to do a quick recce before committing ourselves to mooring up, contrary to our usual practice of diving straight in to the first available space before it gets nabbed by some sneaky German or Russian interloper. We slowly approached the quay bow first and gazed intently at the forward-looking sonar. As we had suspected, this showed the sea bed falling away steeply from the quay. Well, when I say '*steeply*' I actually mean '*bloody near vertically*'. Twenty metres from the quay, the sonar showed the depth as greater than the range setting, and that was sixty metres.

The rule of thumb[46] for laying out an anchor is to deploy three to five times as much chain as there is depth where you drop the anchor. We had a hundred metres of chain. This is a lot for a cruising yacht, but it was still nowhere near enough. If we got ourselves into position with the stern almost touching the quay, our bow was already in thirty metres. The system works best when the anchor is pulling as near as possible to horizontally. Here it would be pulling down nearly vertically.

I devised a cunning plan. We turned and steered away form the quay until the bow was in an estimated depth considerably greater than 100 metres. I then dropped the anchor and all 100 metres of chain, having first double checked that the inboard end of the chain was securely fixed to the boat [47]. Then, with the anchor dangling vertically 100 metres down, we slowly went astern towards the quay, waiting for the anchor to snag on the rising seabed. It finally caught when the stern was about fifteen metres from the quay. I took up any slack in the chain and Liz took us gently astern, biting the anchor in. We hoped.

Once the stern was near enough to the quay, I ran back, picked up the two ropes and leapt ashore with them. A little bit of adjustment fore and aft and we were set up.

We were set up, but not relaxed. I didn't have a lot of faith in the anchor being able to hold us off the quay if the weather picked up from the north east. This wasn't forecast, but you never know in the Med. We decided to get the paperwork done, provision up and set off for Turkey early the next morning. Well, that was the plan.

The provisioning and paperwork were easy enough, if a bit time consuming. When we returned to the boat, we found ourselves hemmed in on both sides. When we had left *Birvidik* she was on an almost empty quay. Now it was absolutely chock-full. On our port side there was now a tour/tripper boat, twice the length of *Birvidik*.[48] On our starboard side there was now a solid raft of mainly charter boats, all packed in cheek by jowl.

Even from the quay, we could see that their anchor chains were all over the place (and all over ours). Once on board it became even more obvious. I dug out mask and snorkel and slipped into the water to have a look. It was not a pretty sight. Ours, being a good little anally retentive anchor chain, ran dutifully out at ninety degrees to the quay and disappeared into the gloomy depths. The others' chains were laying in all directions and criss-crossing each other. The whole lot of them were over ours. Such is the penalty for being first in.

Although all the anchors were too deep for me to see, I could work out the order in which the boats had arrived by seeing which chains were over and under which. It was apparent that there was only one way to sort out this mess and that was for the boats to leave in the reverse order to the way they arrived. I jotted the recommended order on a scrap of paper and went around the surrounding boats to suggest a plan. Most skippers were accommodating and grateful for the suggestion but there were, as always, a couple of flies in the ointment.

One Dutch skipper proclaimed from his high horse that he intended to leave at his scheduled time and if any idiot had been incompetent enough to drop their chain over his then he would lift their chain with his and drop the offending anchor wherever he saw fit. It didn't seem to occur to him that he had demonstrated equal incompetence by laying his chain across at least four others.

More of a problem was the tour boat. The skipper wasn't on board, but the crewman I came across said that the boat was not intending to leave until two days' time, when they were due to set off with a new group of passengers. I didn't fancy being stuck in this barely tenable mooring for nearly three more days, especially as the weather was forecast to deteriorate. I asked when the skipper was likely to be back on board and was met with an apologetic shrug.

The exodus started the next morning. At first everything went well and according to plan. To make things even better, the skipper of the tour boat turned up and said he would weigh anchor, move off to let us out and re-moor. What a nice chap. The first three boats left in the correct order, lifted their anchors without incident, and headed out of the harbour. All that was left now was one charter boat, then our modest, sympathetic Dutch friend, to be followed by the tripper boat and then us. That's where things started to go wrong.

There was a slight delay on the next boat in the queue. He was waiting for a delivery from the local wine shop. When this hadn't arrived by half an hour after the agreed time, the skipper set off on foot to chivvy them up a bit. This was all too much for our impatient Dutch friend, who announced that he wasn't going to wait any longer 'for some alcoholic's booze supply', and he intended to cast off and leave right then.

He was true to his word. He started his engine, cast off his stern lines and started pulling in his anchor chain. The inevitable happened and he snagged the other boat's chain. Despite the protestations of the assembled yotties, he made no effort to disentangle the two. Rather, he continued to make things worse by pulling in more chain with his windlass. This did not have the desired effect. Instead of separating the two chains, he only knotted them further. Still he continued too apply more force with the windlass. All that this achieved was to bring the two boats closer together until they were almost touching, bow to bow. The exhortations and expletives from the other skippers rose to a falsetto crescendo.

Albert Einstein is (probably incorrectly) credited with the aphorism that insanity is defined as 'keeping on doing the same thing over and over again and expecting different results'[49]. Under stress, though, this sort of behaviour appears to be an almost universal human characteristic. Consider the hurried, impatient executive repeatedly jabbing the lift button despite logic and experience amply demonstrating its total futility.

In a desperate attempt to break the impasse, I clambered onto the other boat and made my way to the bow where I was able to utter the six sweetest words in the English language: '*I told you this would happen*'.

Luckily, in addition to my smug, smart-arse attitude, I had also brought my secret weapon, my anchor-thief. This is a highly cunning device and every yottie should have one. It is a large metal hook with a strong eye at the top and another at the bottom. To these eyes are attached two differently coloured ropes. The hook is lowered, suspended from the rope on the top eye. This keeps the hook in normal position, and it is manoeuvred so as to snag the top chain. It is then would up tight on a winch. This took the strain off the manic Dutchman's chain. Once his complexion had changed from a mottled purple to a slightly less lethal shade of merely deep puce, I indicated for him to lower his anchor so that it was free of the suspended chain and then to back gently out before raising his anchor. It was intensely rewarding to see him meekly comply. Such opportunities for smug self-satisfaction are as rare as rocking-horse shit and should be deeply savoured whenever they arise.

I pulled up on the second rope on the anchor thief and the hook promptly capsized and dropped the chain back in the water. I modestly acknowledged the ripple of admiring appreciation that spread through the assembled onlookers and struck a noble, but unassuming, pose on the bow.

Pity I spoilt the effect by stubbing my toe on a cleat as I made my way back and hopped, whimpering pathetically, across to *Birvidik*.

After that, all we had to do was wait for the other two boats to move off and we were free. We crossed Symi town off our list of possible stops for next season and headed off to Marmaris.

The Second Turkish Winter – Yat Marine, Marmaris.

October 17ᵗʰ 2010.- April 15ᵗʰ 2011

On arriving at Yat Marine for the winter we were directed to pontoon B where we moored up. Opposite us was a large power boat, *Tickety-Boo*. Once we had tied up and snugged all the lines down, the skipper came over. I was fully expecting one of the opening gambits from the Introductory Coded Exchange, but instead got a conversation opener that was so totally unexpected that it threw me completely.

"Can you ride a motor bike?" he asked.

"Done a bit" I replied warily.

"You can use mine for the winter if you like" he said, pointing to a 175 scooter parked at the root of the pontoon.

"All you have to do is keep the battery charged and pay the road tax in January."

Yat Marine is about five kilometres away from Marmaris proper, down a poorly maintained, pothole bestrewn excuse for a road. I thought about his offer for all of five picoseconds.

"Done!" I said. Thus were we introduced to the sublime subtleties of Turkish driving.

I had noticed that as we went further East in the Med, there seemed to an increasing degree of fatalism in the national psyche. There's a phrase for it in Arabic - *in shā 'a llāh,* the literal translation of which is 'If God wills'[50]. This fatalism reaches its apotheosis in Turkish driving. If Allah wants them to crash then crash they will, irrespective of how safely they drive. Conversely, if Allah doesn't want them to crash then they won't, even if they drive like bloody maniacs. Which they do. I don't think they've quite got their heads round the concept of probability theory.

For the foreigner, lacking the reliance on divine will, driving in Turkey is an interesting experience, as we had already discovered on those rare instances we had taken a taxi or hired a car. In theory the Turks drive on the right and give way to traffic approaching from the right. In practice they drive down the middle and give way to no-one. Lane discipline is an alien concept to them. On the rare occasions that the lanes are marked the Turks take no notice of them whatsoever. If road markings are changed for any reason, they leave the old markings as well, just to add a touch of a frisson to proceedings.

Overtaking seems to be carried out, for preference, on the brows of hills and approaching blind corners, of which there are many. Failing that, approaching a complex junction makes a good alternative. Red traffic lights are not even just regarded as advisory, they are totally disregarded. During a five-hour drive to Antalya airport and back, we were virtually the only car to stop at any red light. There we sat doing our 'couple of pensioner' impressions (impressions?). *"Pass the thermos dear. Oooh - look at her, what does she think she looks like? Have you got any of those peppermints?"* Cars screamed past us on both sides kicking up clouds of dust which obscured the still red traffic lights, their drivers giving us quizzical and disdainful looks.

I had been under the impression that the purpose of road planning was to facilitate the flow of traffic and to reduce the risk of accidents. Turkish road planning seems to be part of a grand design to reduce population growth. Lane markings appear and disappear without reason. The right-hand lane will suddenly just peter out leaving you with a choice of barging into the high speed pack to your left or careering right down a steep bank into a dried up river bed. If lanes do merge, they usually do so just over the brow of a hill followed immediately by a sharp right-hand bend. The Turks have also reintroduced the concept of the three-lane road, an innovation that caused such carnage that even the

Portuguese phased them out. These have one lane going in each direction separated by an overtaking lane which serves for both directions. This ensures that when the inevitable head-on collision occurs both cars are travelling really, really fast and the resultant bang is really, really satisfying.

At first, we were somewhat nervous about riding the bike, what with the *in shā 'a llāh* attitude to driving exhibited by most Turkish drivers. In addition, the tiny wheels are not the best design for the Turkish roads which, with their many deep potholes and nasty adverse cambers, are better suited to trials bikes.

Unfortunately, I didn't seem to take long to get the hang of it and I went native. I began to drive like a Turk, which Liz found a degree disconcerting. I started suddenly turning left across busy roads, executing U turns on dual carriageways, driving the wrong way down one-way streets and taking short cuts through pedestrian precincts. I didn't quite get around to driving into the supermarket or off the pontoon into the marina, but it would only have been a matter of time. Having begun driving it sedately and remaining primly upright, steering round corners without so much as a degree of lean, I ended up slinging it into corners with gusto, only to be noisily reminded by the grinding noise as I grounded the stand that it was not designed to be Barry Sheened.

I may have gone native in the matter of Turkish driving techniques, but I continued to have trouble integrating into yottie culture as far as alcohol is concerned. The problem is that most of them start so early.

Now don't get me wrong; I like a drink as much as the next man. Unless the next man's Oliver Reed. It's just that most yotties seem to start drinking around mid-afternoon[51]. We, by contrast, rarely if ever fancy a drink before about eight o'clock at night.

This is compensated for by the fact that we finish a lot later than your average yottie. Most of them are cosily tucked up in bed by nine p.m. whereas we're just getting into our stride. The overall level of consumption probably balances out, but there is a very short overlapping time window during which we and they can socialise over a drink.

Yotties' drinking habits are partially explained by their innate stinginess, as the marina bar serves cheap beer between 6 o'clock and 7:30, but that only exacerbates an existing tendency.

"*Do come round for a drink*" they say to us (usually before they really get to know us).

"*Love to*", we say, "*What time?*" - expecting a sensible time such as eight to eight thirty.

Oh no. They suggest ridiculous times like 5 o'clock or even earlier. At that rate we stumble back to *Birvidik* at about nine o'clock and blunder incoherently about the galley in a usually spectacularly unsuccessful attempt to muster something to eat.

We now try to negotiate times along the lines of haggling prices with a Turkish merchant. The other yotties start off with some ludicrous time like 3:30 in the afternoon. We counter by suggesting two o'clock in the morning. They snort at this and spin a pitiful tale of the disastrous effect such a late night will have on their mental health and already fragile family life, but magnanimously concede a start time of 4:15. We respond with harrowing descriptions of sclerotic livers and malnutrition, but generously suggest midnight.

Entering into the spirit of things, they come up with 6 o'clock on the strict understanding that we take personal responsibility for the collapse of their marriage, the decline of their children into a life of delinquency and the rapid worsening of their irritable bowel syndrome. We come down to 9:30 on the condition that they sign a waiver on the irritable bowel syndrome and meet us halfway on the costs of the liver transplants. We usually end up on about 6:45, which pleases nobody, but at least it's fair in that we're all equally pissed off.

The social activities in Yat Marine that winter were legion, and we threw ourselves into things wholeheartedly. Liz went to yoga at 8:30 in the morning three days a week and I was beautifully outmanoeuvred by Justin from *Belle Helene*. Justin used to be a headteacher. Demonstrating an impressive mastery of Senior Management Skills, he publicly volunteered to take on the organisation of the Turkish language classes and then cunningly engineered things so that someone else (in this case Muggins here) was conned into doing all the actual work. Absolutely brilliantly done. I resolved to spend time at the feet of the master - watch & learn, boy, watch & learn.

As a result, I spent half the winter giving Turkish lessons to around 30 yotties twice a week, which is a bit rich seeing as my mastery of the language was (and is) about on a par with that of the average Turkish foetus. Luckily, I had the assistance of the lovely Zaza, a native Turkish speaker. I worked on the system of staying just ahead of the class - about ten minutes ahead, in fact, by the end of each lesson. No problem really - it's a system that served me well for the previous 30 years.

I have made singularly unsuccessful attempts to learn a raft of different languages over the course of our travels, but Turkish stood out as the absolutely least successful. It wasn't the vocabulary, or the slightly different alphabet. The Greek alphabet is significantly more alien to western eyes and ears than is the Turkish, and I got a tentative grip on Greek.

No, the problem with Turkish is its syntax. Forget German and its irritating habit of always the verb at the end of the sentence putting. Turkish is an agglutinative language. It takes the German penchant for sticking smaller terms together to make great blockbusters of words and puts it on steroids. Whole complex sentences with conditional clauses jostling for position end up as one word with a plethora of suffixes and prefixes tacked higgledy-piggledy onto the root word. It's totally incomprehensible to a set-in-his-ways like me who has grown up using word order to determine meaning. Soddit – I'll stick with the romance languages.

Another advantage of wintering in Marmaris was that, being a larger town, it was much easier to buy stuff and to get work done. This gives the yottie a deeper insight into two defining characteristics of Turkish culture, namely their astonishing work ethic and the pivotal role of tea in Turkish social intercourse.

Let us start with the latter. Tea is the essential social lubricant that facilitates, structures and modulates almost every aspect of Turkish life. It does the job that in British society requires not only tea and coffee, but alcohol, celebrity gossip and talking about the weather. It is the communal ritual that formalises business, commerce, leisure, family, friendships and neighbourhoods.

This is far more formalised than the stereotypical British notion of looking upon a nice cup of tea as the universal panacea to all of life's ills. It permeates all corners of Turkish life.

All of this works fine for Turks, habituated to it from an early age, but it poses one, significant problem for strangers such as yotties; Turkish tea is vile. It has emetic and purgative properties beyond the dreams of a celebrity snake oil nutritionist. Forget any preconceptions you may have of nice, reviving cups of English Breakfast tea with just the right amount of milk. Banish from your mind fond memories of a sophisticated Earl Grey or a rich, smoky Lapsang Souchong. Think more of neat vinegar lightly diluted with battery acid and bitter aloes.

Turkish tea is a highly corrosive liquid of such astringent awfulness that it is not humanly possible to even contemplate so much as a sip unless you have just washed your mouth out with a 50-50 mixture of drain cleaner and embalming fluid and you desperately need something to take the taste away.

Despite all this, there is no getting away from it. Unless you avoid all contact with the local populace then somewhere, sometime, you're going to have to drink some tea. Go into any shop and a glass of tea is thrust into your hand before you've so much as opened your mouth. Want to discuss with a craftsman the job you want done? Not 'til you've had a glass of tea you won't. Haircut? Tea first. Meet your prospective in-laws to ask for their daughter's hand in marriage? Nope – important stuff first, get that glass of tea down you.

There is a tacit contract involved in all this, a *quid pro quo* that is based on underlying human psychological traits regarding the reciprocity of gift-giving and the sharing of food and drink. If you take tea with someone, the relationship changes subtly. An implied rapport is established. You are no longer strangers, but now acquaintances or even friends.

If you keep an ear out, you can pick this up by noticing changes in the terms of address. *Efendim* or *Bay* (Sir) will be replaced with honorifics denoting family relationships. The exact choice gives an indication of the esteem in which you are held and closeness of the perceived relationship. If the relationship is new and perceived as somewhat distant you will be addressed, respectfully, as *Kızı* (cousin). As things develop, the address can change to the more familiar term *Abi* (big brother). If you are older, or of significantly higher status than your new-found friend, then you will be addressed as *Amca* (uncle on the father's side) and if you are addressed as *Baba* (father) then you've really hit the jackpot.

With these changes in status come different responsibilities and obligations. Respect must be shown and attention must be paid. It is considered very rude to peremptorily end a conversation or leave the room. Indeed, it feels very rude even to a non-Turk and few can bring themselves to do it. This puts our yottie in a quandary. He doesn't want to seem rude, but he lacks the Turks' defensive adaptation of a mouth lining and tongue tempered by a lifetime of tea drinking until they are as leathery as a geriatric buffalo's scrotum that has been pickled in a mixture of neat tannin and formaldehyde for 20 years.

There is an almost unvarying pattern to the yottie's first experience of the Turkish tea ritual. It usually starts with our yottie being in search of goods or services of some kind. As an example, let us say that he is in the *sanayı*, trying to get a price for a rebuild on his (now out of production) 64cc 1954, Featherweight Seagull outboard motor.

The sanayı is a Turkish institution that is found in, or on the outskirts of, virtually every Turkish town. It's a sort of light engineering ghetto. Here you will find all the craftsmen; the metalworkers, mechanics and electricians; the canvas workers, glaziers and plumbers. If you want anything repaired or made from scratch, then this is where you head. Turkey is probably one of the last strongholds holding out against the modern 'chuck it out and fit a new one' culture.

Each trade seems to congregate in specific areas. On the surface this would appear illogical as you surround yourself with your competition, but I suppose it must work. After all, we do the same. How many doctors are there in Harley Street or tailors in Jermyn Street?

Our gallant yottie successfully negotiates the sanayı and finds the desired premises. He tentatively enters the dark recesses of the cluttered workshop and waits a few minutes for his eyes to become accustomed to the gloom. He is startled from his reverie by a polite touch on his elbow and a low voiced "*Efendim?*". He pulls out the translation of his requirements that the marina office kindly wrote down for him and begins to prattle on in something that is almost, but not quite, totally unlike Turkish. The engineer (for it is he) puts his finger to his lips and ushers our yottie to a corner where there sits a low table surrounded by scattered cushions. "*Otur lütfen*" he says quietly and motions him to sit down. Mr Yottie complies and starts to explain his requirements again before realising that the engineer has disappeared.

Some minutes later the engineer re-appears carrying two tulip shaped glasses filled with an ominous brown liquid looking like slightly thinned varnish. "*çay!*" he says in a tone that will brook no argument. He sits down opposite Mr Yottie. "*şerefe*" he says and raises the glass to his lips. Mr. Yottie does likewise and cautiously sniffs the steaming glass.

The smell, repulsive though it undoubtedly is, gives no real indication of the horrors to come. It is relatively benign, consisting as it does of an underlying base aroma of turpentine, enhanced by notes of used engine oil and paint stripper, finally topped off with delicate hints of insect repellent. The engineer sips appreciatively at his glass and looks encouragingly at Mr. Yottie, who reciprocates and instantly regrets it. The human body is not designed to drink this sort of material. In fact, it has, over millions of years, evolved an arsenal of defensive measures, an army of reflexes and physiological responses all designed to avoid precisely such an occurrence. These measures kick in immediately.

The first response is to try to get rid of the stuff before it goes any further and does any more damage. His mouth goes into convulsions and his tongue shrivels and ties itself into a rolling hitch in a vain attempt to escape the taste sensation of having just chewed a mouthful of a mixture of dried hops and drain cleaner. His lips purse and his cheeks pinch in, rapidly followed by an overwhelming urge to spray the offending liquid all over the table.

Biologically speaking, this is by far the most sensible thing to do. Sociologically speaking, it has certain drawbacks. Bowing to the social pressure, our yottie summons up a supreme effort of will, screws up his eyes and swallows. His system reacts with incredulity as this insult and deploys stage II defences. This consists of waves of nausea and the knotting of the stomach, rapidly followed by dry heaving.

The usual tactic in these situations is to gaze around and look for somewhere that the offending liquid can be surreptitiously discarded. In the absence of suitable receptacles, desperate yotties have been known to furtively pour it into their trouser pocket, having decided that, on balance, they would prefer a reputation for incontinence to subjecting themselves to more such agony.

There are only two things that give Turkish tea a run for its money in the awfulness stakes, and those are Turkish coffee and ayran. Even then they come in a poor joint second.

At first sight (and smell), Turkish coffee seems to hold out the promise of offering a rather pleasant and satisfying sensory experience. It is served in small cups, little bigger than thimbles. It is a rich, dark colour and gives off a flavourful, full-bodied aroma which tantalisingly teases the nose as you raise the cup to your lips. The coffee is extremely hot, so you take a delicate sip form the top. It is, indeed, exquisite - if perhaps just a little on the bitter side for western tastes. You replace the cup on the table and leave it to cool for a few minutes.

After a short interval, you raise the cup to your lips and take a good, healthy swig. This is a mistake. Instead of the ambrosial liquid you were expecting you have a mouthful of concentrated coffee grounds which cling tenaciously to your teeth, palate, throat and, most importantly, your tongue. These grounds have the consistency of bricklayer's mortar and the taste of concentrated seagull shit.[52] A cup of Turkish coffee is about 90% grounds with a two millimetre layer of drinkable coffee floating on the top.

Turks seem to have a penchant for disgusting drinks. They must have evolved different taste buds to most other races. What else could explain the fact that not only do they have Turkish tea and Turkish coffee, but they rub salt in the wound by coming up with Ayran.

Ayran is easily mistaken for milk. It looks like milk. It's the same colour as milk and it has the same consistency as milk. It's kept in the fridge like milk. It's even sold in the same containers as milk.

Just don't, whatever you do, put it in your tea.

I did.

Ayran is made by taking a particularly sour plain yoghourt, diluting it with iced water and adding salt. This process changes its taste profile from 'violently emetic' to merely 'vile'. If you add it to tea the mixture instantly curdles and the taste profile changes to 'obnoxiously repulsive'. Adding ayran to Turkish tea achieves the seemingly impossible task of making Turkish tea taste even worse than it does normally.

All in all, it's probably best to stick to beer.

That advice, of course, is predicated on the assumption that it's still available. President Recep Tayyip Erdoğan is no fan of the demon drink.

The Turks make recompense for the horrors they have inflicted on the world of beverages by working harder and longer than almost anyone else on the planet.

The Turkish work ethic has to be seen to be believed. Actually, even then belief is difficult. *"Turk! Work Hard!"*

---

exhorted Kemal Ataturk, and by God they did as they were told. The Turks make the Plymouth Rock Puritans look like a bunch of dope-addled sixties drop-outs by comparison.

They work all the hours God sends and then throw in a few He was keeping in reserve. Shops are open from sparrow-fart to gone midnight or even longer. Bulvar, a small to medium supermarket in Finike was open 24/7. You could saunter in at four in the morning for a bag of crisps, a bottle of diet coke and a pack of incontinence pads, and be served by a bleary-eyed Turk slumped over the checkout. [53]

We needed to have all the old antifouling taken off the hull while we were in Turkey. This is a laborious and tedious undertaking, involving hour upon hour of contorting yourself into awkward positions and scraping off poisonous paint from a curved surface with a tiny blade on a wooden handle. All of this had to be done while encased in the equivalent of a Gulf War noddy suit, complete with respirator, goggles and gloves.

When restricted like this, the maximum we could manage was about an hour and a half before we had to take an hour off to recover. It would take the two of us about a week to do the job. We decided to get a quote from Ali, the local general factotum and Marmaris's answer to Faik.

The price Ali quoted was very reasonable, nowhere near as eye-watering as we had anticipated. He put two men on the job, and by God they grafted. They started before it was fully light and worked through until it was too dark to see to do the job.

If a Turk pays people to do a job, he lets them get on with it. After serving them a cup of gut-scouring tea he buggers off and comes back when the job's done. Not so us. Being British, we are consumed by guilt at the prospect of two people grafting away on our boat while we sit on our arses drinking tea and reading the paper. The guilt was ratcheted up several notches by their complete failure to take any precautions against the toxic effects of the scraped off antifoul.[54]

We ran around after them like a couple of mother hens. We offered them overalls, gloves and respirators, all of which they declined. We fussed over them with glasses of fruit juice at half-hourly intervals, tutting disapprovingly when they didn't drink enough. We force-fed them cheese sandwiches, surreptitiously brushing flakes of antifoul off the bread.

They did a grand job, but I strongly suspect that it took them twice as long as it would have done had we just kept out of the bloody way.

Marmaris Yat Marine (in case you'd lost track of where we were) is an excellent place. It has everything an overwintering yottie could wish for - Swimming pool, bar, restaurant, sauna, shop, artisans, chandlers...

...and a gym, and that's where the trouble started.

The presence of the gym triggered a rash of good intentions regarding improvements in general fitness. We vowed to work out four times a week. I entered into the spirit of things wholeheartedly (possibly rather too wholeheartedly) and gave all the apparatus a good seeing to. Forty-five minutes on the runner were followed by a further 45 minutes humping heavy weights about and pulling and pushing an assortment of bars and levers.

I approached the end of the session - just the stretches and abs to do then. At which point I spied something out of the corner of my eye. *Oooh look - an inclined bench. Must give that some wellie; do some sit-ups on it. No sense in doing things by half measures. Let's do them with a couple of 5 kg weights on the chest.* On the 5th sit up there was a grunt, followed by two popping noises and an exclamation of 'Oh Bugger!' as a couple of fetching little bulges popped up in my groin.

I was now the proud owner of a bilateral direct inguinal hernia. *'How did you get on and off the boat?'* I hear you ask. *Very carefully* is the answer, thank you for asking. I tried the usual male trick of doing nothing for a while and seeing if it went away. After about ten days it became apparent even to me that it wasn't going to do the decent thing and clear off of its own accord. A visit to the local private hospital and, 65 quid lighter, the diagnosis was confirmed.

All of which attention-seeking and needy, sympathy-soliciting whingeing brings us to the point, such as it is, of this digression; namely medical care and the long-term cruiser.

Illness and injury are rarely a barrel of laughs, but at least for those with a more conventional lifestyle, the process is relatively well understood and easy to put into motion. You go to your GP and explain the problem. (S)he then either treats you, or surreptitiously adds the cryptic note '*TF Bundy*' [55]on your file, or refers you on to an NHS specialist who will see you at his or her clinic, hopefully some time before judgement day. Unless you are filthy rich or insured, that is, in which case you get to see the same specialist next Tuesday, at which point the specialist's secretary will surgically remove the contents of your bank account before you get halfway across the deep-pile carpet.

No such simplicity for the cruising sailor. The choices are so many, so varied and so nuanced that in order to make the right decision you would need an algorithm more complicated than Google's, Amazon's and Facebook's combined.

Some choices, of course, are relatively straightforward. All the algorithms will start with the question "*Is it immediately life-threatening?*" If the answer to this is "*Of course it is you bloody idiot – I can't breathe and there's blood pouring copiously out of my every orifice!*" then you call an ambulance, go straight to the best hospital in the vicinity, get done whatever needs to be done, and deal with the financial fallout later.

If it's not immediately life threatening but is nevertheless pretty bloody urgent then the first thing you do is look to see if you've got insurance cover or an EHIC if you're in the EU (Use it while you can, folks).

However, if your problem is not life-threatening or urgent but still debilitating and potentially a bit nasty, such as – Oh I don't know, a bilateral direct inguinal hernia to pick an example purely at random – then you're spoiled for choice.

To wit, you can:

1. Pay a small fortune and have the op done next week in a local private hospital. (Preferably with the competence of surgeon and general hygiene and nursing standards of the hospital having been ascertained beforehand).

2. Get yourself back home and get the job done on your home health service. This is by far the cheapest option but it does involve writing off at least a year's cruising while you sit around waiting for appointments and theatre dates, which get cancelled and rescheduled at the last minute because some idiot's crashed a car into a bus queue or the beds are all full of well but frail pensioners who can't get the place they need in a care home because their local council has been effectively bankrupted by a mixture of central government politicking, rapacious development consortia and its own incompetence and hubris.

3. Get yourself back home and go private. We had expected that by the time we had factored in the travel costs and the cattery bills this would probably have been the most expensive option but it did promise to avoid the problems of (2) while still ensuring a familiar and Anglophone environment. We also expected it to take a lot longer than (1). We were pleasantly wrong on both counts.

This is where the financially prudent among you will smugly proffer the opinion that we bring this upon ourselves and that all these difficulties would have been avoided had we bothered to take out travel health insurance.

I counter this with the following tightly reasoned argument:

Would they Bollocks.

Let me expand my argument.

a) It is virtually impossible to get health insurance that meets the requirements of the cruising sailor. Most only cover shortish trips abroad, certainly not a year or more. Combine that with trying to get cover for a more mature demographic, usually with pre-existing medical conditions and you're on a hiding to nothing.

b) Related to (a), Almost without exception, travel insurance policies cover emergency treatment and repatriation only. With a condition such as I had, they just tell you to get yourself back home and line up behind that queue of pensioners. They don't cover non-urgent conditions.

c) Most insurance policies are so tightly worded that if something is at all likely to happen to you then the odds are that you're not going to be covered for it. Conversely, as the odds of your being infected with the Ebola virus as a result of having been unexpectedly ravished by a lust-crazed hippo whilst taking a midnight skinny dip in the Zambezi are so infinitesimal, they'll happily commit to cover for that. Although they might quibble somewhat if you'd had a few drinks beforehand and might be regarded as having led it on a bit.

In the eleven years' of cruising up to the time of writing, our policy had been not to take out health insurance. Instead, we put the premium money into a savings account and used that account to pay any medical bills as they arose. This has covered several medical interventions including the hernia repair currently under discussion and thus far we're still in profit. However, as we are getting older and we're driving more, we feel the risk of bankruptcy-inducing serious illness or accident is increasing. Intensive care can easily run to over a grand a day. So at the time of writing we have managed to take out insurance to cover such an eventuality – for peace of mind if nothing else.

All that was required now was to assess the options. The surgeon at the Turkish private hospital said that they could do it there, laparoscopically, at a date and time of our convenience. "*How much?*" we asked? He sloped off for a clinical conference with his cardiologist, anaesthetist and financial advisor. He returned with a scrap of paper with some scribbles on it. Just as he was about to hand it over he paused, pulled it back sharply, and said "*You are insured, aren't you.*"

"*No*" we replied succinctly.

He went off into a further huddle with the aforementioned specialists and returned with a fresh set of scribbles – five thousand quid. God knows how much it would have been had we been insured.

One of the problems with medical treatment in foreign cultures is that there is no easy way to assess the quality of the surgery and care. We decided to investigate going back to Jersey to get it done. It would still have to be private but at least we would have inside information on the care there.

I recounted this saga in our blog, which prompted a flurry of responses, most gloatingly sarcastic, one sympathetic and one useful. The useful one was from Chris Sutton. Having read the blog prompted a synaptic flash of recognition when he later saw an advert for the British Hernia Centre in London. This is a very highly specialised private clinic which churns through hernia repairs like an assembly line. He passed on the contact details to us.

I had an electronic consultation with them, during which they asked for a measure of the size of the hernia. They used an interestingly idiosyncratic system of measurement, asking me to choose from pea, egg, plum, lemon, orange, grapefruit, melon and football. My thanks go to Mr. Malcolm Denham of Guildford for sadistically suggesting that the scale should be extended at the upper end by 'pumpkin' and 'space-hopper'.

I expressed my admiration for their ingenious measurement scale, but suggested that it required finer discrimination, especially at the lower end. I proposed that they insert 'marrowfat pea' and 'quail's egg' between pea and egg. I also offered to further refine the entire scale for them for a very reasonable fee, but they declined. In the end they confirmed our existing feeling that going down the laparoscopic route was not the wisest course of action. They also said that they could do the op in London for two thousand seven hundred quid, compared with the five thousand the Turkish hospital was asking.

We put them on hold while I contacted our GP in Jersey and got a referral to Jim Allardice. We'd still have to go private but at least we had inside gen on the quality of care and surgery. That's the advantage of having inside information – Jim was very highly regarded. Within days he had phoned and we discussed the case. He suggested that he did one side and looked at the other to decide if bilateral repair was indicated. He also quoted a price of two thousand all in. Bargain - under half the price quoted in Turkey for what would have been an inferior procedure.

So, we arranged flights to Jersey via Istanbul and London so that I could go under the knife once I'd stopped the warfarin for a week so I didn't squirt all over the table.

In the interim I managed to acquire a cracking cold which went to my chest, causing a hacking cough which went on for days. This is not something you want when you have a double hernia. Every time I coughed my hand shot down to my groin in an attempt to stop the bulges running the gamut of egg, through plum, lemon, orange, grapefruit, to melon and even (God forbid) football. The effect was to make me look like a consumptive rapper.

The worst was when it waited until I had both hands full and was, for example, halfway down the companionway steps. I would look around frantically and see that there was no way I could put the things down in time. In desperation I would raise both hands, bend forward, slightly bend my left knee and bring my right knee up to my chest in a passable impression of Bruce Forsyth. This never failed to reduce Liz to tears. Of laughter.

All went well with the op, and after a few days of hobbling around as if I'd been kicked in the balls by a donkey I was back to my usual morose self. We stopped off at Istanbul for a few days before returning to Marmaris where we bailed out Einstein from her month's incarceration in the cattery. That'll teach the little bastard to keep circumventing our Alcatraz-like defences and going off clubbing with the local ferals.

We learnt two significant lessons from our visit to Istanbul: Don't go in February and don't expect it to be representative of Turkey as a whole.

Remember my comments earlier regarding the Turks' ability to cope with extreme heat? That was only half the story. They seem impervious to extremes of cold as well. Istanbul in February is bloody freezing.

Everywhere.

Inside and out.

It's impossible to get warm.

There are hardcore purists (bloody idiots more like) who maintain with boring, pompous, smug regularity that there is no such thing as bad weather, only bad clothing.

Hah!

Most societies that for some unfathomable reason choose to operate in cold climates realise that clothes alone will not cut the mustard. All clothing does is slow down the rate of heat loss from the body to the bloody freezing environment. It's down to the laws of thermodynamics; don't even think of arguing with them. They take no prisoners.[56] Stick around in a cold environment for long enough and your core temperature's going to drop eventually. Unless you can whack some heat into you that is. You can try hot drinks and chocolate, but these are mere holding actions.

For that reason, the abovementioned societies all work on the same general principle of having nice, toasty-warm mini-environments such as homes, offices, restaurants, shops, cars and busses. These get your core temperature up to a level capable of sustaining life before you venture out to the next mini sauna, wrapped up like the Michelin Man playing Nanook of the North.

All of them except the Turks that is. In Istanbul in February, nowhere is warm. Not the hotel rooms – not in the sort of hotel we were in, anyway. If you override the pathetic central heating for twelve hours you might just about get the ambient temperature above freezing. Step outside for more than eight nanoseconds and the maids will have been in, made the bed, turned the heating back to arctic and opened the windows wide to give the place a good airing. By the time you get back there are icicles hanging from the curtain rails and the temperature's low enough to give an Emperor

Penguin chilblains.

Restaurants are no better, most of them maintaining a temperature on the cool side of nippy. The accepted response to low temperatures in Turkish restaurants is not to turn the heating up but to supply blankets. We huddled round tables dressed in fleeces and jackets and wrapped in blankets looking like a bunch of Patagonian peasants on a picnic.

The major tourist attractions posed similar thermodynamic challenges. Aya Sofia? – could double as a Smithfield chill room. The Blue Mosque? – named after the colour of visitors' extremities, I reckon. Topkapi Palace? – bloody freezing, especially the Harem area. Can't imagine groups of languorous young concubines drifting elegantly around in diaphanous pantaloons and delicate chemises here. They were more likely to be found wrapped in horse blankets and huddled round a smouldering pile of camel dung. Very erotic. Dolmabahçe Palace? – Supposed to be stunningly ornate, but I couldn't see a thing through the haze of hoar frost on my glasses.

These were just the indoor attractions, where there were at least doors and windows to provide some discouragement to the ever-present icy blasts. The Grand Bazaar and the Spice Bazaar are colourful and fascinating shopping opportunities which just happen to be sited in a labyrinth of interlocking wind tunnels.

We valiantly persisted in our sightseeing until our core temperatures approached critical and hypothermia became imminent.

You might as well brace yourselves here, for what follows is possibly the only actually useful information in the whole series of books. Should any of you be deranged enough to visit Istanbul in the middle of the winter, here is a trick that will stave off the onset of hypothermia and frostbite without the horrendous expense of booking into a five-star hotel.

Ready?

Here it is...

Take a ride on the tram.

The Istanbul tram system is a life-saver for the hypothermic visitor. The trams are comfortable and as warm as toast. The T1 line runs for a whisker under 20 kilometres and cost you a flat fee of 2.3 Turkish Lira (45 pence). Trams run every two minutes in peak times and every 15 minutes outside peak periods. You buy a ticket from a machine at the tram stop, validate it when you board the tram and then ride up and down to your heart's content until you come out of your cryogenically induced coma and sensation returns to your hands and feet. That should give you enough residual heat to make it back to the hotel.

So much for my first recommendation of not going in February, but what about my second suggestion of not expecting Istanbul to be representative of Turkey as a whole? On the surface, it should be. After all, with a population of around fifteen million, it accounts for nearly twenty percent of Turkey's 78 million population. Compare that with Greater London's 8 ½ million accounting for just 13% of the UK's population.

No Brit[57] would seriously contend that London was a representative microcosm of the whole UK. Few capital cities are.[58] Most people, in most countries accept that such cities are special cases and are qualitatively different from most of the rest of the country. In fact, a lot of people actively resent what they see as the disproportionate influence their capital city and its resident movers and shakers have their lives, on the body politic and on other institutions of the country as a whole.

There is a school of thought that Brexit referendum result and the election of Donald Trump are manifestations of a polarisation of Western societies and that the political and philosophical middle ground is being lost to two extreme, diametrically opposed and aggressively conflicting world views. Well, compared to Turkey, the British are a homogenous mass of cloned sheep all called Brian.

Turkey's divisions go back to the founding of the republic in 1923 when Mustafa Kemal Atatürk raised the modern Republic of Turkey from the smouldering remains of the Ottoman Empire.

His aim was to establish a modern, secular, westernised, educated, emancipated society in a country primarily composed of conservative, Islamic, eastward-looking, predominantly illiterate, patriarchal peasants.

Well good luck with that. He obviously liked a challenge.[59]

And he didn't sit on his arse twiddling his thumbs. In a few years he had transformed Turkish society. His reforms included the emancipation of women, the abolition or control of all Islamic institutions and the introduction of western legal codes and the western calendar. He set up a committee of linguists, educators and writers and told them to come up with a new Latinate alphabet to replace the Arabic script in use at the time, and not to hang about. They did it in a year and it was implemented in three months. This, combined with his 'Campaign against ignorance', rapidly raised the literacy rate from around 10% to over 90%.

He wasn't all sweetness and light, though. People who get a lot done rarely are. Ali Kemal, one of his more influential critics, was intercepted by an ally of Atatürk who armed and incited a mob to lynch Kemal, a job they did most thoroughly with cudgels, stones and knives before hanging him from a tree with a rude notice pinned to his chest with a hunting knife[60]. Demonstrations of intent such as this, coupled with the fact that Atatürk was in charge of the army and so had most of the guns, swords, artillery, bombs and aeroplanes, tended to discourage overt resistance to his reforms, which went ahead apace.

It's one thing to discourage overt opposition, but changing hearts and minds is another matter. A large proportion of the Turks did sign up wholeheartedly to Atatürk's ideas, but an equally large number found them anathema. Some of this opposition was philosophically and ideologically driven, but I'm sure the Imams and Madrassas weren't exactly thrilled with their loss of power and influence once they were effectively taken under government control.

The dividing lines between the two camps were not drawn only on religious and political grounds, but also on material and geographical ones. The secularists tended to be more liberal, better educated, wealthier, more influential and to live in the big cities and the western and southwestern coasts. Those in the other camp tended to be conservative, pious, poorly educated, impoverished, disenfranchised and they lived predominantly in the central and eastern parts of the country. They are also, probably, marginally greater in number than the secularists.

The secularists, though, have got the army on their side. Historically, should any uppity Islamist politician get within sniffing distance of power and so pose a threat to Atatürk's legacy, the army would step in with a gentle little coup as a reminder of who's actually in charge[61].

All this elicits cognitive dissonance in the minds of wishy-washy liberals such as me. On the one hand the democratic will of the majority, especially the disadvantaged, should prevail. On the other hand, the measures they want to implement are so fundamentally wrong and repressive that they should be avoided at almost all costs.

All of which brings echoes of the English Civil War as described by Sellar and Yeatman in '1066 and All That', where the Cavaliers were 'Wrong But Wromantic' whereas the roundheads were 'Right But Repulsive'. Who do you side with when the good guys do bad things and the bad guys do good things?

Turkey also serves as a model for possible developments in other western democracies where polarization seems to be occurring.

Conventional wisdom has it that power in liberal democracies goes to whoever wins the battle for the middle ground. This model is based on the premise that the electorate's attitudes on any matter (e.g. left vs right) are distributed in a bell curve. Very few have extreme left-wing views and very few are extreme right-wingers. Most voters' views are bunched around the middle. This leads to more or less consensus politics where the majority of people think that government policy, if not exactly in tune with their thinking, is at least not too far from it. This encourages participation, engagement and debate. OK – it's not perfect but it's about the best we'll get in terms of peaceful co-existence.

A highly polarised electorate paints a very different

picture. The distribution graph is no longer a dromedary's hump, but now looks like the twin humps of a Bactrian camel; a couple of mountains with a valley between them. There is very little overlap in the middle. As a result, it becomes pointless for a politician to court the middle ground. In practical terms, there isn't any. Instead, power now goes to whoever successfully panders to whichever is the biggest of the two humps which lie at the two extremes. This goes by the rather clumsy title of a majoritarian dictatorship.

Government policies will now be sorely resented by the nearly 50% of the population in the losing hump who will now, with considerable justification, feel voiceless, disenfranchised and run roughshod over by a government that treats them and their views and feelings with dismissive contempt. The winning side, meanwhile, stands a good chance of further inflaming the situation with arrogant crowing, taunting and metaphorically rubbing the losers' noses in it. The old virtues of graciousness in defeat and magnanimity in victory fade and die. This will hold true whichever side wins.

Such polarisation is not an automatic precursor to civil strife, but I suspect it is an important prerequisite. Perhaps one of the most important tasks currently facing liberal democracies is to address this polarisation starting with trying to determine its causes.

I'll start the ball rolling. Why do so many feel angry, frustrated and impotent when they have to suffer the consequences of the self-serving shenanigans of the political, financial and business classes. And remember, to misquote H.L. Mencken:

"To every complex problem there is an answer that is easy, neat, simple, plausible and wrong."

Meanwhile, back in Marmaris Yat Marine, the time was rapidly approaching for *Birvidik's* annual lift out. This involves hoiking sixteen tonnes of boat out of its natural habitat and propping it up on concrete, supported by a patchwork mêlée of acrows, old planks and assorted bits of tree.

In this precarious position, the hull is subject to

considerably different stresses than it is in its design environment. The hull flexes under these changed circumstances, making doors, drawers and cupboards either stick or swing open of their own accord. Sometimes both.

All this just adds to the joys of living 'on the hard' as it is known. The full irritations of this have been described in full tedious detail in 'An Idiot Aboard', so I won't labour the matter other than to point out that, although we had by now become accustomed to the difficulties of living on the hard, we now had an extra factor to take into account, namely the cat.

More precisely, having a cat whose co-ordination, balance and agility are so indescribably awful that the adjectival phrase 'cat-like' could not be applied by any stretch of the imagination. This did not, however, have any effect on her delusions of competence in this department. As a result, an arms race developed. She kept trying to get onto adjoining boats by jumping gaps several metres up in the air and a metre or so beyond her capacity. We employed increasingly desperate (and expensive) measures to prevent her.

Surrounding the boat in 40 quid's worth of netting was easily overcome by her climbing determinedly up the netting, balancing precariously on the 1-inch stainless steel handrail at the top and hurling herself at the adjacent superyacht in a whirling flurry of fur and claws. Raising the netting so that the boat appeared to have been cocooned in a web constructed by an outsized spider after a rather large spliff fared no better so we resorted to bondage and tied her up in a harness attached to a short lead. Too short as things turned out, so we lengthened it with a length of elastic. This, we hoped, would enable her to roam the deck, but discourage her from jumping onto the adjacent boat. It didn't. We were, however, able to reel her in like a game fish and so we chalked it up as a partial victory.

We failed, however, to anticipate her retaliatory strategy. By taking the most tortuous and circuitous routes she could around the deck she created a literal cat's cradle entangling every obstruction she could find (which were many). If this failed to trip us up, she expressed her displeasure by whining and complaining until one of us came out and disentangled her. This occurred at approximately ten-minute intervals. On top of this she managed to create some knots that would have taken me 45 minutes, two pairs of hands and an eight-page set of explanatory diagrams. She also validated a memorable quote from Tony Jennet, my first sailing instructor - "*Any fucking idiot can tie a knot that won't come undone!*" He was a bluff, no-nonsense sort of bloke, Tony.

Nevertheless, we persevered.

We had tied her up and were working at ground level when we heard the by now familiar sound of her launching herself at the neighbouring superyacht. Unfortunately, she had failed to take into account the series of loops and knots she had already tangled in the elastic. Mid leap, her eyes glistening in manic determination, she was rudely and unexpectedly brought to a jerking halt by the lead. The whirling claws made desperate attempts to latch on to the pristine bodywork of the superyacht, but it was an unequal struggle and she slid over the edge of its deck with an expression and performance that would have done credit to a Tom & Jerry episode. Her eyes were now like saucers as she viewed the rapidly approaching concrete. We braced ourselves for the sounds of splintering bone and bursting spleen.

About a metre and a half before ground zero the elastic began to tighten and her rate of descent slowed. I couldn't have calculated the length of elastic better if I'd had a Cray supercomputer. She came softly to rest as her paws gently brushed the concrete. The pupils started to contract a little. She then adopted her customary air in such circumstances, namely a smug "*I meant to do that all along*" sort of air. Smug lasted about 3 milliseconds until the tension in the elastic came into play and she accelerated up into the air again. This confused her somewhat. She's never really managed to come to grips with the concept of conservation of energy. She stared disconsolately and bemusedly as the ground receded.

The elastic pulled her up to about three-quarters the height of her original drop. Obviously thinking that she had somehow miraculously gained the power of flight she windmilled her paws in a desperate (and ultimately futile) attempt to climb back on board before her superpowers disappeared as suddenly and mysteriously as they had come into being. Then gravity took over again. The damping action continued for a minute or so, with ever diminishing oscillations until she finally came to rest hanging forlornly about a metre up in the air like one of those floppy rubber toys on elastic. She had to hang there, terminally embarrassed, for about five minutes until we managed to stop laughing, wait for the ache in our stomachs to subside and untie her.

Serves her right.

Greece

(again)

The plan was simplicity itself – leave Marmaris and check back into Greece and the EU on Symi before making our way across the southern Aegean before the Meltemi kicked in. Then we could spend a leisurely season pottering around the Peloponnese before making our way down to Crete for the winter.

We should have known better.

It started off well. We had decided against the harbour in Symi town after the shenanigans of our previous visit the year before. We planned to anchor in Panormitis, a secluded bay on the south of the island, and take the bus to Symi town to complete the paperwork.

Things went fine at first. We doped ourselves up with Stugeron to counter the fact that we had almost certainly lost our sea legs over the winter and then turned to the problem of the cat. We had consulted a number of vets who all confirmed our previous advice that stugeron doesn't work on cats.

What did work, apparently, were sedatives. With these the cat may well have still suffered from sea-sickness but it would have been so zonked it didn't give a toss. There were a number of available sedatives, all being more or less equally effective once you'd managed to get them into the cat. It was the getting them into the cat that posed the problems. The choices seemed to be tablet, gel, oral liquid, suppository or injection.

This is one of the few instances where having a dog would have proved less troublesome than having a cat. Dogs are by nature social animals; their survival depends on membership of the pack. As a result, they are so pathetically eager to please and desperate to fit in that fooling them is a piece of piss. Things are helped along by the fact that life in a pack has a lot of similarity to school dinners. Eating is a communal activity that is effectively a free-for-all version of Devil take the hindmost. If you don't fight your corner and wolf down food when you get the chance, then you're going to go hungry.

The cunning owner of a boat dog can utilise these potential weaknesses when preparing Fido for a possibly lumpy trip. Frequently, mission can be accomplished by the simple ruse of pretending that the tablet is a tasty morsel which, if he's lucky and quick, Fido will get before it goes to someone else. Waving it about, accompanied by excited and friendly cries of *'Here, boy – look what I've got for you'* will have the poor sap jumping and slathering with enthusiasm. Once you've got him into a frenzy of excitement, just flick the tablet in his rough direction. He'll catch it and swallow it in one before there's been any time for him to taste the thing. He may look slightly pained and reproachful when the lingering aftertaste hits, but as he has the attention span of a fruit fly this phase rarely lasts long.

In the unlikely event of this strategy failing, then the fall-back position is almost infallible. This involves hiding the tablet in food. Almost anything will usually do – dogs aren't picky. They can't afford to be – the pack is a source of both co-operation and competition. If you want to ensure the success of this strategy, have another dog standing close by before putting the doctored food down. The fear of losing out to a rival will guarantee that the dumb mutt hoovers the lot down in short order.

All of this is dependent on cynically manipulating the dog's naïve trust and insecurity. Cats, on the other hand, are suspicious buggers. Not for them the blind sycophancy of the pack. They are solitary ambush hunters. Wary scepticism is their default mode. Getting a sedative into them requires guile of the highest order or the drastic imposition of brute force. We tried an escalating scale of methods over the first few trips until we hit on one that worked.

Attempting the simplest tactic of just offering her the tablet was so eminently absurd that we dismissed it out of hand and moved straight on to phase two.

We dug out her favourite treats. We normally use these to reward her for good behaviour and limit them to around three at any one time. I put six in her bowl and hid the tablet in the middle of them.

She approached the bowl gingerly and gave it a suspicious sniff for a minute or so before poking it about with her paw. She followed this by taking the tablet distastefully between her canines and dropping it dismissively on the carpet. Then she gobbled down the treats and went for a kip.

We moved on to tactic two, which involved trying to emulate the vet's trick of pushing the tablet to the back of the throat and then holding the mouth closed while massaging the throat to encourage swallowing.

It always looks so easy when the vet does it.

The first problem is to get the cat's mouth open in the first place. Vets seem to achieve this effortlessly by pressing the forefinger and thumb to the sides of the mouth near the jaw hinge. They seem to be able to do this with the gentlest of pressure. If the cat is particularly recalcitrant, they sometimes augment this action with a light downward pressure on the lower incisors.

Compare and contrast this idealised technique with our clumsy and amateurish efforts. The domestic cat has one of the lowest Bite Force Quotients of all carnivores[62] but it still seems to require inordinate amounts of brute force, sometimes augmented by a jemmy, to get its mouth open against its will. I tried to emulate the vet technique, but Einstein's mouth remained obstinately shut, despite my increasing the pressure to the point where there was a real risk of her lower jaw coming away in my hand.

Liz, by now fed up with having her thighs shredded by the cat's claws, came up with a cunning plan. She put her finger over the cat's nose. Even Einstein's legendary stubbornness couldn't overcome the asphyxiation reflex and she opened her mouth with a gasp, just before she passed out. I took advantage of this by pushing the tablet down her throat. She immediately hawked it up, spat it out and then threw up on my hand.

We moved on to oral gel, designed to be rubbed into the gums. This presented all the problems of tablets and then some. Once we had finally got her mouth open, we had to try and rub a measured amount of slippery, obviously foul-tasting, gel on her gums. She spat most of it out and made it impossible to titrate the correct dose. We gave up on that.

Administering an oral liquid involved getting the mouth open with all that entailed and then squirting a syringe full of liquid down the back of her throat. All this succeeded in doing was nearly drowning her before she coughed, spluttered and sprayed it all over us.

We decided to pass on the suppository on the grounds of dignity and good taste and brought out the big guns – injection. We had left this until last as we had feared it would be the most difficult and distressing. How wrong we were. We should have gone for the jab first.

Using Liz's clinical skills, augmented by close observation of vets at work, we found the jab to be the easiest, cleanest and quickest method, and the least distressing to both her and us. Grab her by the scruff of the neck, stick the needle in subcutaneously and squirt. She didn't even flinch. We used that method thenceforth.

Having finally managed to drug the cat into comatose acquiescence, I fired up all the navigation and communications gizmos. These are many and varied, having multiplied exponentially since we set off from Jersey. Nowadays we get our weather forecasts ('mets' in the parlance) over the internet via the mobile phone network. These are updated every three hours or so. Our position is shown by GPS. This still has a circle of uncertainty, but nowadays you'd have trouble fitting an office desk in it. This position is then relayed to a chart plotter which shows a cute little boat shape trundling its way across the chart.

And so it was that *Birvidik*, bristling with technology and creature comforts, sailed jauntily from Marmaris *en route* for Symi. We motored into Panormitis, the aforementioned beautiful secluded and protected bay on the South of the island, and dropped the hook. Then it started.

I switched off the autopilot. This action, for some

inexplicable reason, offended the GPS in the chartplotter which bleeped twice in annoyance and promptly switched itself off in a sulk. Nothing could coax it back into service. Not to worry, we still had two backup GPSs. We're nothing if not cautious.

I decided to get a met, so I fired up the computer and attached the dongle. Merely having this arrangement was a triumph in itself. After much bureaucratic wrangling we had finally managed to get an internet contract with Vodafone Greece in Corfu in 2008. This was a process so entangled in labyrinthine, Byzantine complexity that we kept paying the monthly subscriptions even whilst we were in Turkey, just so that we could have it immediately available whenever we returned to Greek waters. The program chuntered about for a bit and then protested that it couldn't find a network. This was surprising given that we were moored in the shadow of a bloody great comms mast and our ordinary Greek mobile phones showed maximum signal strengths. In addition, our fluorescent lights thrummed and pulsed like something out of 'The Twilight Zone'. Even the cooker gave off a dull glow and emanated snatches of ghostly Greek conversations. What do you mean 'network not found'? There was so much electromagnetic radiation around that if you stood on the saloon table, equidistant from the toaster and the steering compass and spun round with your arms in the air the computer gave you a whole-body scan.

As we were in the middle of nowhere, we decided to head on to Nysiros the next day and see if we could sort things out there. We set off using the Garmin GPS to check our position and headed for Pali on Nysiros. Halfway across I noticed that the Magellan, the 'backup, backup' GPS had suffered sudden onset Alzheimer's and kept forgetting where the satellites were. We were now down to one GPS and panic started to set in.

Nysiros is a lovely island, with a protected harbour, picturesque villages, friendly locals and a stunning, and still active, volcanic crater. Its population, though, is a tad on the small side at around 2000 souls and so it's not exactly a hub of commercial activity. In fact, apart from tourist shops, tavernas and basic food shops, business is so slow that absolutely nobody keeps any stock at all. Whatever you want needs to be ordered from Athens and can take weeks to arrive. This can pose problems if, for example, you suddenly find yourself running low on colostomy bags. Unsurprisingly, therefore, we were spectacularly unsuccessful in our proposed tasks of getting the chartplotter fixed, buying a replacement backup backup GPS and getting the internet setup working again.

We were, though, given a contact number for Vodafone which I duly rang. I was shunted through a succession of operatives and exposed to enough of 'My Way' being played on a Rolf Harris stylophone to be justified in claiming my treatment as being in obvious and blatant breach of the Geneva Convention. Eventually, I was informed that the account had been unilaterally closed. Despite my pleas, the laughingly termed 'customer services agent' was either unable or unwilling to elucidate why this had been done, instead stalling by asking for increasingly obscure pieces of data. I hung in there and managed to wring multidigit numbers for IMEI, IMSI, and ICCID from the computer when, in desperation, she stumped me by asking for my Greek tax number.

"*I haven't got one*" I said, my voice about half an octave higher than usual.

"*You must have*" said she with an air of self-satisfied finality. "*If you don't have a Greek tax number, you're not allowed to have an internet contract*". QED - game set and match to Greek bureaucracy.

Further investigation revealed that the only places in Greece that you stand a snowball's chance in Hell of getting anything done, ever, are Athens, Corfu, Kos and Rhodes. Rhodes would have taken us back where we started. Athens and Corfu were miles away and so, as soon as the gale force Northerlies blew themselves out, it was back to Kos to sort it all out.

So much for an early start to the season.

Mind you, if we had been proper hairy sailors I'd have sharpened my pencils and ploughed on regardless, relying on trad nav.

If.

Kos started off well and then slid inexorably downhill. Those with long memories will remember our previous, unsuccessful, attempts to get into Kos marina last year. So before we left Nysiros (and with an ominous sense of *déjà vu*) I rang them and asked if there was the slightest chance of getting a berth for a few days to sort out our little problems. "*Of course*," they replied. "*When do you want to come and for how long?*". I should have been suspicious straight away.

We reversed direction and set sail for Kos at sparrowfart on the Monday and got in about midday. I went over to reception and booked in for three days. While I was there I asked the receptionist if there was an at least halfway competent electronics bod in the vicinity and she gave me a mobile number. I reckoned that Dejan Sevic didn't sound authentically Greek, but I rang the number and by 1:30 we had a fluently multilingual Serb on the boat poking around with the electronics. After about ten minutes of this he demonstrated that his diagnostic skills were at least on a par with mine by pronouncing that "*Your GPS engine is knackered*". I told you he was fluent.

Even in Kos there was nowhere with one of these in stock. The Greeks seemed to have got the 'just in time' school of logistics down to a fine art. Either that or their credit rating was now so low that no-one would supply them with so much as a paperclip unless paid up front. Apparently, he had actually held three in stock (GPS engines, not paperclips), but these had all been used up in the aftermath of a recent thunderstorm which had wreaked havoc with electronics across the Dodecanese. "*Not to worry*" he assured me, "*I can order one from Athens and it'll be here by tomorrow*". Impressed and reassured by his confidence I set off to Kos town to get Vodafone sorted out.

This proved somewhat more problematic, with a repeat of the demands for more numbers that I didn't have. They were, at least, different numbers that I didn't have from the ones previously demanded over the phone, but I still didn't have them. The absence of a Greek tax number didn't seem to bother them at all. I'm sure they just make these things up to relieve the boredom of spending eight hours a day selling pointless accessories and irritating ringtones to hordes of gormless, vapid adolescents. It transpired that the only way to sort things out was to set up an entirely new contract from scratch. This only took three days and five visits to the shop.

The next day was notable for the absence of any visit from Dejan. When I finally phoned him, he said that the main agent in Athens didn't have any in stock and he couldn't give a date when he would. It was looking like the 'poor credit rating' theory was gaining strength. On the bright side, though, the hand held GPS seemed to have done an Ernest Saunders and made a miraculous recovery from Alzheimer's. It will be interesting to see to whom Saunders' apparent miracle is attributed. I'm half expecting the beatification procedure to kick in for Bernie Madoff and Fred Goodwin soon - probably before they're even dead.

Taking solace from our partial success we set off for Kalymnos and made fast to a buoy in Emborios. We hired a scooter for a couple of days and toured the Island. The road from Emborios south reminded me of when we rode a motorcycle down the Croatian coast in the early 1970s. It winds its way precariously halfway up between the soaring limestone crags and the sea, giving a breathtaking view over the many islets and bays. Occasionally they've erected a token crash barrier, but usually the road is edged with about a metre or so of loose gravel and then it falls precipitously onto the rocky shore below.

Travelling in on the bus to pick up the bike, we were somewhat less than encouraged by the fact that the locals had a habit of crossing themselves whenever the bus approached a bend. This faded into insignificance when we had to get a taxi back after dropping off the bike. The driver gave a passable impression of Peter Sellers impersonating a gangster in one of the Pink Panther films - drastically overweight, wedged into the driving seat of his Merc, slicked back dyed black hair and shades. He had obviously trained at the same school of taxi driving as the stunt drivers in 'The Italian Job'. He threw the Merc into one corner after the other with such enthusiasm and speed that we spent the entire journey with our faces pressed flat against alternate windows. Tyres squealed and gravel flew. We sank into our seats and nervously tightened the seatbelts. He did all of this with one hand, leaving the other free for doughnuts, mobile phone and, as he approached any particularly circumflex bend, crossing himself. Does crossing oneself with a doughnut in one's hand have any particular theological significance I wonder?

These terrors notwithstanding, I've got a soft spot for Kalymnos and the Kalymniots - they hang on in there come what may.

The island used to have a thriving economy based on sponge diving. Sponges were big business as far back as the Mycean era. According to no lesser authority than Lawrence Durrell, the servants in 'The Odyssey' swabbed tables with them. They were used by artisans to apply paint. Soldiers used them to transfer wine from amphora to mouth. Burnt sponge served as a cure for various illnesses and sponges soaked in olive oil were used as contraceptive pessaries. Indeed, in the argot of modern Athenian prostitutes the word 'sponge' has a number of colourful translations.

Getting hold of them, though, (sponges, not Athenian prostitutes) was a phenomenally dangerous activity involving grabbing hold of a large rock and throwing yourself off a boat into 20 metres or more of water without so much as a pair of goggles or a swimming costume. On hitting bottom the diver took the iron bar from between his teeth and started prizing sponges off the sea bed and depositing them in a basket tied to his waist. Just before he expired from hypoxia he would head for the surface (no fins) and, if he was lucky, still be conscious enough to breathe when he got there.

The advent of hard hat diving suits should have increased available working depths and improved their life expectancy no end. It did the former but as for the latter it brought its own little limitations. For a start the air was supplied by a couple of bored matelots working a see-saw bellows a bit like those hand trucks they used to use on the railways in the old west. They had to pump constantly and at increasing rates as the diver descended. If their attention wandered, or they stopped for a fag or sloped off for a dump, not only could the diver not breathe, but the pressure in the suit dropped off. This caused the suit to compress under the higher water pressure. Brass helmets, though, don't compress very well. The only entrance available to equalise the pressure is the neck of the helmet. Can you see where this is going? At 30 metres the total force on the body of the suit is equivalent to around 2500 newtons (about a quarter of a tonne). The low pressure (which is where the water wants to push stuff) is in the helmet.... It doesn't bear thinking about, does it?

Even if they survived all that, there was the small matter of decompression sickness. No-one told them about nitrogen saturation curves. Hardly surprising, since no-one at the time knew anything about them. Divers crippled by the bends became a familiar sight around the island. Between 1886 and 1910 some 1 000 divers died and another 2 000 were crippled.

After the privations of the second world war, the advent of scuba gear and decompression tables should have done wonders for the Kalymniot economy, but the double whammy of mysterious sponge diseases attributed to pollution and the advent of cheap synthetic sponges killed off the fledgling recovery. Undeterred, the island succumbed to the siren promises of the package holiday industry and the west coast was transformed into the Benidorm of the Dodecanese. The tour companies stayed just long enough to ruin both the local ambience and what local commerce there was before suddenly pulling out completely, ostensibly because their poor pampered punters couldn't face a 20 minute boat transfer from Kos and the Kalymniots baulked at blighting a significant proportion of what was left of their island with the construction of an international airport.

So they dusted themselves down and started again. They promoted Kalymnos as a walking and climbing venue, making good use of the island's geography. This took off in a big way and they now have a thriving industry which, according to some with whom we spoke, is bringing in more income for much less disruption than the not sadly missed bucket, spade and lager brigades ever did. Of course, now the Greek economy's imploded...

Despite all their troubles the island continued to develop, to the point where Kalymnos town is now the second largest in the Dodecanese, having overtaken Kos. This made us think that it might be worth trying to get our GPS sorted out there, and so it turned out. It was still the 'order from Athens' syndrome, but the guy in the shop phoned Athens there and then, ascertained that the model we had was obsolete and advised us of a compatible replacement. This arrived in three days (over a weekend) and I fitted it and had it working within two hours.

Now we could continue across the Aegean.

Except for the fact that we'd now missed the weather window.

We left Kalymnos on the 25th of May. Ah! - Spring in the Southern Aegean! The sea and the air were warming up. Relaxing summer days and balmy summer nights beckoned enticingly. Shorts, T shirts and sandals were the order of the day.

Were they bollocks. We were swaddled in enough foul-weather gear to survive the Southern Ocean. We were wearing lifejackets for Christ's sake.

Missed weather window or not, after a week in Kalymnos it was definitely time to move on. The forecast wasn't too bad, broken cloud with a force four fine on the starboard bow. So it was when we started out on the ten hour trip to Naxos. We trimmed the sails and set off on a cracking motor sail, making about eight knots. Einstein was drugged up to the eyeballs and slumped on a beanbag in the cockpit. The sun shone most of the time and *Birvidik* cut cleanly through the water, riding the low swell with an easy motion.

This lasted all of 40 minutes.

Then the wind swung round dead on the nose and freshened to a force 5. The sky clouded over and darkened, and it started to rain. The wind built to a six, still dead on the nose, and proceeded to build up a short, steep sea into which

Birvidik slammed with stomach-jarring regularity. We had eight hours of this until we decided enough was enough and stopped early, pulling into the isolated overnight anchorage on Dhenoussa. This gave us short relief as the weather was forecast to deteriorate even further, with the Northerly six increasing to North Westerly eight, so we left early the next morning to try to get into the anchorage on Paros before it really hit.

Coming out of the bay involved turning into the swell which the wind had continued to build up overnight. The wind and waves were funnelled into the channel between Dhenoussa and Naxos and really threw *Birvidik* about. Fortunately, we had had the foresight to drug everyone on the boat (Stugeron for us, sedative for Einstein) before setting off.

Things continued to fail to improve.

About halfway there, Liz took over the con and I went below for a bit of shuteye. No more than ten minutes into my off duty, an alarm started beeping continuously, which brought me up to the cockpit in short order. It turned out to be the autopilot, which displayed the terse and, I thought, rather unnecessarily cryptic message 'DRIVE STOP'. No-one can think with all that beeping noise going on, so I turned the autopilot off and reverted to hand steering. Well, perhaps the phrase 'attempted to return to hand steering' would have been more accurate. The steering was locked solid.

There are many systems on a boat that, in a pinch, you can get away without or bodge some sort of substitute for, but steering is not one of them. If you lose your electronics you can revert to trad nav. If you lose your echo sounder you can use a lead line. If you lose your engine you can use the sails. If you lose the mast you can usually jury rig something to provide some sort of propulsion. But if you lose your steering you're definitely knackered. Unable to control your direction you are left at the mercy of the sea. If it's in a bad mood, and it was definitely a bit grumpy this day, the sea makes Judge Jeffries look like Mahatma Ghandi.

Without steerage you can't control the aspect of the boat to the waves, nor can you guide it away from nasty hard sharp things, like rocks, of which there were plenty in the narrow straits in which we found ourselves. Although on a lee shore we at least had a modicum of sea room. At a rough estimate we had about half an hour before a close encounter with one of the sharp pointy things surrounding the East coast of Paros. Our first thought was that the violent motion had dislodged something which had then fallen into, and jammed, the steering mechanism.

The most likely place was right at the stern, where the steering mechanism operates the quadrant which turns the rudder. I dived into the aft cabin, pulled out the two drawers at the back and threw them onto the bed, scattering the contents. I slung on a headlight and wormed my way into the steering space behind the drawers, no mean feat when the room you are in is lurching randomly about. I couldn't see anything obvious, but I called to Liz to try turning the wheel to starboard while I kept my hand on the torque tube to see if I could feel anything. To our surprise, and relief, it turned and then freed itself completely. Everything now worked perfectly.

This, of course, was good news, but slightly worrying as we had no idea what had caused the problem in the first place. Had it gone away completely, or would it decide to come back at the most inopportune moments, such as when undertaking some close quarters manoeuvre between Scylla and Charybdis? We thought about attempting to track the entire steering system to find the fault. This, however, would have involved dismantling half the boat, which is difficult enough on a calm day in a marina. We decided to work on the assumption that it had sorted itself out and re-engaged the autopilot.

Just as the adrenaline levels were tapering off, we came out of the Northern end of the channel and into the full force of the wind and sea. The boat pitched violently and threw itself from side to side. We also needed to change course here and that posed another problem. Currently, we had the sea on the bow, unpleasant, but cope-able with. The course we needed would put the seas on the beam, which would have made an even worse motion, despite the steadying effect of the sails. I decided to continue beating into wind until we had enough sea-room to tack down wind and sea to our destination. This took a very unpleasant forty minutes during which Liz managed to rick her back when an unexpected lurch of the boat coincided with her attempt to pump out the toilet.

Then came the next little challenge. I hoped that once we were on our new course we would have the wind and sea on the starboard quarter and the motion would ease. To get there though, I had to turn through 100 degrees to port, which involved taking us through having the seas beam on. With a nice regular pattern this is doable. You judge the pattern of the waves and turn just before the crest. Then with any luck you'll pass through the beam on position and be on your next course before the next wave hits. With a confused sea such as we had, gauging this becomes far more difficult, but I gave it a go.

I blew it.

A big, irregular wave appeared out of nowhere mid-manoeuvre. It hit us square on the starboard side and knocked us on our beam ends (that's flat on your side for the non-yotties out there). I saw it coming a fraction of a second before it hit. I just had time to shout a warning down to Liz to grab hold of something and looked across to see Einstein, still in a drugged stupor, and still slumped on a beanbag on the starboard cockpit seat. Clutching the wheel, I braced myself with my left leg and stuck my right leg out like a geriatric Jackie Chan in a futile attempt to keep her on the seat. No such luck. The beanbag, complete with cat, slid off the seat and hung, momentarily, in mid-air before plummeting to the cockpit sole with a muffled thud. She raised her head, and one eyebrow, sighed and collapsed back on the bag like a deflating balloon.

Another hour and a half of downwind tacks, luckily unaccompanied by any steering failures, led us into the calm waters of Naoussa anchorage in Paros.

Which is where we bloody well stayed until the winds decided to behave themselves.

We used the time to clear up the unholy mess in the all

the sections of the boat and to search for the cause of the steering problems. No luck - everything still worked perfectly.

We waited for a stable weather window and set off for Syros, where we moored up against the town quay after a satisfyingly smooth and uneventful trip. We moored stern-to, dropping our main bow anchor and motoring astern to the quay and tying to it. Traditionally, we have moored bows-to in these circumstances, as reported in tedious detail previously. As is usual in cruising, the final choice is a compromise between conflicting factors. In this case the balance was tipped in favour of stern-to by two main considerations. Firstly, the holding was not reported to be the best and the pilot murmured dark warnings about ferry wash. We reckoned that our vastly oversized main anchor would hold us off the quay better than the lighter and less efficient stern anchor. Secondly, it also warned of unpleasant smells originating from the large quantities of raw sewage discharged into the harbour. This also explained the sloppy, gooey bottom and resultant bad holding. The stern anchor and chain would have had to have been lifted by hand when we left, and I didn't fancy ending up coated in a sticky culture of every pathogen known to medical science. So stern-to it was.

Our crew roster is the opposite of that usually employed on cruising boats where the bloke poses on the helm while the poor woman runs around doing all the grunt work. When we approach a stern to mooring Liz assumes station at the helm. I then put out fenders at the required height on both sides of the boat. Next, I dig out the mooring ropes, uncoil them, run them through the stern fairleads, tie them off on cleats and then re-coil them ready for heaving. After that I lower the stern platform and secure it in position prior to fixing the access ladder in place. I then run to the bow, slack off the anchor windlass and heave the anchor over the bow roller. Liz then starts to go astern toward the quay, and I drop anchor and release the windlass to allow the chain to run free. Once the chain is running freely, I need to run back to the stern to see if there are any helpful passers-by to whom I can throw the stern lines. No luck in this case.

Plenty of ghouls, but no assistance.

Undeterred, I then guide Liz in going astern until the shore is within reach and make a desperate leap for the shore whilst simultaneously holding on to the two stern ropes. If by some miracle I reach the land unscathed and still in possession of the two ropes, I make them fast to the quay somewhere (anywhere) and then frantically fend the boat off in a generally unsuccessful attempt to stop it crashing into the concrete quay and spilling the café frappés of the assorted beautiful people at the waterside tables. At this point, Liz goes ahead to try to minimise the destruction wrought by the quay whilst I simultaneously scrabble back onto the rapidly receding stern platform before I need to demonstrate a claim to being the reincarnation of Jesse Owens in order to get back on. Once back onboard I run to the bow and take up the anchor chain until it is bar-tight and the anchor has bitten. All that now remains to be done is spend half an hour adjusting the stern lines and anchor chain alternately until the boat is nicely snugged at a convenient distance for getting ashore.

During all this, Liz sits on the helmsman's seat waggling the wheel and playing with the girlie buttons (bow thrusters).

After the previous two weeks of quiet, isolated anchorages, Ermiopoulis, the capital of Syros and erstwhile capital of the Cyclades, made a stimulating change. The town quay was the social centre of the town, abuzz with cars, motorcycles and pedestrians. The far side of the road from the quay was lined with shops and, primarily, cafes, bars and restaurants. The last-mentioned three businesses had spread to occupy the quay space opposite, which they had covered with tables, chairs and sun awnings. Waiters and waitresses traversed the no man's land of the main road, carrying an endless procession of food and drink in one direction and the detritus of consumption in the other. They negotiated the chaotic traffic, side-stepping and pirouetting with easy, practiced grace. The whole area, already busy throughout the day, reached its climax in the evening when what seemed like every soul on the island either paraded up and down in the evening *passeio*, or watched unselfconsciously from the myriad café tables. Einstein sat on the stern with her eyes out on stalks.

Rapidly going native, we repaired to the café nearest to *Birvidik* for a drink before dinner. Halfway through I nipped back on board to pick up some money. While down below, I heard the rumble of a ferry's engines echoing through the hull. I mentioned in the previous book how ferries came to occupy a special place in Greek society and how, as a result, ferry skippers came to consider themselves God, or if not God then at least on a par with the Archangel Gabriel. I braced myself for the inevitable ferry wash, and I was not disappointed.

Birvidik, in common with all the other boats on the quay, lurched, bucked, surged, pitched and rolled, straining at the lines holding her to the rusted fittings on the quay which were, by now, definitely not looking man enough for the job. Clinging on to the mizzen mast like a drunk round a lamppost, I cast a worried glance around me. There are a range of unpleasant possibilities in a situation such as this. The most obvious is that the surge will carry you back and crash the stern repeatedly into the rough concrete quay. It got close, but the fenders we had deployed at the stern managed to avert that. The second is that the anchor is pulled free and the boat swings sideways, crashes across the neighbouring boats and proceeds to pound its whole side repeatedly. The anchor held. Failing that, the violent rolling motion of the boats could result in the mast crashing into next door's mast and ripping off shrouds, crosstrees or worse still losing the mast completely. OK there. We'd thought to position the boat so that the masts didn't align with those either side. If you survive all those, the next problem is if you and the next boat roll sideways and manage to catch the capping rail or the join between the deck and the hull. At best you'll lose the capping rail and at worst the deck will peel away from the hull like the top of a sardine can.

We just scraped through on all counts and after about ten minutes it all settled down enough for me to get off the boat. With a sigh of relief, I sat at the table to finish my drink.

Did I mention that these ferries have a very short turn-around time?

Fifteen minutes later we were on the edge of our seats as the whole thing started off again. Luckily the wash from a leaving ferry is not as bad as that from when it arrives. Neither was this the only ferry creating havoc, although it was by far the worst. We reckoned we could manage to put up with it for a few days, but the next Met I got indicated that if we didn't leave PDQ we'd be stuck there for another week or so. The prospect of enduring that ferry wash for a total of about ten days concentrated the mind wonderfully, and we set off for Kithnos the next day. Once again, the sea was flat calm. We looked forward to a peaceful and uneventful trip. And so it was, for the first couple of hours.

After those first couple of hours, we glanced astern and saw a couple of faint dots on the horizon. A few minutes later this had clarified and increased to several quite large dots, chucking out a considerable amount of smoke. When we glanced behind about ten minutes after that the dots had metamorphosed into four Greek navy destroyers steaming line astern at high speed - damned near 30 knots according to the radar. I thought Greece was skint. Where do they get the money to burn fuel at that rate? They were catching up on us alarmingly quickly. Never mind, I thought, they're navy ships, crewed by highly trained professionals. They'll know the colregs inside out. The colregs, in this situation, stipulate that as the overtaking vessels it was their responsibility to keep out of our way. We held our course and speed. They came progressively closer. Two rather worrying possibilities occurred to us.

1 The skippers of the destroyers had delusions of grandeur and thought they were ferry skippers, or

2 Warships are excused colregs because they have a note from their mum, namely the Government.

In the end, they hammered past about 200 metres on our starboard side. However, 4 x 8 000 tonnes of shipping travelling at nearly 30 knots produces an awful lot of wash. Then there is the interaction between the sequence of bow and stern waves of each boat. By the time these primary waves had reached us they were probably no more than about a couple of metres high.

I suspect that a detailed explanation of constructive interference would lose us what few remaining readers we may have, but believe me, when four sets of waves like that reinforce each other they can produce some real mothers. By the time the effect of the interference had become apparent there was no time to turn into them and they hit us square on the beam. This threw us into possibly the most violent rolling I think we've ever experienced - worse than Biscay and worse than the recent bit of unpleasantness around Naxos. We swung like a metronome, from almost flat on our port side to almost flat on our starboard side and back again. And again, and again. Luckily, it only lasted about four minutes. The effects though were spectacular. Once stability had returned, we spent the next half an hour clearing up the carnage below. The destroyers faded into the distance

So, with the day's excitement comfortably out of the way we continued heading due West, towards the Northern tip of Kithnos. As we approached Kithnos I glanced over my shoulder to see another faint dot on the horizon, also chucking out smoke. This turned out to be the NEL ferry from Syros, making about 20 knots according to the radar and dead on course to hit us smack up the jaxie. A quick bit of mental arithmetic suggested that it would be a close-run thing as to whether we reached the tip of Kithnos and turned left before it played steamroller with us. To give us a sporting chance I increased the revs. After ten minutes of cat and mouse it became apparent that we'd make the corner first, which we did and turned to port, heading South, close along the west coast of Kithnos.

We looked behind, expecting to see the ferry, by now only some 500 metres behind us, steam past heading for the Greek mainland. Unfortunately, it did no such thing. Instead it executed a sharp 90-degree left turn and steamed straight toward us, still at full speed. There was little we could do. The colregs said we should hold our course and speed and that the ferry, as overtaking vessel, should take avoiding action. So we held our course, speed and breath. Still it bore down on us, heading straight for our stern. I tried calling them on the VHF so that we could agree on a course of action but got no reply.

The colregs also state that, if a collision looks likely, the stand-on vessel (that's us) should take (and I quote) "*such evasive action as is appropriate under the circumstances*". They make no effort to explain what such actions might be, but I was pretty sure that going hard astern wasn't one of them. Trying to outrun it wasn't much of an option either - at best it might give us another 15 seconds before impact. That left us with turning to port or to starboard. There wasn't any sea room to port as we were close to the steep-to cliffs. If turning that way didn't drive us onto the rocks then the wash from the ferry, at such close range, probably would.

That left starboard. The problem with turning to starboard was that, should the ferry skipper suddenly wake up and take avoiding action, then turning to starboard is exactly what he would do, thus still succeeding in liquidising us, only in slightly deeper water. A final radio call elicited no response and with the thing towering over us less than a hundred metres away I said "*Oh sod it!*", threw the wheel hard to starboard and gave the engine everything it had

The ferry carried on blithely across our stern, missing us by less than 50 metres. The wash picked us up and we surfed out of harm's way before turning in a wide circle to get back on course through the turbulent water that marked the ferry's passing. Ignoring my slurs on the parentage, mental capacity and onanistic tendencies of its skipper the ferry sped on regardless for Kithnos town. I suspect it has a route plugged into its chartplotter and that is the route it takes, and bollocks to anybody else who happens to be around.

It was at this point that paranoia struck deep. There was no doubt about it, they were definitely out to get me. If the weather couldn't do it then the Greeks would have a damned good go.

I must look up and memorise the Greek for "*Oi - Shit for brains!*"

From Kithnos it was but a short day's run and we were back in Poros and the Saronic Gulf. It was here that the human cost of the Greek economic crisis could be seen in its full misery.

As we blundered our way around the Med, we were not usually fully aware that we were also blundering our way through other peoples' lives. It is very easy to make only a superficial acquaintance with the people of the countries we visit. Certain travel books and some blogs, however, seem to detail an endless procession of invitations into the homes and workplaces of a litany of colourful local characters.

They then go on to describe how they managed to hold deep and meaningful conversations by means of a mixture of sign language and what they describe with nauseating feyness and false modesty as their 'rather basic' Greek/Turkish/Proto Indo-European/Old Icelandic etc. They're usually the ones who pepper their accounts with completely unnecessary, italicised foreign nouns (never verbs, note) as a means of showing off. You know the sort of pretentious tosh: "*Caramba*!" shouted the *campesino* as he threw his *azuela* to the *piso*. I sat in the *sombra* and sipped my *cuba libre* unconcernedly. One had to show sufficient *cojones* in these circumstances."

As a result of this cross-cultural anthropological fertilisation, hitherto unfathomed insights are gained into the true nature of the societies visited and the hidden depths of the lives of members of other cultures. These gems of cultural understanding and discovery can then be transmitted to less adventurous and sensitive souls, such as ourselves, with an air of such smug, self-regarding superiority that, even as a Guardian reader, I find the whole experience violently emetic.

Never bloody happens to us. - most of the time we're approached by locals it's usually because they want to sell us something. We have on occasions been invited to take tea with Turks, but have usually politely refused on the grounds that

1. They're usually trying to sell us something
2. Even if they aren't, Turkish tea is of such agonisingly

astringent awfulness that it strips away the lining of the oesophagus and stomach and immediately induces oesophageal varices, perforated gastric ulcer and irritable bowel syndrome.

3. *Pace* the irritating toe rags mentioned above, our sign language skills certainly make us no Marcels Marceaux and it's impossible to hold any proper sort of conversation when your entire vocabulary consists of *'yes', 'no', 'good morning', 'no thanks', 'how much?'* and *'HOW MUCH?!!'*.

Things were a bit different, though, as we cruised the Saronic gulf, where a good ¾ of the population speak reasonable English and about a half speak better English than did most of the kids I used to teach. As a result, we struck up conversations (and acquaintanceships) with more locals around here than we have in all the preceding areas put together. This also coincided with the inexorable decline of Greece into an economic basket case. The effects of this decline were visible everywhere.

Considering the circumstances, foreign tourism in Greece as a whole seemed to have held up reasonably well, but this area is dependent primarily on Greek, mainly Athenian, custom. And it showed, as could be seen from a stroll around Poros or Epidavros.

This was August, the peak of the season and even the most popular tavernas, those situated on the seafront with stunning views, were half empty. All the others, those that would normally have picked up the overspill, were either empty or had just one or two punters in rattling hollowly around. Every third shop front was boarded up and those that were open had little stock on display. When we talked to locals, employees or business owners, we got the same story. They put a brave face on it, but you could tell they were hurting.

It was bad enough having businesses close, staff laid off, pensions cut and all the other hardships imposed by the IMF and ECB, but what really seemed to get the goat of the everyday Greek was the plethora of petty-minded, vindictive comments made in the foreign, especially British, press. These were reported frequently in the Greek press as they proclaimed self-righteously that it was all average Johnny Greek's fault, and that the Bubbles had been the architects of their own downfall. If only they'd paid their taxes, lectured the Telegraph, Mail & Express, then none of this would have happened.

Strange then that these papers, and their devoted readers, are the very ones that rail against taxation in Britain and regard tax avoidance as bordering on a sacred duty.

"Hypocrisy is the homage vice pays to virtue." (Francois de la Rochefoucauld, 1613 - 1680, since you ask)

"We'd save how much tax if we moved our office from Dublin to The Netherlands?" (Paul David Hewson, 1960 - present)

Oh, don't get me started.

Despite the glitches and holdups, we had made good time crossing the Aegean and had time in hand before we made our way down the east side of the Peloponnese and across to Crete for the winter. We also had quite a few visitors booked to come out and so we decided to potter around the Saronic for a month or so before moving on. The idea was that this would enable to get the hang of the area, its attractions and its anchorages and so be able to give our visitors a more interesting time. What we didn't know at the time was that this decision would lead to our encounters with the Four Norsemen of the Apocalypse.

The liveaboard cruising fraternity is cosmopolitan, but hardly diverse; you're most unlikely to see a black, brown or yellow face. What you are most likely to encounter are middle class mores and white faces. Except in the case of the Germans, of course, when you will also be exposed to most of the other distasteful parts of their pendulous, mottled anatomies. It gives the impression of a boat crewed by a pack of albino Shar Pei nudes as painted by Francis Bacon.

Even within this fairly narrow subcategory of humanity, representation is not evenly distributed. Things vary from cruising area to cruising area and from season to season. The Ionian in August, for example, is overwhelmed by a deluge of Italians who swarm into every harbour and anchorage. They manage to cram six boats into a space so small that I wouldn't even attempt to squeeze in an oiled bar of soap, an image that brings tears to the eyes if one thinks about it too much. Having executed this enviable feat of seamanship and three-dimensional legerdemain they go below for a quick preen, slap on a pair of microscopic speedos and then pose around on deck with effortless style and élan. All other cruisers retire below, crippled by dysmorphic self-doubt, self-loathing and a complete collapse of self-esteem. The Germans even put some clothes on.

We, however, were cruising the Sardonic (© K. Saint) Gulf where things were somewhat different. Italians were rare here. The majority of cruisers were German, French and British. Also strongly represented were the Austrians, Swedes and Norwegians. Closely following them came the Aussies, Kiwis, Americans and Canadians. Occasionally popping up were a smattering of Russians, Finns, Swiss, citizens of assorted Baltic states and a very few Danes.

Ah yes, the Danes. There aren't many of them but, by Christ, they punch above their weight. They have an effect that's out of all proportion to their numbers. To put this (possibly surprising) statement into context I will need to digress slightly.

The fact that there are so few Danes cruising is hardly surprising when you look at some details. For a start there are only 5.5 million of them, about the same as Singapore or Slovenia and half the population of Portugal. On top of which, it really is a tiny country. If you take Scandinavia as a whole to comprise Denmark, Norway, Sweden, Finland, Iceland and Greenland, it has a total land area of just under 3.5 million square kilometres. That's halfway between India and Australia. Denmark has an area of 43 000 square kilometres, which makes it fractionally bigger than Switzerland and well under half the size of Portugal. And yet until 1400 the whole of Scandinavia as described above was ruled by Denmark, which comprised a tad over 1% of its land area.

Nowadays, though, the Danes are not the stuff of which empires are made, they're far too sensible. If any of their subjects wanted independence from the Danish crown all they had to do was ask nicely. Well, OK, the Swedes had to fight a bit from 1521 to 1553, but not much.

The Danish character, if there is such a thing, appears to be sober sensibleness tempered with a puckish streak. The Progress Party, which became the second largest party in the 1973 general election vowed to slash public spending. Among the ways it proposed doing this was to replace the entire department of defence with an answering machine primed with a recorded message saying "*we surrender*" in Russian.

However, to drag myself reluctantly back to the point:

A characteristic of the Sardonic Gulf is the almost complete absence of totally secure moorings. Other than around Athens, marinas are about as common as rocking horse shit. Most of the time we had to free anchor or lie stern to a quay with our anchor holding us off from pounding the stern to fragments on the concrete. This is where the Danes come in.

Despite our hopes and expectations, the weather hadn't exactly been over-clement in the Sardonic. We frequently had to take shelter from strong winds by going stern to quays. In each case we hi-tail it to a harbour that should offer reasonable shelter from the forecast wind direction. Once in we choose the best available spot, drop the hook and back up to the quay. Having tied the stern securely to the concrete with as many ropes as we can find (which is a lot on *Birvidik*) we wind in the anchor chain with the windlass until you can play a top F on it. If we can't get it to do this, we untie everything and do it again until we can. We then find more ropes and tie them out from the sides to stop the boat slewing sideways, settle into the cockpit and wait for the weather, and disaster, to strike.

We did this in Ermioni on the North quay, next to a Danish boat. After exchanging pleasantries, we settled into the cockpit with a cup of tea. The wind rose steadily on the beam, but everything held snug and firm. Once the wind had got up to a nice force six, forecast to rise to force eight, the Danish boat decided it wanted to leave. Why it waited until then is beyond me. "*Never mind*" I thought, "*Viking*

ancestors and all that - seamanship must be in their genes".
Was it buggery.

As they pulled out of their berth the wind, predictably I thought, dragged them sideways across our anchor chain, making a noise like Erik Bloodaxe laying into a tin bucket full of spanners. Hauling themselves into wind with their windlass they managed to get their anchor partly up. Instead of continuing to motor into wind and lift the anchor completely they then proceeded to motor randomly round the harbour in a state of panic with the anchor hanging down two metres in the water. Unsurprisingly, they managed to snag our anchor chain and drag it halfway across the harbour, lifting our anchor in the process. As we now had nothing to hold us off the quay we slewed sideways and only avoided some serious cosmetic damage by the rapid deployment of our entire stock of fenders.

The etiquette in situations such as this is for the offending boat to lift and untangle the anchors, and then take the other boat's anchor across to its original position and drop it back in place with apologies. What they did was to drop our anchor half the correct distance out and diagonally across the anchor chains of three other boats, then swiftly hack out of the harbour at high speed, resolutely refusing to make eye contact.

We pulled out, relayed the anchor and re-moored.

The next day another Danish boat came in, laid its anchor diagonally across several other anchor chains (including our, obviously) and proceeded to drag them all over the harbour, doing the nautical equivalent of 'knit one, purl one'. We gave up at this point and once we had extricated ourselves moved round to the south quay, which was deserted. We dropped the anchor and veered out 60 metres of chain as the bottom dropped off steeply. We had just moored up and snugged in when our spirits sank. Coming in was yet another Danish boat which proceeded to try and moor up next to us despite there being about 300 metres of unoccupied quay stretching invitingly into the distance.

They dropped about 15 metres of chain in 20 metres of

water then expressed astonishment when it failed to bite. So, of course, they blew sideways, T-boned our bow, snagged on our pulpit and lifted our anchor. After we'd helped them untangle they expressed their gratitude by dropping our anchor about five metres from our bow and buggering off. We waited until they were out of the way and walked *Birvidik* sideways to tie her up alongside to the quay. This way we had no need of an anchor to hold us off and so could view the approach of other boats, even Danish ones, with something approaching equanimity.

Over that summer we had our anchor lifted by other boats a total of six times; once by a Greek boat, once by a German boat and four times by Danes.

Bloody Danes - I'm sure they're out to get me as well. I suspect it's a simmering resentment over their being routed by Aethelstan at Eamont in 927 A.D. but holding a grudge for 1027 years is a bit extreme even by Scandinavian standards. Well, it's either that or they're using a pack of rather surrealist heavies in an attempt to collect over a thousand years' worth of unpaid Danegeld. It got to the stage where I was half expecting Sandi Toksvig to appear under the boat with scuba gear and a large drill.

Cruising is a mixture of the novel and the familiar. One of the most familiar refrains we hear goes along the lines of *"Ooh, the weather's not usually like this at this time of year mate! This is the [Worst/windiest/wettest/coldest/foulest] [Summer/winter/spring/autumn/month/year] [in twenty years/since records began/ since time immemorial]* And so it was with our time in the Saronic.

The received wisdom, as promulgated by the pilot books, internet, almanacs and weather gurus was that the Meltemi weakened in the western approaches of the Aegean and that in the summer the Saronic and the eastern coast of the Peloponnese had relatively benign sailing conditions and only suffered the occasional windy episode. Well someone forgot to tell the weather about that.

We spent the whole of the summer and early autumn dodging from one hidey-hole to another, nervously sitting out thunderstorms, katabatic winds, squall-lines and

Meltemi after Meltemi. Our last visitor of the season, our friend Chris from Jersey, endured the grand finale at the end of October, which was a stormy and windy bout of Biblical proportions. Appropriately, then, here follows today's reading, which is from the Book of Lamentations:

And so it came to pass that the *Birvidik*-ites did forsake the lands of the Eastern Aegeanites, crying unto The Lord *"Verily this Meltemi wind business is getting right on my tits, let us bog off to the land of the Western Aegeanites, who call themselves the Atheniites but whom everyone else calls the economic-basket-case-ites."*

And the *Birvidik*-ites did consult with graven images, known as In-ter-net and found that the land of the Atheniites was truly blessed, with good cheap wine and no Meltemi wind business and not much smiting and so they did hie themselves thence forth bloody with.

After much tribulation they did arrive at the land of the Atheniites at the place called Por-os and they saw that it was dead good and that In-ter-net had not lied about good cheap wine and so they did rejoice and sent notice to others of their tribe to come to Por-os and join them in celebration. And others of their tribe came, even unto multitudes. Well, five to be precise.

And the *Birvidik*-ites did consult again with In-ter-net, who said *"Verily, ye Birvidik-ites are in deep do-do for the Meltemi wind business will come down to the land of the Atheniites like the wolf on the fold, even unto eighteen days solid, which is most unusual for this time of year squire."* And so it did come to pass, and the *Birvidik*-ites were seriously pissed off.

And just to put the tin hat on it, once the Meltemi wind business did finally withdraw, a mighty tempest arose, with thunderbolts and a deluge from the skies, and the *Birvidik*-ites were sorely afraid and, in their terror and distress they cried out to In-ter-net saying *"What the bloody Hell's all this? You didn't mention anything about being smitten by bloody thunderbolts."* And In-ter-net said *"Oh, didn't I? - Sorry about that, I've been a bit busy recently. Won't happen again."*

And Chris of their tribe, who was hiding in the

forepeak, said "*Sod this for a game of soldiers. I'm off back to the Land of Obscure, Only Slightly Dodgy, Financial Products, which is known as Jer-sey*". But he was sorely delayed because all the Atheniites were on smite.

And lo! the meltemi wind business came back again, yea even unto the eighth degree on the scale that is known as Bo - For and the *Birvidik*-ites did wail and gnash their teeth crying "*Will we ever be delivered to the promised land that is known as Crete?*"

"*Buggered if I know*" said In-ter-net.

We dropped Chris off from Ermioni on the 22nd of September, which left us a month to travel down the eastern Peloponnese to Crete and then along its North coast to our wintering hole at Agios Nikolaos. This was 225 nautical miles in total, which even at our leisurely pace should have been no challenge at all – four to five travelling days.

We were looking forward to a much more laid-back experience than that. We envisaged short hops down to Elafonisos, taking in Leonidhion and Monemvassia on the way before going on to north west Crete via Kithera and Antikithera. Once in Gramvousa we planned short trips of a few hours each to Chania, Rethymnon and Iraklion before a gentle potter to the anchorage at Spinalonga lagoon, where we intended to relax for a few days before nipping round the corner and tying up in Agios Nikolaos for the winter.

The Weather Gods had other ideas and served up a veritable feast of delaying tactics.

As an *amuse-bouche* they delivered gale force Meltemis for eight days. Once those had finished, we took advantage of the temporary lull to make our very lumpy way round to Porto Heli, where we anchored in very different circumstances – bright sunshine, no wind and blistering hot. We relaxed on board and admired the blue-tinged mountains rising from the flat-calm sea.

The more attentive amongst you will recognise these conditions from the description of the antics in Fethye. We, however, failed to make the connection, and lolled around on deck, revelling in the change in weather. Then our

Eumenides served up the *entrée*.

By early evening the sun had just started to go down and I was laying out the table in the cockpit for dinner. It was pleasantly cool after the rather oppressive heat of the day and I felt a welcome zephyr of wind on my cheek, warm and gentle to the touch.

Still we didn't twig.

The zephyrs became stronger and more frequent, still warm as if someone had just opened an oven door. A slight, inchoate uneasiness began taking form in my subconscious. We turned to each other simultaneously and both said "*You don't think that this is the start of a...*"

Before we could say 'katabatic' we were hit by a blast of hot air that swung the bow off violently, pulled the anchor chain bar-taut and knocked the boat on its side. Cutlery and crockery scattered onto the cockpit sole.

Our first task was to play 'catch' with the cushions and other assorted soft furnishings that were flying haphazardly in the wind. Our second was to try to drop the sunshades, which were acting like huge sails, magnifying the effects of the wind on the boat. This was like having a wrestling match with an epileptic octopus. Every time we managed to smother most of the shade by screwing it up and wrapping our bodies and arms round it, the wind would catch another bit, tear it from our grasp and start thrashing us round the face and shoulders with the metal fittings festooning its edges.

Once we had finally subjugated the shades and thrown them into the aft cabin, things calmed down a little, despite the wind steadily increasing. We were well dug in, in good holding. We let out our full hundred metres of chain and we were still well clear of all the other boats. Just to be on the safe side I ran a couple of chums down the chain[63]. We reckoned we'd probably be alright but decided to mount anchor watches until either the wind went down or the sun came up. We cleared the decks and prepared the cockpit for action.

It was just as well we did, as the main course arrived at just before midnight. We had been worried, not so much that we would drag our anchor, but that another boat would drag down on us. The prime threat was a large motor boat which was swinging wildly off our port bow. It did drag, but passed well clear of us to port. We saw the crew frantically scurrying about on deck and silently wished them luck.

The *pièce de résistance* of that night came at about two in the morning when a boat motored into the anchorage (God knows where from). Despite our having switched on every light we could, he came straight across our bow, missing us by no more than a couple of metres. Our anchor chain was bar tight at a shallow angle so, of course, he caught it on his keel and ripped our anchor out. And he wasn't even Danish[64].

We started to slew backwards. Liz leapt into the cockpit, started the engine and went ahead, holding *Birvidik* into the wind as best she could. I, meanwhile, enabled the anchor windlass, fought my way onto the foredeck and started to haul in the anchor. The last thing we wanted to do was to snag another boat's anchor and end up with the two of us careering through the anchorage picking up others like a snowball rolling down a hill.

Having a hundred metres of anchor chain has many advantages, but it has one big drawback. It all has to go in an anchor locker. Preferably of its own volition.

Systems where the anchor chain obediently tucks itself away in the anchor locker when you haul up your anchor are known as 'self-stowing'. These are a fantasy; they don't exist in the real world. Well, certainly not in anything smaller than a cross-channel ferry.

In small boats, when you haul in the anchor chain it is fed via the hawse pipe into a laughably small space unaccountably unincorporated into the rest of the boat's stowage system. The chain gets fed in by gravity; its own weight pulls it down into the anchor locker where it piles up pyramid-like until the pile reaches the outlet of the hawse pipe. This usually happens when you've pulled in all of about 12 metres of chain. At this point the chain in the whole caboodle jams solid; hawse pipe, gypsy, windlass – the lot.

This is bad news for the crew on the foredeck as he has

to rush below and manhandle the accumulated chain so that it is more evenly spread throughout the anchor locker. Then he has to find his screwdrivers and Allen keys so that he can rush back to the foredeck and remove the inspection plate on the windlass in order to free the jammed chain from the windlass gypsy before pulling in more chain. The whole process repeats itself at exponentially decreasing intervals until ether all the chain is in or you've rammed into another boat.

Liz did a sterling job holding station and I managed to get all the chain in and the anchor hanging off the bow. All we had to do now was to re-anchor, preferably without ploughing into any other boats or lifting their anchors and chains. It's difficult enough to do this in bright sunshine and light winds. In the pitch black and a gusting katabatic it's bloody murder. We seemed to manage it, although it took us about an hour and a half before we were satisfied.

Once we were reasonably sure that we were securely lying to our anchor, Liz retired to bed and I went back on watch. Then Einstein joined in. A ginger and white blur shot across the cockpit and up the mizzen mast, where she clung precariously to the swinging sail cover. Strong winds seem to induce a form of mania in her. Her eyes go like saucers and her hair looks as if she's just been given a blow-dry by Sweeny Todd. Her breathing takes the form of a series of asthmatic snorts and her eyes shoot glances in all directions as if she's dropped a serious dose of psilocybin. She screeches and bounces erratically about the boat at full tilt before suddenly freezing and staring in disbelief at whatever hallucination her overwrought brain cells have conjured up.

This does little to ease the difficulties of an already stressful set of circumstances. It's hard enough trying to cope with the darkness, the wind, the waves and the other boats, without having to worry about a manic, unco-ordinated cat charging around the boat, especially a cat that usually can't walk down a two-metre-wide pontoon without falling in. If she went over the side in these conditions, that would be it. She would be swept away and we wouldn't have stood a chance of finding her. By the time we'd launched the dinghy she'd have been over the other side of the bay.

Attempting to pick her up and lock her down in the saloon merely resulted in hands and arms looking like I'd tried swimming through razor wire or I was seriously into self-harm. All I could do was to ensure that the cat rescue net was ready to hand and keep an eye on her. Luckily, after about a couple of hours of this the katabatic blew itself out and so did the cat's manic phase. I tempted her down to the saloon with a bribe of cat treats, shut the door and crawled thankfully to bed.

There was no katabatic the next evening. It was too cold and wet. And so it remained for the next six days. Looking at the met, I discovered a projected three-day weather window where the Meltemi took a short break before teaming up with a couple of thunderstorms and wreaking havoc over the area. This prompted moving on to Monemvassia in a lumpy, confused sea left over from the previous crap weather.

Remember that mysterious event off Paxos when the jammed steering miraculously cured itself? Remember that nagging worry that it might come back unannounced and unwanted?

You're ahead of me here, aren't you.

The approach to Monemvassia lies behind an isthmus and consists of an open anchorage partially protected by the isthmus and two large breakwaters. Tucked into the corners of the anchorage are two well protected, but very small harbours. We headed for the northern one. About 400 metres off the entrance, as you have probably by now anticipated, the steering locked solid. Good game, good game.

I rushed to the foredeck and deployed the anchor, allowing the wind to take us back until we had enough scope out. I locked off the windlass and Liz took *Birvidik* astern to bite the anchor in. We were now in a very vulnerable position, in an exposed anchorage with no steerage and little dragging room. I set about trying to trace the steering fault.

No job on a boat is local. Any repair or diagnostic

investigation, however apparently localised, inevitably involves dismantling half the boat. So it was with the steering. This runs half the length of the boat and getting access involves opening up and emptying the steering locker in the saloon, the port cockpit locker, the heating exhaust locker, the hanging locker, the dressing table cupboards and all six stern cabin drawers.

Stage two is to strip to a pair of rather unsavoury skimpy Y-fronts, don a headlight and liberally grease the body with goose fat before contorting and squeezing yourself into the aforementioned spaces and attempting a close examination of the steering mechanism, trying to identify the cause of the jam.

This task is not made any easier by the loss of focussing power which develops in the more advanced-aged demographic typified by the average yottie.

In this respect I am very much the average yottie. Unaided, I can focus on anything exactly 31.4 centimetres away. No more, no less. Any closer or further away, I need glasses. Different glasses. I am therefore the proud possessor of six pairs of glasses, not counting spares. These comprise (in increasing focusing distance): reading glasses, computer glasses, saxophone glasses, television glasses, general purpose glasses and driving glasses. For really close examination I also carry a magnifying glass.

"*Ah Bob, you Silly-Billy*" I hear you cry indulgently, "*Why don't you get yourself some varifocals?*" I did. Varifocals work fine when you still have some accommodation left. Then you've got a reasonable area of lens for each focal range. By the time you get to my state, the varifocals are covering such a range of distances that, in order to focus at any given distance, you have to ensure that you are looking exactly through a horizontal strip of lens that's no wider than a pencil lead. Doing this requires head and neck contortions that would have guaranteed getting the Linda Blair part in The Exorcist.

A good place to witness this phenomenon is in the supermarket. Let us say that our yottie wishes to replenish his supply of Fray Bentos steak and kidney pies.[65]

The varifocalled yottie can first be identified as he attempts to home in on the right area of shelving. He walks slowly down the aisle with a peculiar slow nodding of the head. This scans the shelves through the range of focal lengths on his glasses and gives him a fighting chance of homing in on roughly the right section to find what he's looking for.

Once he gets there his behaviour changes. He now needs to read the small print. This is easiest if the item is on a shelf at about chest height as then he can look through the close-range strip of the varifocals. What he wants is rarely so conveniently sited.

If he wishes to look at stuff higher up, he has to tilt his head right back until he gets a crick in his neck and then make his extraocular muscles ache as he tries to look through the bottom of his varifocals. Passers-by notice this strange aspect and all stop and look at the ceiling, trying to identify whatever strange phenomenon has attracted his attention. An alternative strategy for this situation is to lean in closely and lift the glasses so that the bottoms of the lenses are in line with the eyebrows. This facilitates focus but makes him look like a particularly pompous, pedantic and supercilious schoolmaster. Which in my case is quite appropriate.

Items on lower shelves pose even more of a challenge. He can try squatting down and employing the top shelf technique but with his knees he's likely to have to call in one of the supermarket's hydraulic pallet trucks to get him up again.

Another possible technique is to bend forward with the hands on the knees and the head tilted back, thus reading through the bottom third of the lenses. While far from perfect, this makes the label at least guessable, unless it's in Greek script.[66] The drawback to this tactic is that it also requires the backside to be pushed out as a counterbalance. This may give the wrong message to passing aficionados of musical theatre.

If his target item is on the bottom shelf, then he's going home empty handed. Reading anything at that height would entail lying spread-eagled on the floor with the head tilted right back, somewhat reminiscent of a stranded turtle. Even a yottie has some residual decorum.

By the time eyesight has deteriorated to my standard, varifocals have usually been forsaken in favour of a range of specialist glasses as described above. This arrangement, though, comes with its own set of challenges, the greatest of which is where do you put the bloody things. Many imaginative solutions to this problem have been devised but the two favourites seem to be 'Put them on spectacle lanyards and hang them round your neck' or 'Stick them on top of your head'. The former gives our yottie the appearance of a maiden aunt that has gone a bit overboard on the jewellery. The latter, meanwhile, makes him look like a gigantic wolf spider that has escaped from the Island of Doctor Moreau.

Both pose problems in the confined space of a boat locker. If he hangs them round his neck they tangle up and he gets his arm stuck through them while wriggling into the far end of the locker. This effectively hog-ties him with his nose pressed into the most inaccessible corner of the oubliette in which he finds himself. The subsequent panic-stricken, claustrophobic struggles usually result in the lanyards breaking and the assorted glasses are then scattered onto the floor of the locker where they are knelt and sat on until reduced to a scree of glass and plastic.

If worn on the top of the head, they are repeatedly banged and scratched into a state of opacity but at least they don't truss you up like a turkey. I favour the latter.

Once in the confines of the locker a further set of challenges become apparent. The incompatible 3D geometries of human bodies and boat lockers usually dictate that it is impossible to look directly at the area you wish to inspect. Accordingly, our yottie ends up squinting at it through the corner of his eye or lying on his back and trying to peer myopically at the point of interest through his eyebrows. Both these angles lie outside the field of view of most glasses. To compound matters, once in this position the headlight brightly illuminates the only corner of the locker unencumbered by anything he might want to look at.

Further contortions are required. Firstly, the headlight is augmented by a pencil torch held precariously in the teeth and then the glasses are removed from the face and a ludicrously optimistic attempt is made to hold them in the direct line between at least one eyeball and the item under investigation. This is just about achievable, but if he wants to use a screwdriver, spanner or socket as well, then he's on a hiding to nothing.

Given these vexatious obstacles that life and *Anno Domini* delight in throwing at us, it's a miracle that jobs such as this meet with any success at all. However, in a state of unbridled optimism we just keep on keeping on and, once in a while, we meet with success. So it was in this instance. After nearly three hours of sweat, contortion and no little amount of profanities I identified the problem. One of the retaining bolts for the cover plate on the autopilot drive motor had worked loose. It had then jammed between the drive sprocket and chain, thus effectively locking the whole thing up.

It only took me another hour to free the bolt, slap a dollop of loctite on it and screw it back in with the biggest socket wrench I could get into the available space. We were on our way again. Elafonisos and Kithera beckoned.

Unfortunately, Elafonisos didn't beckon hard enough, and Kithera just managed a feeble wave. The weather Gods stuck their oar in again, with the met giving us just a short weather window of a couple of days before another set of fronts rolled in, dragging their associated winds, waves and rain with them. We decided to head to Kithera for one night and then make the 60 nautical mile trip to Chania on Crete. This would enable us to take advantage of any short weather windows to make the 100+ miles along the north coast of Crete in a series of short hops.

The First Winter back in Greece – Crete

October 19th2011 - May 5th 2012.

In common with their counterparts in many other countries, many non-metropolitian Greeks regard city dwellers, especially those from their capital city, as arrogant, snobbish dilettantes; self-absorbed and out of touch with the harsh realities of everyday life. In return, many Athenians look down on non-metropolitan Greeks, especially islanders, as uncultured hicks, quaint anachronisms in the modern world[67]. Like most stereotypes, in some instances there is a grain of truth in both of these viewpoints, but they are mostly wrong, especially in the case of the Cretans.

Crete is a sod of a big island – the 88th largest in the world, in fact. It's the fifth largest in the Mediterranean (after Sicily, Cyprus, Sardinia and Corsica, since you ask) and it's the largest and most southerly of all the Greek islands. It's damned near the most southerly in the Med, but a little spindly bit of Cyprus just pips it to the post.

It's very long and thin, 260 kilometres from East to West, but only 60 kilometres North to South at its widest point, reducing to twelve kilometres at its narrowest. Its population is near as dammit the same as that of greater Athens and it proudly retains its identity and culture, including its own poetry, music and dance. It makes a significant contribution to the Greek economy and an even more significant one to the whole cultural heritage of Greece.

Crete was the centre of the earliest known civilisations in Europe, the Minoans, who not only developed a sophisticated society, but were also responsible for introducing the first known attempts at written language in Europe, a script known as Linear A. Unfortunately, no-one understands a word of it. The one thing that everyone seems to agree on is that it was nothing like Greek.

We wintered in Agios Nikolaos, having stopped off at Rethymnon, the island of Dhia and the lagoon at Spinalonga on the way. There were a lot of overwintering yotties at Ay Nik and the whirlwind of social activities soon reached fever pitch. The usual stalwarts of quizzes, barbecues, travel and technical talks, exercise classes, guided walks and group meals at various restaurants were supplemented by a music group, Scottish dancing, art classes, yoga, Pilates and a computer workshop.

Pontoon politics also raised its ugly head but this time it wasn't so much the usual factional in-fighting between various cliques of yotties as their having to tip-toe tactfully around the turf war between the marina authorities and the local sailing club. This schism centred on a dilapidated two-story building in the marina grounds. This was at the time under the aegis of the local sailing club and was used as a base for dinghy sailing activities for the local kids.

This had traditionally been subsidised by the local municipal authority, but funds had dried up after the already precarious Greek economy had finally gone tits-up following the financial crash of 2008. Maintenance had stalled and the building was starting to fall into disrepair. The club struggled on, but the marina management had its eye on the building. The marina offices and the washing and toilet facilities were housed in a couple of portacabins. The management reckoned that the sailing club building could be far better used to house some swanky new offices and facilities than to keep a bunch of spotty adolescents off the streets. The municipality had not yet taken a stance on the matter and so there was a stand-off, with the yacht club in *de facto* charge as they had the keys and the marina management didn't.

This put our yotties in a delicate situation, requiring tact, diplomacy, subtlety and sensitivity to the needs and feelings of others. These are not qualities that come easily to your average yottie, but it is surprising what he can pull out of the hat when push comes to shove. Especially when his self-interest is involved.

The problem centred on the fact that the yacht club was happy for the yotties to use the clubhouse as a social centre excepting for the few occasions when it was in use by the dinghy sailors. To do this, of course, the yotties would need a key, which the yacht club officials readily made available on the strict understanding that it should under no circumstances be allowed to fall into the grasping clutches of the marina management.

This led to an elaborate game of pass the parcel in which the key was shunted from the organiser of one activity to the next without its being intercepted by any member of the marina staff. This generally worked fine except in the case of first thing in the morning.

On sailing vessel *Spirit Chaser*, Barbara Bodytemple, the organiser of the 07:30 Morning Mindfulness and Pilates Pump & Tone class would leap sprightlily from her bunk at 05:00, having retired at eight the previous night after a refreshing herbal infusion. She would then down a delicious glass of pureed sprout and savour a nourishing bowl of quinoa and raw shredded carrot before going for an invigorating cold shower. On her return she consults the timetable she sellotaped onto the skipper's chartplotter screen to find out who last used the clubhouse and therefore has the key. I don't know why she bothers because this is invariably Barrie 'Bloodshot' McManus of sailing vessel *Tactical Chunder*, who runs the midnight to 3 a.m. meeting of the ouzo appreciation society. The arrangement with Bloodshot was that he would leave the key in one of the wellies on *Spirit Chaser's* foredeck before staggering back to his boat. Inevitably, he has forgotten.

Barbara sighs in mild irritation at her karma being compromised so early in the day and set off for *Tactical Chunder*. On arrival she taps politely on the foredeck and waits. No response. All she can hear is deep, rumbling 120 dB snoring. This is hardly surprising as Bloodshot is in an alcohol induced coma that even a consultant neurologist would have had difficulty differentiating from a Persistent Vegetative State. After what she deems to be a decent and polite interval, she knocks again, a little louder, and calls out "*Barrie – Coo-ee*" in a polite, singsong voice. The snoring continues. Stage three involves thumping the foredeck with a clenched fist raising the voice to a shout: "*BLOODSHOT! WAKE UP PLEASE!*" No answer.

Further attempts, progressively increasing in frequency, duration and intensity continue to have no effect.

Eventually she loses all self-restraint (and self-respect). She is now late for her first class and her ladies will be waiting. Her mindfulness goes out the window. The blood vessels in her temples start to throb visibly. She picks up the winch handle that was lying abandoned on the foredeck and starts hammering it on *Tactical Chunder's* stainless steel pulpit. She goes a delicate shade of purple and an apoplectic, spittle-sprayed stream of invective echoes round the marina.

"Wake up, McManus, you gin-sodden, kebab-scoffing barrel of fucking lard. Stop snoring like a chainsaw on fucking steroids, get your pendulous arse out of your stinking pit and give me the bloody key!"

By this time the only person not out on deck witnessing this spectacle of pathetic loss of control is Bloodshot himself. In desperation she redoubles her winch handle related efforts, raining a frenzy of blows on the pulpit, forestay and windlass in a performance that would have done credit to Ragnar Skull-Splitter in musth. After reaching a crescendo she collapses on the pontoon in paroxysms of heaving sobs – a broken, hollow shell, a wraithlike parody of her former calm and assured self.

At which point Bloodshot appears in the cockpit, bleary eyed and confused, and clad only in a pair of saggy Y-fronts that may once have been white. He shuffles forward, holding up his Y-fronts with one hand and scratching his unkempt hair, beard and genitalia with the other, in which he carries The Key. He passes it to the whimpering broken woman on the pontoon.

"Sorry Barbara" he says in a cracked, hoarse voice *"I forgot."*

She takes the key, makes a mental note to soak it in a bucket of bleach overnight, stands to her full height and, with a supreme effort of will reclaims her dignity.

"Thankyou Barrie" she says in a calm and controlled voice. *"Please be so kind as to try to remember next time."* She looks round at the assembled onlookers, gives a short, dignified nod and walks slowly and graciously down the pontoon toward the clubhouse as if nothing had happened.

You have to admire the woman.[68]

Despite all the pontoon politics, yotties can pull together for the benefit of others, especially when their furtherance of their own self-interest is sheltered behind a comforting veneer of apparent altruism. The key and yacht club business at Ay Nik gave just such an opportunity. Since the funding source from the local council had dried up, the whole building had fallen into a sad state of disrepair. Tiles were cracked and missing. Electrical fittings dangled forlornly from their power supplies. Cracked windows were held together with parcel tape, which only partially moderated the icy blast howling into the rooms. Floors were uneven and potholed and great chunks of plaster had fallen off the walls and ceilings.

Things were getting serious. It was bad enough that the local kids had to put up with the likes of this, but how were sophisticated yotties such as us to function in such barbaric, primitive conditions. Something had to be done.

Cometh the hour, cometh the idea. And the idea came into being toward the end of a boozy social evening in the yacht club on a particularly foul night

It is a frequently quoted truism in educational circles that the average secondary school staffroom has a staggering range of different skills and expertise. This is even more true of the average crowd of overwintering yotties. The major difference is that the yotties' skill sets were far more practical and less esoteric than those of the staffroom. OK, they may not have been able to rustle up a quick critique on the role of allegory in mediaeval spiritual education, or calculate the area under the curve of function $f(x) = ax^n + bx - c$ where $a \neq 0$, but they could produce artisans and tradesmen by the busload; electricians, plasterers, builders, glaziers, tilers – the list is endless. On top of this, almost any yottie worth his or her salt could turn his or her hand to carpentry, GRP repair, plumbing, canvas work and diesel engine maintenance and repair. This is a virtue born of necessity, not volition.

Once the idea had been conceived it spread like wildfire. We had the technology and the expertise. We could rebuild it. The cost of raw materials would be minuscule spread among a hundred plus yotties. All we needed to do then was to plan the project out and match the talents of the assembled yotties to the jobs to be done.

And so it came to pass. Cement was mixed, plaster applied, windows repaired, and electrical circuits made considerably less lethal. Uneven floors were levelled, screeded and tiled. Potentially dangerous stairways were made safe. A quick lick of paint and the place was as new.

We held a ceremony where the renovated building was officially handed back to the yacht club. This ritual was more symbolic than anything else, seeing as we used the building much more than they did. The key was handed over with full pomp and protocol before being handed straight back as we needed the place for yoga first thing in the morning.

It could easily appear from my cynical descriptions that yotties are, without exception, a marauding bunch of self-centred, parasitic, miserly, antisocial borderline-criminal sociopaths whose over-riding motivation is to screw the bejeezus out of every living being in a 100 km radius.

This is, of course, a vile, libellous and totally unfounded calumny; a hyperbole based on little more than the antics of a conspicuous but totally unrepresentative sample of the tribe, whose personal foibles I have extrapolated to the level of stereotype without so much as a shred of justification.

In fact, many yotties make a point of giving something back to the communities in which they find themselves for the winter. A favoured technique here is for each boat to have a plastic water bottle into which they deposit all the small denomination coins that would otherwise clutter up their pockets or sideboards before ending up in the engine bay and jamming the bilge pump or engine controls. Toward the end of the winter these are collected, and a counting evening arranged. Here, the pots are tipped out and an army of yotties count the coins out and bag them up by denomination. Considerable amounts can be raised in this manner, the highest we have personally experienced being over 2000 euros.

Before you can convince yotties to take part in this sort

of exercise, though, you need to have decided on which charity is to be the lucky recipient. In an echo of natural selection, there will always be more deserving charities than can be supported by the carrying capacity of the donor environment. Further echoing natural selection, the lucky winners are chosen mainly by random chance and not by reasoned design or moral imperative. In the case of distributing the yotties' largesse, as in most instances of charitable giving, the choice of recipient is driven by emotion, by the lottery of personal contacts, and by serendipity.

In most cases the favoured charity will be associated with huge round eyes and pleading expressions, which usually means either children or animals. We're hard-wired to feel protective toward anything displaying these characteristics.[69]

In fact, the whole winter business can get a bit much. Most people, if they think about it at all, which is unlikely, think of the cruising life as being one of non-stop activity throughout the summer, charging from one exotic exploration to the next, contrasted with five months of languorous recharge in the winter.

Nothing could be further from the truth.

Summers start off with the best of intentions - pledges to keep exercising, runs in the morning, bike rides to explore exotic sites, mental stimulation by exposure to ancient cultures and high art. This gradually fades as temperatures climb inexorably upwards until, by the beginning of July, the hours from 14:00 to 17:00 are written off - fit only for lolling on the boat in as much shade and breeze as we can find. By the end of July, and lasting until the middle of September, physical activity (or mental activity for that matter) is a Sisyphean struggle from about half an hour after sunrise to about half an hour after sunset. Physical effort is akin to trying to run through neck deep molasses wearing diving boots whilst any attempt at mental exertion makes you suspect someone's laced your tea with a shovel full of rohypnol.

The Greeks have evolved a very effective way of dealing

with this. They go to sleep. The hours between 14:00 and around 17:30 are denoted 'The hours of common peace' or more commonly Το μικρό του ύπνου (To mikro tou hypnou) the little sleep. Technically the use of any noisy equipment, from motorcycles to power tools, is forbidden during this time. The time is set aside for a leisurely lunch, a relaxed chat with family and friends and gentle snooze for a couple of hours.

They make up for this by going back to work around 18:00 and staying at work until most normal people have been in bed for at least two hours. Then they go out and party. Eating, drinking and socialising last until the early morning, when they nip back home for half an hour's kip followed by a shit, shower and shave. Then they go to work. Greeks have the longest working hours in Europe but are the second least productive per capita. No wonder.

We did try to adapt to this eminently sensible system, but we couldn't get our Northern European body clocks to synchronise with it. Anyway, it never seems to really be worth starting anything productive in the half an hour available between sunset and drinks starting. Then we go to bed just as the first Greek shops are closing their shutters and the taverna staff are relaxing in the two-hour gap between the last tourists and the first Greek customers.

As a result, we are, by the end of the summer, in a state of effete, raddled dissolution. We have the muscle tone of Stephen Hawking and the aerobic capacity of Pete Docherty. Our mental acuities are about on a par with those of the late, lamented Jade Goody at her intellectual peak.

Come winter, though, all that changes. There were about a hundred liveaboards in Ag. Nikolaous the winter we were there, and the number of activities increases exponentially as the number of liveaboards goes up. Liz started a yoga group three times a week. We went on organised walks every Thursday. These were led by Tony and Tessa, who were so frighteningly fit they could almost have passed for Kiwis. Scooping up the stragglers was Dave, who didn't even break into a sweat while carrying exhausted yotties up near vertical scree slopes, despite apparently being fuelled by a mixture of whisky and roll-ups. Mind you, he is from Yorkshire. The walks started off at the Ranulph Fiennes level and became progressively more demanding. By halfway through the winter we had progressed to crampons and karabiners and we fully expected to be issued with oxygen cylinders for the last couple.

Not content with doing the equivalent of the three peaks challenge every week, I decided to get myself properly fit that winter. Those who remember the previous winter's gym fiasco will be coming to a justified diagnosis of either early onset Alzheimer's or terminal stupidity. Having buggered up my hip running on tarmac every day for a fortnight I joined the local gym and just about managed to avoid ending up with a football sized bulge poking through my abdominal wall.

We still had about 28 minutes of the week unaccounted for, so I joined a band and inflicted the tenor saxophone on anyone within a kilometre radius twice a week. In between all this I tried to fit in an hour of Greek language every afternoon and the list of undone boat jobs grew by the day. On top of all that I had promised Liz that I'd knock off a best-seller by Easter. We didn't have time to draw breath. How did we ever manage to hold down full-time jobs?

In fact, even writing about it has tired me out. I think I'm going to have to go and have a lie down for a bit.

While on the subject of The Little Sleep, it is noticeable that while this custom is eminently sensible in the summer, when the weather is blistering hot, the days are long and evenings are warm and balmy, it doesn't seem such a good idea when the Greeks insist on carrying it over into the winter.

Mediterranean winters are nothing like the fantasies that inhabit the popular imagination. The daylight hours are a tad longer and the temperatures fractionally higher than they are in Northern Europe, but that's about it. In the depths of winter, depressions and their associated fronts abound. These bring strong winds, steep seas and driving rain. The sun drags itself out of its pit at about half past seven and gives up and goes back to sleep at about a quarter past five. That's only about 35 minutes more daylight than

London and even that assumes the watery sun manages to struggle its way through the grey 8/8 cloud cover.

All of this makes shopping in the winter in Greece one of the most depressing experiences known to man. The shops open at around ten in the morning only to shut at one o'clock on the dot.

The rational thing to do here is to plan ahead and draw up a shopping schedule the night before, so that the shopping expedition can swing into well-oiled action at the crack of ten the next morning. Such rationality is not an option for most yotties. The Barbara Bodytemples amongst them are only halfway through their morning 5K swim by the time the shops shut and the Bloodshots won't surface until the sun is about to dip below the horizon. The likes of us, meanwhile, are so disorganised that despite having got up at a quarter past seven we're still wandering around in our jim-jams at eleven o'clock, absent-mindedly munching on toast and wondering where we left the shopping trolley.

Yotties, therefore, have to shop in the evening shift, which usually starts around five thirty to six p.m. This is a grey and joyless experience, even for women. Our hapless yotties, hands in their pockets and hunched against the wind and rain, make their way slowly up the dark and almost desolate main street. The wet cobbles shimmer with pale reflections of the feeble lights emanating from the empty shops. The wind tears the last few leaves from the trees leaving them silhouetted stark and haggard against the watery moonlight. Eddies whirl the leaves half-heartedly around the feet of the few shoppers foolhardy or desperate enough to brave the desolation and soul-sapping misery.

The shopkeepers either stand in the doorways emanating an air of dignified resignation or bow to the inevitable and sit behind their counters, reading a book or playing solitaire on the computer. It's costing them more in electricity than they're making on the few sales they may be lucky enough to complete.

The sheer pointlessness of the whole exercise is enough to make St. Monica weep with frustration. No-one wants to be here, shopkeepers or customers. The contrast with the summer is striking and therein lies the rub and the irony. There's no need for all this spirit-sapping misery. If only they could bring themselves to change the shop hours on a seasonal basis. In the summer, keep them as they are. That makes sense. Winter shop hours, however, should be nine until five, with no break for lunch. That way everyone's happy; shopkeepers concentrate their efforts into the profitable times when there are likely to be enough punters to make it worth their while and the punters can get their shopping done without twiddling their thumbs all afternoon and then wasting valuable drinking time. That shouldn't be beyond their wit – after all, they change their bus timetables every three weeks or so[70].

Winter isn't all bad news on the shopping front though. There is one aspect that comes into its own in the winter and that is shopping online.

Despite any reservations one may have about Mr. Bezo's shameless attempts at world economic domination and his company's dubious employment practices, it has to be admitted that Amazon is irresistibly handy for the cruising yottie. He can get almost anything he wants delivered to almost anywhere on the globe. OK, this comes at a cost, both in terms of delivery charges and in terms of the decimation of local businesses and economies but the average yottie, like Oscar Wilde, can resist anything but temptation.

Our yottie can only take advantage of this cornucopia of shopping opportunities in the winter though. In the summer, he moves on every few days or so, rarely staying as long as a week unless forced to by weather or technical problems. This does not give time for delivery, even with Amazon's ruthlessly efficient logistics. Mind you, the way things are going, it won't be long before he can get his multi-coloured LED toilet bowl light dropped off by drone 12 miles offshore.

In the winter, however, our yotties are in one place for several months. Add to this the fact that most overwintering marinas are fully prepared for yottie postal requirements, with efficient arrangements for receiving and holding deliveries, and it's hardly surprising that most winter marina offices end up looking like Mount Pleasant sorting office on a busy Wednesday before Christmas.

Liz went for this in a big way. Memorably, she decided it was time she dragged the pair of us kicking and screaming into the 21st Century. She wanted a smartphone.

I should never have married a younger woman.

However, I put on a brave face and bowed to the inevitable. *"Shouldn't be a problem (other than financially)"* I thought. *"I'll look it up on the internet. I'm pretty computerate. I'm down with the kids."*

Hah!

Technological progress has leapfrogged over me and leapt into the future, pausing just long enough to turn round and give me a two fingered salute on the way. Motor cars were the advance guard. There was a time when I could open the bonnet, look inside and identify each component and what it did. Not only that, but I could take the whole thing apart, service and repair every bit (even down to manually regrinding valves) and then put it all back together. Sometimes it even worked again.

Not now. Even if I finally manage to work out how to lift the bonnet of a modern car I'm no longer confronted with a comforting array of hoses and wires, carburettors, radiators, water pumps, gearbox, rocker boxes and camshafts. All I can see now is a sinister, hermetically sealed, grey box looking for all the world as if it's just escaped from the set of the Death Star. Frequently it will be plastered with warning stickers, designed specifically for anachronisms like me, which shout *"WARNING - NO USER SERVICEABLE PARTS INSIDE!"* in blindingly fluorescent upper case. These are usually followed by another screaming *"DON'T EVEN THINK ABOUT USING THAT SCREWDRIVER!"*

At first sight this would lead one to suspect that repairing a modern car requires an array of highly sophisticated tools, a Tardis and a PhD in quantum mechanics. Nothing could be further from the truth. All it takes is a spotty YTS trainee, a bottom of the range laptop and a courier service. Diagnosis is made by connecting an umbilical between the engine and the laptop, which will then chunter away for a while, during which time the car takes on a life of its own. The engine starts and stops. Lights flash on and off, wipers make a few desultory swipes across the windscreen, the suspension pumps up and down a couple of times and the horn plays 'Colonel Bogie' in B flat. Eventually everything settles down again and the laptop flashes up a message along the lines of "*Front nearside ABS sensor failure. Remove component trs(ii)/27/xplt#/@$$ and replace. To order part press f12*" Our spotty trainee then hits f12 which sends a message to the main depot and the courier service ordering part trs(ii)/27/xplt#/@$$. Then he tells you to come back on Thursday.

Come Thursday he connects the laptop again and punches in a highly encrypted code. This is a sort of electronic screwdriver or tyre lever and the sinister grey box opens as if by magic to reveal a matrix of smaller hermetically sealed grey boxes. He unplugs one of these and replaces it with its clone. Then he slaps a bill for £457:23 + VAT in your hand and waves you goodbye.

The same thing, only worse, has happened with computers themselves. I never could take a computer apart and fix it, but I had a rough idea how it worked. I knew what RAM, BIOS and a load of other acronyms were and what they did. I could use spreadsheets. Hell, I could even set up a database in Access. So, with just a slightly swaggering smile I winked at Liz and confidently typed 'iPhone' into google.

It was gibberish. What is it with these people - why can't they give things sensible names? WTF is 'Android'? And why does he like ice cream? What am I supposed to make of 'CDMA model: CDMA EV-DO Rev. A (800, 1900 MHz)' or '802.11b/g/n Wi-Fi (802.11n 2.4GHz only)'?

And then, apparently, you can get something called 'Apps'. It turns out that 'Apps' is not, as I first suspected, an unpleasant suppurating skin condition, but a contraction of 'applications' which turned out to be little mini programs. There are thousands of these things. Five hundred thousand to be precise. Well, there were yesterday. Christ knows how many there'll be tomorrow.

Among them are such useful little items as *'Where's my iPhone?'*. If you've lost your bloody iPhone, how are you going to use the app to find it? There's another one that shouts at you until you've done a hundred push ups. Or you can wind up some cartoon birds until they're incandescent with rage and then poke them around a screen. Why? What you really want are useful things - apps that will serve deep seated human needs. Apps such as *'Where are my bloody car keys?'* or how about *'What did I come in here for?'*

I'll tell you what would be a really good app - one where you pointed the phone's camera at the couple you think you recognise, and it tells you their names and where you last met. The *'Who the Hell are you?'* app. This could be used in combination with *'Just how mind numbingly boring is this jerk?'* to give you a chance to hide under the table or glug down a litre of hemlock before they get to you and pester you about whether you've found Jesus yet. *"Afraid not - sorry. Where did you last leave him?"*

A few more apps like that would increase the sum of human happiness. Unlike those that enable you to send yet another photograph of your bloody cat to the one person on the planet who's interested and about four thousand others who would rather stick needles in their eyes than open another of your irritating attachments.

I'm going back to clay tablets and an abacus.

Another recurrent bugbear in the winter is, as previously mentioned, the annual lift out. This is always a nervous time, entailing as it does, entrusting your beloved boat cum home cum container of all your worldly goods to some bloke you've never met before and don't know from Adam.

Naturally, you would prefer the operator of the travel hoist (or, Heaven forbid, the crane) to be competent, trained, tested, certified and conscientious with an unblemished record and a comprehensive insurance policy.

You can prefer it as much as you like but there are a couple of glaring flaws in this otherwise admirable and reasonable aspiration. The first is that there is no way of checking. This is probably for the best as far as your peace of mind is concerned. The further South and East you go, the less likely it is the operator has had any form of formal training whatsoever. By the time you get to Greece or Turkey the best you can probably hope for is that he once spent half an hour idly flicking through a fuzzy photocopy of a user manual printed in Bulgarian and, with a bit of luck, has been at the game long enough to have learnt from the mistakes he has inevitably made on other peoples' boats.

The second flaw is that even if you could check up on him it would do you no good as there's no-one else to go to. So it boils down to either hand your boat over to your local cowboy or up sticks and sail day and night for a week so that you can consign your pride and joy to some other cowboy who's probably no better than the one you left and could quite feasibly be even worse. You might as well save yourself the effort and stick where you are.

There are, of course, a few honourable exceptions to this sorry state of affairs but unfortunately Roussos, the lift operator in Crete, didn't appear to be one of them as things turned out.

We approached lift-out day, as always, with a growing sense of unease and trepidation reaching fever-pitch as we backed into the lifting bay and Roussos tightened the straps and lifted *Birvidik* slowly out of the water. I usually remain on board during this procedure although precisely what a 97-pound weakling armed only with a sausage fender and a flimsy telescopic boathook could have done if 16 tonnes of boat decided to surrender itself to gravity is a moot point.

Contrary to our fevered imaginings, the lift-out went without a hitch and *Birvidik* was propped up on the concrete.

An uncharacteristic flurry of activity enabled us to complete all our planned jobs and we left *Birvidik* propped up on the hard and flew off to Portugal for an ill-deserved period of recuperation.

After we'd been gone about a fortnight, we received an email from one of our fellow yotties in Ag. Nik, informing us that *Birvidik* had had an altercation with the travel hoist and had, unsurprisingly, lost.

Travel hoists, as has been mentioned before, are

remarkably functional, if hardly elegant, pieces of engineering. They are also very large, very heavy, and very, very powerful; festooned as they are with a labyrinth of hydraulic piping powered by a diesel engine originally designed to pull a 2 000-tonne freight train. They are also remarkably manoeuvrable, with each of their four wheels independently steerable. Experienced operators can manoeuvre one of these things with balletic grace, even while it is cradling a 25-tonne boat in its arms. They coax it through tortuous paths into spaces only centimetres wider than itself. Not only that, but, as the hoist is so tall the operator has to think in three dimensions while extemporising this mechanical *pas de deux*.

And this is where our Ag. Nik operator, Rousso, fell down. Apparently, he was moving a large catamaran into the space alongside and behind *Birvidik*. He was concentrating so closely on the 10 mm gap between the hoist and *Birvidik's* hull that he forgot about the 20 cm overhang at the top of the hoist, which snagged on the main mast cap shroud (one of the wires holding the mast up).

The wire in question is eight-millimetre 1 x 19 stainless steel. It has a breaking strain of over 5 ½ tonnes. You or I couldn't help but notice these sorts of forces if we came across them or, more pertinently, they came across us. So would the average family car, which would probably stall if trying to pull that sort of a load. Even a small truck would labour. Not a travel hoist – the engine didn't even change tone as the hoist pulled the wire back like a bowstring.

Witnesses reported that the mast, appropriately for the last simile, bent over like a bow. Something had to give, and it wasn't going to be the travel hoist. Nor, as it turned out, was it going to be the wire. What eventually gave was the bottle screw, AKA the turnbuckle. This is a robust chunk of stainless steel which is used to adjust the tension in the wire. It parted with a thunk and the mast sprang back upright with a twang that could be heard halfway across town. Yotties all over the marina poked their heads up and stared around like a clan of startled prairie dogs.

This news left us in a bit of a quandary. It was

impossible to tell at a range of just over three thousand kilometres what ancillary damage might have been done. At worst it could have permanently bent the mast, buggered up the in-mast furling gear, strained and weakened the other rigging wires, loosened the chainplates (which attach the wires to the hull), or even weakened the hull from pressure against the props that held the boat up.

Which, it was generally agreed, would be bad.

We contacted our insurers and pointed out to them that, should such damage become apparent during the forthcoming sailing season, the likely outcome would have been the rapid descent of *Birvidik* plus crew to the bottom of the Mediterranean. They concurred that such an event would knock a significant hole in their profit and loss account for that year and arranged for a surveyor to nip across to Crete from Athens and give the boat a quick once over.

Which was good.

He reported back:

The cap shrouds had indeed been damaged and strained by the incident, and would need to be replaced, as would their bottle screws. (Bad).

Nothing else seemed to have been damaged. (Good).

The rest of the rigging, although undamaged by the incident, was looking tired and would need to be replaced in its entirety very soon. (Bad).

At our expense. (Badder)

The insurers came back to us. They argued that:

The cap shroud damage was an insured risk. (Good)

We had a £500 deductible on the policy and the total cost of the cap shroud replacement was unlikely to be significantly more than that. So we'd end up paying most, if not all of it. (Bad).

The legal costs section of our policy entitled us to claim assistance in recovering our associated expenditure from the hoist operator. (Good)

We contacted their recommended rigger and arranged for him to come over from Athens and replace all the rigging. He said he could do it for about three thousand quid. (Not bad.) (ish).

But he couldn't get over to do it until the 9th May, nine days after our winter contract with the marina expired and we had intended to set off sailing. (Bad)

We arrived back on *Birvidik* at the end of April and he arrived on the ninth of May with two assistants. They knocked the job off in one day and, as they had managed to get another job in the same marina, reduced the price a tad by splitting the travelling costs. (Good).

Following the repairs, we entered into extended correspondence with our insurance company. It turned out that, of the nearly £2 000 we paid out for re-doing the standing rigging, the insured damage (i.e. that directly caused by the travel hoist) amounted to about £800. This was only £300 above our excess of £500, so it wasn't worth losing the no-claims for that amount. We resigned ourselves to forking out for the lot.

Our insurer, however, pointed out that we had legal cover included in our policy. This entitled us to the services of some purportedly big-shot lawyers in order to sue the arse off either the marina or the hoist operator (or both). As a bonus, claiming on this did not affect our no-claims. We contacted them and sent off the reams of documentation they subsequently requested.

After a few weeks and a series of learned umms & ahs, we received a communication in what appeared to be almost, but not quite, totally unlike English. Working my way through the periphrastic, circumlocutory tautologies I teased out the underlying meaning:

I am a specialist in International Litigation.

Translation: I joined this firm as a YTS trainee last Tuesday and have never been abroad, but my sister married a Lithuanian.

I have been passed your file by your legal expense insurer.

No-one else could be arsed with this piddling little claim so the tea-lady told me I had to deal with it.

I have reviewed your case in detail.

I got as far as the second paragraph before giving up and going out for six pints and a Balti.

I believe your claim has reasonable prospects of success.

You've got a rock-solid, cast-iron, copper-bottomed case.

I am concerned about the length of time it will take to settlement.

You're more likely to get a telegram from The Queen first.

Levels of responsiveness in Greece can in no way be compared to those in England.

This lot can make the Bloody Sunday enquiry look like summary vigilante justice.

We do not yet know whether the marina or hoist operator are (sic) insured.

They're almost certainly not.

Due to the Greek financial situation we are experiencing a number of insurers going bankrupt.

Even if they were insured it wouldn't make an iota of difference.

This case will be uneconomic, with costs several times the value of your claim.

Hang on - we could end up losing money on this.

The estimated value of your claim is £1085 and the unrecoverable legal expenses are estimated at £2000 to £3000 or more.

Holy Shit! How do we get out of this one?

Lawyer strikes and court strikes are currently very common in Greece.

We'll start by putting the frighteners on him.

If you were a private, fee paying client...

If you were I might give a flying fuck

I could not advise you to spend more in unrecoverable legal fees than you could hope to recover in damages.

I'd crawl over broken glass on my hands and knees to get you into court.

As obliged under your policy of insurance...
As I can't work out how to wheedle my way out of it...
I have advised your insurers....
I told them we could be in deep doo-doo here
They have instructed me to make an offer to you.
They said 'buy the bugger off'....
The amount I am instructed to offer is £750.
As cheaply as possible.
I could have summarised it in two brief paragraphs:
Dear Sir.

You are completely in the right, both morally and legally, but that's totally irrelevant. The chances of you getting any money whatsoever from anyone, anywhere in Greece at any time before Armageddon are so infinitesimal that you'd be better off paying your life savings to that nice gentleman who emailed you from Nigeria. You know, the one with the idiosyncratic spelling and grammar.

Accordingly, we want nothing to do with the entire enterprise and with our years of experience we reckon we can get you to forget the whole business for seven hundred and fifty quid.

Yours etc
Vicky Pollard
Asst. Beverage Dispensing Officer
Weasel, Ferret, Polecat, Stoat & Partners.

And do you know what?
They were right.
We know when we're beaten.

Crete to the Ionian via the Peloponnese.

May 5th 2012 – October 10th 2012

We left Ag. Nik and retraced our steps westwards along the North coast of Crete. The problem with retracing your footsteps is that it makes you slack and blasé. Correction: it makes *me* slack and blasé.

The trouble is that I think I know it all. I get overconfident and take my eye off the ball. It was particularly the case in this instance as we were retracing our steps precisely: same route same stopping places. I knew we had travelled this exact track on the way east and so I didn't pay close enough attention to the chart. I knew there were no problems on this route, so I just punched in the waypoints and off we went.

Well, I thought I knew.

As we began to cross Souda bay, we were slightly disconcerted by a distant boom followed by a high-pitched whistle, and even more disconcerted by the sight of a high speed military launch closing fast on an interception course.

My General Operating Procedure with military vessels is to say 'hello' very politely and then do exactly what they tell me to. This turned out to be the correct course of action. They pulled alongside and asked if I was aware that we were slap bang in the middle of an operational NATO live missile firing range. I replied that I hadn't been, but I was more than willing to believe them, especially considering that boomy whizzy thing overhead. So that's what that funny dotted red line on the chart meant.

"*Call Range Control on channel 12 and do exactly as they tell you.*" They said.

"*Yes Sir. Very sorry Sir. Won't happen again Sir. Please don't blow me out of the water, Sir*" I mumbled, looking down at my boots.

I called Range Control and began a rambling grovel. I was interrupted, politely, but firmly.

"*Good morning Birvidik. You will steer exactly 310 degrees, making the best speed you can, until you are met by the coastguard vessel. You will then follow them exactly as they guide you out of the range.*"

"*Yes Sir. Very sorry Sir. Won't happen again Sir. Please don't blow me out of the water, Sir*"

They then asked me if I knew the identity of the yacht

eight miles behind me. Quick as a flash, I shopped them. *"The yacht's name is Kiara, Sir. Dutch flag, Sir. They're doing it as well, Sir. It's not just me, Sir. It was their idea, Sir. Honest. They made me."*

Hoping I'd diverted his ire (and fire) somewhat, I set the autopilot sensitivity to maximum (equivalent to 'does this dress make my bum look fat?') and punched in 310 degrees. Twenty minutes later we were met by the coastguard.

The guy on the aft deck waved his arms in that waggly movement that aeroplanes do to mean 'follow me' and it shot off at about 20 knots. *Birvidik* has a 90 horse power engine, but even so, the most we can make is about eight and a half knots. At those revs we produce large quantities of smoke and I didn't want to give them the slightest suspicion that we were laying a smokescreen for nefarious purposes, God knows what they'd have thrown at us then, so we limped after them at about seven knots. Just before they disappeared over the horizon they turned around and picked us up at a more modest speed. We still had trouble keeping up.

Once they'd guided us out of the range to Cape Maleka (this always makes us snigger like schoolboys as 'Malaka' means 'wanker' in Greek) they peeled off and waved us on our way.

They must have reported back as the Greek Range Control Officer came back on channel 12.

"You are free to proceed Birvidik. Thankyou for your co-operation."

"My pleasure" I replied. *"You're the guys with all the guns"*

"That we are Sir" broke in a laconic American voice, *"That we most certainly are."*

In future I'm going to make sure I read the chart properly.

Until the next time.

Once we had rounded Cape Maleka we set course for the isolated anchorage of Gramvoussa on the western end of

Crete. We intended to spend a few relaxing days at the anchorage before making our leisurely way to the island of Kithera where we hoped to stay for a few days and then go on to the tiny island of Elafonisos, which we had missed due to weather on the way to Crete the previous season.

It was not to be.

One of the fundamental truths of sailing is that although the wind can, and does, come at you from all points of the compass the weather systems themselves almost invariably come in from the west. There was a cracker of a weather system sitting out there right then, straddling Sardinia. This would take a few days to get to us and blow our socks off. At that moment, there was no wind at all where we were. This, however, did not stop our friendly little depression from sending in an advance guard.

Right, now pay attention.

In deep water, the speed of a wave = $\sqrt{gL/2\Pi}$ [71]

Glad I told you that? Thought you would be.

What it actually *means* is that the longer the wavelength, the faster the wave travels. That's why tsunamis travel so quickly, crossing oceans in a few hours. A storm generates waves of many different wavelengths, but the long wavelengths rush ahead, travelling much faster than the actual weather system generating them. So they arrive several days ahead of the nasty stuff. A sort of oceanographic *"Woo oo - we're coming to get you!"*

Which is what we had - a nasty big swell with no wind to fill the sails and stop the boat from throwing itself all over the place.

We were heading straight in to the swell and so were pitching up and down violently. Einstein took umbrage at this. She began by salivating and progressed to vomiting and crapping. Liz, seeing her about to demonstrate projectile vomiting over the saloon carpet, lifted her up to put her in her litter tray. Einstein repaid this concern by crapping down Liz's front and all over her feet. After a quick wipe down, Liz employed our new cosy cat bag, which we bought with this in mind. Einstein is zipped into the padded bag and suspended from Liz's shoulder so that Liz acts as a sort of hammock, minimising unpleasant motion. Einstein demonstrated her gratitude by crapping in the bag and then pissing in it, which soaked through the bag and into Liz's fleece, T shirt and trousers.

Fortunately, a change of course eased the motion and Einstein stood down from DEFCON 5 to DEFCON2. We hosed Liz down with a mix of neat bleach and Jeyes fluid and started to relax, but not too much.

There was no mobile signal at Gramvoussa so we couldn't get a more up to date forecast, but the long swell had posted a warning that we would have been foolish to ignore. We re-jigged our plans and decided to head to Kithera the next morning. With a bit of luck, we could sit out the coming blow in the main port, Kapsali.

Kithera appeared at first sight to have been an ideal place to weather the coming gale. We had managed to secure ourselves a protected looking spot inside the breakwater and the Island was a gem – plenty of interest and small enough to get everywhere on foot. Congratulating ourselves on our foresight and seaman-like decision making we left the boat and set off to explore. Things continued to improve. Apparently, there was a touring orchestra visiting the Island, and concerts were due to be held over the next few days. We returned to the boat full of excitement and enthusiasm.

Then the Port Police turned up. We approached them with beaming smiles and explained our plans. Our explanations elicited that dispiriting official sound of breath being drawn in through clenched teeth.

"*Oh no – you can't stay here after tonight*" they said. "*There's a strong southerly forecast.*"

"*We know that.*" We replied. "*That's why we want to stay here behind this sodding great breakwater.*"

They would not be moved. They deployed the natives' secret weapon – local knowledge. In a strong southerly, they explained, reflected, refracted and diffracted waves interfered with each other and churned up the water behind the breakwater. This made it dangerous for small boats such as ours and very uncomfortable for larger boats such as fishing boats and ferries; three of which were, by odd coincidence, due to arrive in this very spot early the next morning.

Deflated and disappointed we scrubbed the proposed meals out and concerts and retired to *Birvidik* to rehash our passage plan. The choice came down to either a shortish run to an anchorage in the protected looking bay of Porto Kayio or a fourteen-hour trip to Kalamata marina. We chose Porto Kayio. We lived to regret it.

I have a theory. Well, actually I have loads of theories but there is one which seems particularly apposite at this point in the narrative. Like most of my theories, it is unsupported by any reliable or worthwhile scientific research; neither is it underpinned by any empirical evidence, underlying logical analysis or deep philosophical thought. It is, rather, a hotchpotch of random associations based solely on anecdote and personal experience, preferably serving to reinforce my own deeply ingrained prejudices. The bones of it go like this:

Humans are an unusual species in that they are one of the few that has a sense of time. They are able to appreciate the present, remember the past and imagine and plan for the future. Although all humans can do all three to some degree, I suspect that individuals show degrees of preference as to the time zone in which they feel most at home.

Young children live their lives almost exclusively in the present. Unalloyed joy can give way to the deepest despair in microseconds. They laugh more than adults and they cry more. Some blessed souls carry this over into adulthood. They live in the present and they savour every moment. They live life deeply and to the full. I suspect this tendency is associated with the X chromosome, explaining why the mindfulness industry is supported far more by women than it is by men.

It could also be that it is a search for this childlike state that lies behind much of the use of hallucinogens. In a number of studies scientists scanned the brains of people after they had taken LSD. The scans indicated that the subjects' mental states mimicked those of infants, with all the emotional lability associated with infant brain patterns.

Then there are those that live in the past, possibly in a vain attempt to return to the prelapsarian joys and depths of experience of childhood. For these lost souls, the trials, triumphs, responsibilities and rights of adulthood don't hold a candle to the vivid mental picture they hold of the halcyon days of their childhood.

Then we come to the future-fixated, the anally retentive planners and prognosticators, who seem unable to resist forsaking the wonders of the present in order to plot, plan and predict in an ultimately doomed attempt to reduce the dread uncertainty and risk associated with the great unknown that stretches threateningly into the future. I suspect that the gene for this particular characteristic lies on the Y chromosome. I certainly put myself in this category and like most sailors in this category, I do passage planning.

Passage planning, like most human activities that try to second-guess the future, suffers from one fundamental limitation - chaos theory. Life is a chaotic system; it is too complex to predict with any degree of certainty. As such, planning cannot eliminate disaster all of the time, or even most of the time. The best you can hope for is that you can minimise some of the unpleasantness to some degree, at least some of the time. In the grand scheme of things, passage planning is an ultimately futile exercise. But there again, in the grand scheme of things, everything is ultimately pointless[72], so we won't go there. That way, we might be able to retain some shred of sanity.

Take our decision on whether to go on to Porto Kayio or to Kalamata. Choices in passage planning such as this are never cut and dried. There is too much uncertainty applied to too many variables. Wind direction and strength can vary dramatically from that which was forecast, and that's before trying to factor in the local effects of interaction with bodies of land. Wave and swell direction and height can be unexpectedly modified by underwater topography. Holding can be anything between good firm, deep sand through uneven rock to mud the consistency of runny porridge. All in all, planning a passage and selecting an anchorage is about as informed a choice as being bamboozled into investing your newly-liberated pension pot into a dodgy Brazilian debt factoring racket by some iffy, fly-by-night, supposedly independent financial advisor.

Porto Kayio looked pretty bomb-proof on paper. The forecast wind was from the WSW and the only entrance was *via* a narrow channel on the east side. Once through the channel the bay opened up on both sides to reveal anchorages of a good depth, surrounded by protective high ground. We turned into the southern arm of the bay, which looked the best protected, chose our spot and dropped the hook in about ten metres of water. Then we went astern to bite it in before sitting back and seeing what the weather Gods would throw at us. What they threw at us was five days of unrelenting stress.

I frequently deride the oft-expressed Yottie viewpoint that ours is a uniquely healthy lifestyle. I substantiate this diatribe with a litany of counter-arguments, mainly centred around the sedentary nature of yottie life, the artery-clogging diet, the heroic alcohol intake, the melanoma-inducing levels of UV exposure and a tendency to dubious standards of personal hygiene. In the case of stress, though, they're probably on to something.

Before we started full-time cruising, we shared with most non-sailors (and a lot of recreational sailors) many misconceptions about the cruising lifestyle. Prominent amongst these was the expectation of the level of stress associated with the cruising life. This varied wildly. On the arcadian wing were the pathologically optimistic, who imagined a permanently stress-free nirvana, consisting primarily of lolling in a hammock in an idyllic anchorage while sipping contentedly on a grapefruit daiquiri. At the opposite end of the spectrum were the Hieronymus Bosch faction, in whose fevered imaginations Dante-esque visions of monstrous waves, jagged rocks and fearsome sea-monsters jostled for position in an endless panoply of horrors, which could only be ended by a lingering death or sudden, merciful, stress-induced apoplexy.

Both positions are, of course, absolute cobblers. All lifestyles involve some degree of stress. Indeed, it is essential to a happy, successful and fulfilled life. Any humans who unaccountably find themselves in a totally stress-free environment promptly endeavour to rectify this by manufacturing sources of stress, usually in the form of interactions and competition with other humans.

Not all stresses, however, are created equal. There is a qualitative difference between the types of stress experienced in the cruising life and that suffered by the poor average Joe going through the endless, soul-destroying, Sisyphean grind of the everyday, frantic, rat race. Cruising stress tends to be acute. It is high intensity but tends to be of fairly short duration, typically from a few hours to a day or so. For the most part it involves firefighting – dealing with immediate problems, usually those posing an immediate threat to the safety, or even existence, of the boat and/or its crew.

Stress in the workaday environment on the other hand tends to be chronic stress, a constant, low-level, nagging, soul-sapping, debilitating sort of stress. Its source causes are seldom resolvable. Indeed, one of the major sources of chronic workplace stress is being held accountable and responsible for something over which you have little or no control. This situation is frequently brought into being by the likes of managers, politicians, bureaucrats and petty officials (effectively all those self-serving parasites without a proper job), all cynically trying to deflect attention away from their own untrammelled ambition, incompetence, egotism and hubris and onto those poor unfortunates subject to their whims, power and influence[73].

Several studies have shown that there is a strong correlation between autonomy and life expectancy. The more control one has over one's work and outcomes, the less stress one suffers and the longer one lives. Pity the poor Hobbesian souls whose lives are fully scripted by micromanagement. Their lives may not be solitary, but they are sure to be poor, nasty, brutish and certainly short.

The two types of stress evoke very different physiological responses and have very different effects on the well-being, both mental and physical, of those subjected to them. The acute stress response serves a useful biological purpose. It maximises your chances of getting out of a life-threatening situation relatively intact. When your senses pick up information it is sent through to the amygdala, an almond-shaped body deep in the hindbrain[74], to see if any threat is indicated. If there is, the amygdala ropes in another bit of the hindbrain, the hypothalamus, which activates the sympathetic nervous system by sending frantic messages to the adrenal glands telling them to pull their bloody fingers out unless they fancy ending up as garnish on a vulture's *hors d'oeuvres*. Given the options, the adrenals dutifully comply. Adrenaline, noradrenaline and cortisol flood through your system and pull out all the stops on your 'fight or flight' response. This is a bit like holding your body's accelerator pedal down with a brick.

There is hardly a system or organ of the body which is unaffected by this cascade, and all the responses have been honed by evolution to maximise your chances of survival.

Oxygen intake is increased many-fold by increasing heart and breathing rates. This is helped on its way by bronchodilation, the opening up of the airways in the lungs. Adrenaline pushes the liver into flooding the blood with glucose which can be used with the extra oxygen to generate prodigious amounts of energy. The blood vessels to the muscles dilate to divert all this extra energy where it can be put to best use. At the same time, blood vessels in the skin constrict, thus making more blood available to the muscles and minimising blood loss in the event of injury. Hence the frightened pallor. Meanwhile, digestion grinds to a halt as its blood supply is shut off, producing the familiar 'butterflies in the stomach' and the kidneys shut up shop for the duration. No point in wasting valuable blood and anyway you don't really want to stop mid ruck for a quick pee or a dump.

The pupils expand, increasing the eyes' light-gathering abilities. The skin, meanwhile, has another little trick up its sleeve, which in humans has been rendered somewhat ineffective by evolution; it gives you goosebumps. At first glance, making you look like the last turkey in the shop on a wet boxing day would seem to have limited survival value unless it incapacitates your potential predator by reducing it to paroxysms of hysterical laughter.

Goosebumps are a relic of our more hirsute evolutionary past. They are caused by the contraction of the tiny erector pili muscles which are attached to the hair follicles in mammals. This contraction makes the hair stand up on end. On most mammals this has the effect of making it look much bigger and more threatening. We however have lost most of our body hair over the millennia and all the poor erector pili can do now is make us look cold and give us that prickly sensation on the back of the neck when we walk through a graveyard at night

We had become accustomed to the intermittent acute stresses of the cruising life, so we slipped almost unconsciously into threat-countering mode. This involves analysing the situation, determining what needs to be done to minimise the possible adverse consequences of the threat and then doing it.

We looked at our position. On the plus side we were in a protected position in a good anchoring depth with the anchor well bitten in at 1000 revs. On the down side we were faced with strong, gusty winds in an anchorage with restricted manoeuvring room and we were just a smidgeon closer to the rocky shore than we would really have liked. Effectively, we had three choices: stay where we were, try anchoring in deeper water further away from the rocks or make a fourteen-hour run in rough weather to Kalamata marina. Each had its pros and cons, but on balance we decided to stay put, a decision reinforced by watching four other boats limp into the anchorage and then have to make several attempts to get their anchors to bite.

Having made the decision to stay, the worst-case position was having the anchor drag and the boat carried backwards on to the rocks. Should this happen we wouldn't have time to do anything about it before the rudder and transom were pounded into matchwood and the propeller mangled into a lump of metal that could easily have been attributed to later period Picasso. All our planning and efforts, therefore, went into trying to make sure we didn't drag.

We had started off well, with our 35 kg Manson anchor dug well in at the end of 50 metres of 10mm chain. I would have liked to have let out more chain so that the pull was at a shallower angle, but we didn't have the space for that, so I slid two 15kg chums down the chain. This gave us a much shallower catenary and the chums would, in addition, act as shock absorbers giving the anchor some protection from snatch loads.

I still wasn't convinced and decided on a belt and braces approach. I dragged our Danforth stern anchor to the bow, attached it to 15 metres of chain followed by as much multiplait rope as we had room for, and fed it over the bow roller into the dinghy. Liz rowed the dinghy to the designated dropping point while I directed operations from the water with the aid of a facemask and snorkel and dived down to make sure it was well dug in.

We were now lying to two anchors totalling about 120 kg with chain. I still wasn't happy. We had one last string to our collective bow – our second, reserve, backup, Jesus-I-hope-we-never-have-to-use-this, emergency anchor; a 30 kg CQR. This I attached in series to the Danforth.

That was it. We had run out of options, having deployed all of our ground tackle. We had over a hundred and fifty kilograms of ironmongery on the seabed. If that didn't hold us, then we were knackered. All we could do now was wait and hope.

The wind rose to and beyond the predicted force eight and was then augmented by the local topography. The surrounding hills funnelled the wind into acceleration zones which blasted *Birvidik* with gusts of force nine to ten. In addition to this, the shapes of the hills created bistable air flows. The slightest variation in wind direction, or even a puff from the side flipped the flow over the other side of a hill so that it suddenly hit poor *Birvidik* from a completely different angle, leaning her over and making her surge on the anchor chain. Every time she brought up suddenly on the anchor we flinched, waiting for the tell-tale signs of dragging.

It was at this point that stress metamorphosised from acute to chronic. The adrenaline and cortisol kicked in and stayed there for five days – peanuts by comparison with the year-on-year stress experienced by poor wage slaves the world over, but we weren't used to it.

The design spec for the stress response is that it's all going to be done and dusted, one way or the other, fairly quickly. If you're dead and in the process of being lunch, then there's no point in trying any other tactic. If you've survived and are now out of immediate danger then the hind brain invokes the parasympathetic nervous system, which is the physiological brake pedal to the sympathetic system's accelerator and the body stands down and returns to placid normality. This doesn't happen in chronic stress though. The sympathetic system stays in charge and the body remains on high alert. The system isn't designed for this and extended periods of high levels of adrenal hormones have a number of deleterious effects on the body. The constantly elevated blood pressure doesn't do much for your chances of avoiding a stroke or popping an aneurism. Cortisol is the real bugger in chronic stress. Apart from doing more than its fair share of increasing blood pressure it increases blood sugar which raises the risk of diabetes. It also suppresses the immune system and predisposes to clinical depression. Disrupted digestion can lead to malnutrition or, if comfort eating develops, obesity. Just to put the tin hat on things, chronic stress can also trigger acne and decrease libido. All things considered I'd argue that you're better off without it.

By the third day of hardly eating and sleeping fitfully fully clothed, we were beginning to show classic signs of chronic stress, a state of affairs that was exacerbated by my discovery when I dived on the ground tackle to see how it was doing. The unstable gusting had swung *Birvidik* erratically round the ground tackle, which had become tangled in a knotted mass of chain and rope. Although we hadn't dragged, we were now in an even more vulnerable position were we to do so. It would have been impossible to have lifted the anchors, which would have made it impossible to have manoeuvred the boat. If we dragged now, total loss of the boat would almost certainly have followed. I plotted an emergency procedure to get us, and the cat, safely ashore should disaster strike. Stress levels cranked up another couple of notches and we sat and waited, stomachs in knots and teeth clenched, for the wind to abate.

On the fifth night, it did. We awoke to bright sunlight, smooth seas and a flat calm that seemed almost eerie after the trials of the previous five days. Before we could move on to Kalamata, though, there was the small matter of raising the ground tackle, which was now in an even more chaotic cat's cradle on the sea bed.

It was fortunate that I do most of my underwater work with a facemask and snorkel. This meant that both of our dive bottles were still full. I kitted up and went in off the stern platform.

It turned out to be a good job both bottles were full. I'm pretty heavy on air at the best of times, but air consumption varies dramatically depending on circumstance. The biggest factor is depth. Pressure increases by one atmosphere for every ten metres you descend. So, you have one atmosphere of pressure at the surface. At ten metres down you are under two atmospheres in total, at 20 metres three atmospheres and so on. If you double the pressure then your air will last half as long. Triple the pressure, and your air will last one third as long etc. I was working in about 15 metres, which if previous experience was anything to go by should have given me just over an hour on a tank.

Previous experience, however, was noticeable for not featuring the humping around of 35 kg anchors and great lengths of 10-millimetre chain. Exertion at that level could easily reduce my bottom time to half an hour or less per tank. I intended to attempt to mitigate this by transferring the worst of the grunt work to Liz and the windlass. I did this by tying an extra rope onto anything heavy that needed lifting and passing the other end up to Liz. She would then wind it round the windlass and use that to lift the weight. I would then try to disentangle the chaotic web of ropes, chains and anchors.

Despite my offloading all the hard work to Liz, it still took me two hours and nearly all my air to get everything sorted out and lifted to the surface then onto the boat. Even then I had to cut the anchor warp at one point. If we hadn't had dive gear aboard, we'd have been there for another week trying to unscramble the cat's cradle and recover our ground tackle.

We spent the rest of the day washing down and stowing away, before having a welcome shower and settling into the cockpit with an even more welcome drink, the first of either of those for five days.

After a calm and relaxed last night at Porto Kayio we set off at sparrow-fart the next morning to continue traversing the Peloponnese on our way back to the Ionian.

Geographically, Greece is frequently looked upon as being made up of three entities; Mainland Greece, The Islands and The Peloponnese. This last-mentioned is a wild and mountainous region, separated from Mainland Greece by the Saronic and Corinthian gulfs, but just managing to cling on by a narrow isthmus at Corinth. It's a wild and rugged region and its peoples traditionally took after it in this respect. Their loyalties lay primarily with family and clan rather than with the nation state. This is hardly surprising given their geographical isolation compounded by sparse transport links with the rest of the country. In addition, Greece, as mentioned earlier, didn't exist as an independent nation state until 1829 and only achieved its current boundaries in 1947, which makes it fractionally younger than Italy.

If the Peloponnese is a wild, rugged and remote place, its southern three peninsulas take this to the extreme and the middle of the three, the Mani, is the epitome of Peloponnese isolation, both geographically and psychologically. Until the narrow winding road from Kalamata was built relatively recently, many Mani villages could only be reached by boat. In addition to contributing to a definite tendency to piracy amongst the inhabitants of coastal settlements, this remoteness coloured the psyches and culture of the inhabitants, a phenomenon that goes back millennia to the Spartans who inhabited and ruled the area nearly three thousand years ago.

They were a bit of a rum bunch the Spartans, something of a mixed bag by modern standards. In their favour, their attitudes to women were a degree less Neolithic than were those of most of their contemporaries. Don't get carried away here with any silly ideas of gender equality or equal rights. Spartan women had considerable advantages compared with their contemporaries in other local cultures. They were generally better educated, and they were allowed to own and inherit property, which was almost unheard of elsewhere. They were free to travel outside of their homes without chaperones, an unimaginable degree of freedom for women in other tribes.

None of this alters the fact that Spartan women were well treated only because it made them more effective baby machines for restocking the army after its losses due to war, accident, age and disease.

The primary focus of Spartan society was the maintenance and development of an efficient and ruthless army. All Spartan males were obliged to join the army and were trained to this end from the age of seven.

Don't let this highly partisan account mislead you into thinking that Spartan men were a bunch of completely uncultured barbarians. They did like to keep their hair nice. Going into battle scruffily coiffed would have made a laughing stock of a Spartan Hoplite. To avoid this ignominy, they were all allocated into pairs of *very good friends*.[75] The night before a battle the pairs would sit in mutual grooming sessions making sure that their hair was *just right*, and suitably styled for a hard day's slaughtering.

Having the entire male population spending all its waking hours stomping about waving spears and poncing up their barnets instead of actually doing any proper work inevitably led to a bit of a labour shortage. Back at the ranch, the women ran the households but there was no-one around to make the spears, till the fields, build the houses or look after the animals. The Spartans got around this little local difficulty by importing labour.

There were two classes of imported workers, the *Periokoi* and the Helots. The former were tradesmen, free men who lived on the periphery of Spartan settlements and bought, sold and made stuff. If you really had to live in ancient Sparta then being in the *Periokoi* was probably the least bad option.

The most bad option was Helot. These were drawn from conquered populations and did all the work necessary to keep the Spartan state going – they were the farmers, domestic servants and the like, and were treated as absolute slaves. They also greatly outnumbered the Spartans, who seemed to live in constant fear of a Helot uprising. Can't think why. Machiavelli argued in *The Prince* that a vanquished people should be either well treated or crushed. As far as the Helots were concerned, the Spartans went for option two in a big way. They treated them like shit.

They humiliated them in public and Spartans were specifically allowed to kill Helots for being too smart or too fit. Beneath that veneer of martial manliness, did they really have just a whiff of an inferiority complex? Every autumn the Spartans declared war on the Helots so that they could be killed with impunity. Despite all this abuse, some Helots even volunteered to fight in the Spartan army where some of them served with distinction. After one major bloodletting, those Helots that fought best were brought together, ostensibly to be rewarded with their freedom for their valour. Instead, they were slaughtered so that such able soldiers would pose no threat to the Spartan state.

The Spartans, though, had failed to read Machiavelli's fine print. He said 'Crush', not just 'treat like shit'. Well they couldn't wipe them out completely, could they? The whole of Spartan society depended on them. So when Epaminondas of Thebes led an invasion into Spartan territory and liberated the Messenian Helots, who outnumbered the Spartans by seven to one, the writing was on the wall.

They should have gone for option one, really.

A concrete example of the tenacious persistence of bronze age psychology in this area are the many characteristic towers attached to homesteads throughout the area. Although originally set up as defensive measures against the Ottoman Turks, they continued to develop and grow after that conflict ended.

The key to their survival and development was the perseverance until modern times of the Maniote practice of *Maina*, (*μαίῃα*) or vendetta. These were blood feuds between families usually from the same village but sometimes from as far away as Crete. They were highly ritualised with strictly enforced customs and rules. The objective of the feud was the destruction of the opposing clan's tower and the total annihilation of its every male member. Women were granted immunity and took advantage of this by restocking the towers with food and ammunition. Truces were declared at important points in the agricultural calendar, such as ploughing, sowing and harvesting. At such times, combatants would often tend adjoining fields, working in sullen silence.

One of the last major vendettas took place in 1870 and required the combined efforts of the Greek Police, the Greek Navy and the Greek Army to stop it. Even then it needed artillery support.

Now, I appreciate that the reputation and credibility of a government of a modern state supposedly subject to the rule of law is a tad compromised if it is seen to be impotent in the face of open gang warfare and reciprocal mass-murder, but *artillery*? That, surely, is a bit of an over-reaction? And we worry about our police knocking a few thieving adolescent thugs off their mopeds. Given the less than perfect accuracy of late nineteenth century artillery pieces, there must surely have been a lot of collateral damage.[76] Wasn't the cure at risk of being worse than the disease? Never mind though. We are assured by the Greek authorities that all that is now lost in the mists of time and visitors are at no risk whatsoever of being forced to re-live the script of *Deliverance*.

Just don't, whatever you do, let your gaze linger on the lissom daughter of one of the local chieftains.

We had to get to Kalamata to pick up our friend Chris. We

had intended to break the trip into two shorter ones by stopping off at Limeni on the way, but a cursory glance at it through binoculars changed our minds. There was a stubby breakwater which looked as though it might have provided a degree of shelter, but half of what limited mooring space it offered was occupied by a French ketch moored slap bang in the middle of it. We might have just about been able to squeeze in behind or ahead of it had its skipper not rendered these positions impossible by laying a tangled web of lines from his bow and stern to both extremities of the quay. Other than that, there was just a gradually shelving bay. Having just endured the five days in Porto Kayio, we didn't fancy what appeared to be an exposed anchorage with a lumpy swell driving into it. Secure pontoons and lashings of water and electricity beckoned, so we turned out and resigned ourselves to heading on to Kalamata. Enough was enough.

Kalamata is the only large centre of population in the Southern Peloponnese, with a population of 54000. It's the second biggest city in the whole of the Peloponnese, after Patras, but its population is under half that of a town like Maidstone or Rochdale. Never mind, for the Peloponnese, it's big – the sinful metropolis.

Kalamata is a University town, so its age distribution demographic isn't quite as age-heavy as the general Greek population. The Greek age distribution has been changing dramatically over recent decades, due mainly to a combination of declining birth-rate and emigration. This has been exacerbated in many parts of Greece by the exodus of young people from the islands and other remote areas (such as the Peloponnese) to the major cities, notably Athens and Thessaloniki. They left behind shrinking villages with aging populations, slowly dying off. The ten years of grinding austerity following the gigantic financial cock-up of 2008 partly reversed this trend. Unemployment and homelessness are far more prevalent in the cities than they are in rural Greece and so increasing numbers of young Greeks are returning to their ancestral villages and parental farms, where at least they will be fed, watered and sheltered.

After a few days of sybaritic self-indulgence, taking advantage of the plentiful water and electricity, combined with expeditions to the numerous local bars and restaurants, we knuckled down and set off west and north. Our route took us across the bottom of the Peloponnese and up the western coast, calling in at Koroni, Methoni, Navarino bay, Pylos and Kyparrisia before stopping off at Katakolon, from where we intended to visit ancient Olympia, the original site of the Olympic Games.

We approached Pylos with some misgivings, due to rumours we had heard on the yottie grapevine.

Ah, yes, the yottie grapevine. All human societies have communications networks and yotties are no exception. Being mobile and at sea, however, poses particular problems in establishing a comms network, but the relentless, exponential advance of technology has improved matters dramatically over the last few years.

In the ten years since we set out, comms have changed beyond all recognition. Even further back, when I started sailing in the 1970s, VHF radio was a luxury found only on the gentlemen's yachts of the richest of men. Now it is found on every boat from small inflatables upwards. Bigger ships have two or more so that the crewman on the bow can tell the helmsman at the stern what he's just hit. VHF, though, is line of sight. Range depends on antenna height, but typically pans out at around 25 nautical miles or just over 40 kilometres. Even in the relatively enclosed waters of the Channel Islands it's not that difficult to get more than 25 miles from a shore station. If you're halfway across the Atlantic your VHF is about as much use as a chocolate teapot.

That's where Single Side Band comes in. SSB is a high frequency radio that bounces signals off the ionosphere and gives a range of several thousand miles. We fitted *Birvidik* with one of these before we set off and I never got it to work. Not once. This was a shame as it was *via* SSB that the yottie could access the technological wonder of a weather fax and other meteorological data. Without SSB, getting a met involved seeking out a dingy, smoky, seedy internet café in one of the less salubrious neighbourhoods of town and laboriously copying out what you saw on the screen.

Nowadays all that is old hat. Smart phones and dongles allow on-board connection to the internet in coastal waters and with an, admittedly expensive, satellite phone you can browse to your heart's content in the middle of the Pacific and keep up to date with the Eastenders Omnibus collection while anchored in a deserted coral atoll. You can also get weather forecasts for anywhere on the planet, updated every three hours.

Apart from the official and commercial sites on the internet, yotties use a whole range of *ad hoc* arrangements. Virtually every wintering hole has a VHF radio net most mornings and a facebook page, both of which serve to facilitate social organisation and information exchange; advertise bought, sold and given away; conduct clandestine affaires and indulge in increasingly heated arguments about Brexit. In most manifestations, the grapevine takes the form of word of mouth, an anarchic and never-ending game of Chinese Whispers where Y reports that X had been told by Z that P, Q & R had it on good authority that anchorage B was now over-run with Russian jet skiers and thieving vagrants and anything not bolted to the deck would disappear within microseconds. Why, only last week, G told F that H had had his hammock stealthily removed without his noticing and that was while he was dozing in it.

This is where technology is no match for human nature. No matter how sophisticated the technology, it still suffers from the vagaries of human psychology. I.T. professionals have a range of acronyms to cover this (well, they would, wouldn't they?). Prime among these is GIGO – Garbage In, Garbage Out. The most common subsidiary cryptic reports on I.T. job sheets are PEBCAK (Problem Exists Between Chair And Keyboard) and PICNIC (Problem In Chair, Not In Computer).

Whenever two or (preferably) more yotties engage in conversation by any means, ranging from sozzled bar-room discourses *via* radio nets to internet fora, the same pattern emerges. It is a deadly combination of cutthroat one-upmanship and the reinforcement of mutual prejudices.

Each speaker feels constrained to top the previous one with an even more outlandish tale or imagined detail appertaining to the previous report. The charade continues in a bizarre ever-increasing spiral of invention, exaggeration, over-the-top embellishment and downright fabrication. There is no malice here, they just can't help themselves. After a while, they start to believe their own fictions. In such a manner, wild exaggerations, unsubstantiated inventions and blatant absolute falsehoods are accepted as gospel and propagated through yottiedom to a degree that would evoke gasps of envy and disbelief from Donald Trump.

It's little wonder then that yotties retain the 'Here be Sea Monsters' mentality of untold generations of seafarers. It's fear of the unknown. If our yottie has never been to a port or anchorage before, he's willing to believe the worst. There has been some progress. Sea monsters have given way to murderers, thieves, pirates, rapacious officials and dodgy kebab sellers, but the principle remains

If you think communications are fraught with error now, and were even more difficult in the 1970s, consider what things were like in the 1790s.

There was no radio, air mail or telegraph then. Communications, be they ship to ship or ship to shore, had to be line of sight. The most rapid means of signalling was setting fire to something. This was quick, but it had a couple of serious drawbacks. The obvious one is that setting fire to a barrel of molten tar on the deck of a wooden boat loaded to the gunwales with gunpowder was not a completely risk-free tactic. The second problem was that setting fire to something is what information scientists refer to as information sparse. It transfers very little information. In fact, in most cases it transfers just one piece of information, which is usually either *"Help!"* or *"Watch out – the bloody Spanish have arrived!"*.

More detailed information was transmitted by more complex methods, primarily signal flags as even semaphore wasn't invented until the 1800s. They could have used flashing a light on and off, I suppose, but Samuel Morse didn't unveil his famous eponymous code until 1837. All of these difficulties meant that even line of sight comms were about as fluently articulate as a speak your weight machine. Indeed, Nelson's famous signal before Trafalgar had to be changed from '*England confides that every man will do his duty*[77]' to '*England expects that every man will do his duty*' as 'expects' was in the signal book whereas 'confides' was not and would have had to have been spelt out letter by letter.

Despite their limitations, line of sight signals were vastly superior to long distance communication systems because effectively there weren't any of the latter. Ships were away for months or years at a time and were likely to be thousands of miles away. The only way to get information to and fro was by letter carried by another, hopefully faster, ship called a packet boat. This would take about three months each way if you were in Botany Bay. That would mean a minimum gap of around six months between sending the message and getting the reply. And I whinge about a one second delay on Skype.

This was a particular irritation for military commanders wanting to get new orders to distant ships or armies. The delays could lead to hostilities continuing for a considerable time after a war officially ended. The war of 1812, for example, was fought between Britain and its allies against the United States and its allies. It was officially ended by the Treaty of Ghent in December 1814. News of the armistice was still on its way across the Atlantic when the Battle of New Orleans was fought in January 1815 with over 2000 casualties.

The yottie grapevine had hinted that the port police in Pylos were sticklers for the rule book and that they made a point of being particularly officious and unco-operative. This is unusual as Greek maritime regulations are so complex and unenforceable that most Port Police do not understand them, or if they do, they very sensibly decide to tactically (and tactfully) ignore the more ludicrous ones.

One does, occasionally, run into a particularly ambitious or bloody-minded Port Policeman (or woman, true, but it's usually the proud possessor of Y chromosomes and a pair of testicles). If you do, be prepared for an expensive, tedious and seriously inconvenient interlude. Your tormentor will purport to know and understand the Greek Maritime Regulations intimately and in obsessive detail. He is lying. If he did possess the detailed knowledge he professes he would know that the regulations are internally inconsistent, self-contradictory and impossible to apply in practice.

Nevertheless, he will try. He is not really a policeman, remember, despite his title. He may belong to an organisation called the Port Police. He may wear combat fatigues and sodding great boots. He may carry a vicious-looking telescopic baton and pack a bloody big gun, but he is not a policeman. Don't look at his job title, look at his job description. His primary tasks are not arresting people and returning stolen bicycles, they are shuffling paperwork and collecting money. He is not a policeman, he is a bureaucrat, and C. Northcote Parkinson got his number as long ago as 1957.

Parkinson's most famous law was that work expands to fill the time allotted, but he really hit the nail on the head with the law's two axioms:

*An official wants to multiply subordinates, not rivals

*Officials make work for each other.

As a result, the prime objective for any bureaucrat is to expand the empire of his sphere of influence. Creating and enforcing regulations is a cracking way to do this. The practicality or desirability of these regulations is immaterial. In the interests of the sanity of our remaining reader, one example will have to suffice.

The EU has a ship inspection scheme for visiting vessels. It was originally set up to ensure that commercial shipping had some basic essentials such as plimsoll lines, charts, lifejackets, medical kits, fire-fighting equipment and competent officers and crew. This started from the perfectly reasonable assumption that it's not a good idea to have thundering great ships overloaded with dangerous cargoes while staffed with a skeleton crew of under qualified, sleep deprived Filipinos. It's even less of a good idea to have them then charging through crowded waterways without so much as an AA road map, an inflatable crocodile, a packet of band-aids or a wet flannel on board. In 2011, this basically good idea was extended to cover yachts. Typically, though, two archetypal bureaucratic behaviours came into play:

Firstly, the system must be easy for bureaucrats to administer. This means that they measure and record things that are easily measurable and recordable, rather than things that are important. Documents, therefore, take precedence over physical inspection by experts. Secondly, the whole system has to fit a standard form, so no effort is made to modify inspections in order to make them appropriate to the particular vessels being inspected.

As a result, we have the absurd position where, when in Greece, a yacht is technically obliged to adhere to IMO Resolution A.892(21), which requires the documentation of a vessel's movement from berth to berth. This means that if a yacht finds its anchorage or berth compromised by, say, weather change or the arrival of a sodding great gulet full of absolutely bladdered partying Russians, and decides to up sticks and move 200 metres across the bay, this movement must be officially documented in the ship's log, within one hour of arrival or departure. Failure to do so is an offence under the memorandum of understanding. Tot up a few more infractions like this and they can, if they feel like it, detain your boat.

There are hundreds of possible pitfalls like this lurking in the Greek Maritime Regulations but, almost without exception, they are sensibly ignored by the officials charged with their enforcement. Pylos, according to the yottie rumour mill, was an exception. The Port Police there were reported as sullen po-faced jobsworths who went through everything with a fine-tooth comb and imposed swingeing fines for even the most minor omissions, oversights or errors in documentation. This was worrying as Greek regulations are so Byzantine that it is impossible in practice to comply with them entirely. If they really want to get you, they will.

We were tempted to skip Pylos altogether and go straight on to Kyparrisia, but this would have made it a very long day and possibly an overnighter. We only do overnighters if absolutely unavoidable, so we decided to chance our luck and employ our usual tactics reserved for potentially troublesome officialdom.

The usual yottie tactic in these circumstances consists of lying low and hoping to be overlooked. This usually involves turning everything off, gagging the cat with a sock and skulking down below after pinning up a notice in Greek claiming to have decamped to England due to a family emergency. This never works – all it does is pique the interest of the Port Police and almost inevitably guarantees an official going over.

Not for us such underhand tactics. We are far more devious and employ psychology. Firstly, we throw them off-guard by being pro-active and seeking them out rather than waiting to be caught. This confuses and disorientates them. We then compound their discomposure by smiling broadly. This has been known to do the trick on its own. It's the old tribal psychology business again. Humans find it difficult to be nasty to someone who acts like a member of their tribe.[78]

If, despite this opening gambit, we are still faced with a stony face and a large pile of forms we move on to stage two. This involves attempting to win them round with an undignified and demeaning exhibition of crawling, enhanced by exuding an air of jovial, polite bonhomie and demonstrating a hypocritical willingness to enter into a detailed analysis of a football game of which I know absolutely nothing. This last I initiate by dint of close observation. I look around the office for any indication of sporting affiliation. Greek football fanatics just can't resist those little indications of tribal loyalty: An Olymbiakos scarf, an Astromitos paperweight, an Aris Thessaloniki lapel badge or a Man U strip pinned on the wall.[79]

These tactics almost invariably succeed, and we then sail through the paperwork with minor errors laughed off as irrelevances of no real significance. They also frequently have positive and unexpected consequences. We almost always end up positively liking each other. The mere act of smiling, even if forced and duplicitous, triggers the release of dopamine, serotonin and endorphins, all of which improve mood and wellbeing. This effect is compounded by a positive feedback loop whereby seeing someone else smile triggers mirror neurones in the brain which makes the observer smile as well, setting off a similar hormonal cascade. Just to top things off, smiling also releases another hormone, oxytocin, which encourages bonding behaviour by increasing fellow-feeling and empathy. It's a miserable bastard indeed who can withstand our full-frontal smile offensive.

So it was that we moored up against the quay and I immediately set off for the Port Police office, practicing my Duchenne smile [80]on the way, much to the consternation of passers-by, who wondered what the idiot with the manic rictus was doing frightening the children.

I paused at the office door, took a deep breath, and marched confidently in, preparing myself to launch a pre-emptive attack against death by scowl. It was not needed. Far from being confronted by a bunch of vindictive psychopaths intent on bankrupting me and impounding my boat, I was faced by a trio beaming welcoming smiles and ushering me in with heartfelt cries of "*Welcome to Pylos. Please sit down. Would you like a coffee? Have a cigar.*" OK, I lied about the cigar bit.

The trio comprised a grizzled, bearded bloke in his late fifties with lots of chevrons on the epaulets of his threadbare uniform, a statuesque, athletic-looking woman in her early thirties with a more restrained collection of chevrons but a much smarter set of combat fatigues and finally a callow looking youth in a uniform that still had the creases from its packaging. He did not appear to have reached epaulet bling level at all as yet.

I suspected that the older man was nominally in charge, but winding down to retirement, the woman actually ran the place and the ingenue was a very recent addition, who was still learning the ropes. My assessment of the sociodynamics of the group was reinforced by what followed.

Birvidik's paperwork had been selected as a training opportunity for the newbie, to be conducted in an avuncular fashion by beardie. While this was going on, Lara Croft carried on doing all the jobs that needed to be done.

Newbie's induction training continued at a snail's pace, which meant that so did the processing of my paperwork. There was no deliberate obstructiveness or obstreperous officialdom in this, just a typical relaxed Greek attitude to the passing of time. I was obviously in for the long haul here, so I sat down in the proffered comfy chair and sipped my coffee.

The unexpected congeniality of the welcome had taken me aback a bit, but I rallied valiantly and engaged smile mode with the able assistance of the mirror neurones. The three of them couldn't have been more helpful (that's Port Police, not mirror neurones).

All of this triggered a flash of cognitive dissonance in me.[81] My current experience was highly inconsistent with my expectations as from the yottie grapevine. Something had to give. What gave was faith in the yottie grapevine. Frankly this didn't take a lot of effort as I didn't have a lot of faith to start with. The yottie grapevine suffers from the same biases, drawbacks and errors as any reviewing system. Just take a look at Amazon and Google reviews or, for the epitome of these flaws, sites such as Trip Advisor and the like.

The variation in reviews of the same establishment is so dramatic and extreme that it defies the expectations of reason and common sense. The same establishment receives reviews that range from ecstatic hagiographies to scathing damnations with very little in between. Reception staff seem to be suffering from multiple personality disorder, displaying saint-like levels of helpful, tolerant affability to one reviewer while turning on the next with a tirade of snarling, obstreperous obstructionism. The same chef, in the same kitchen prepares the same dish on the same night and receives reviews ranging from "*Sublimely exquisite example of the culinary art*" to "*Inedible, over-priced dog-vomit*". Waiting staff appear to act as if they're auditioning for the lead role in Dr Jekyll and Mr Hyde. Reason dictates that no business would display that degree of extreme variation. The root must lie in the reviewing process.

The causes commonly advanced for these disparities

are incentives, fake reviews and demographics. Incentives are the reasons why people are moved to write a review in the first place. Studies indicate that people are motivated to write a review by events at the extremes. This means that exceptionally good or exceptionally bad experiences are more likely to be reviewed and the bad more so than the good. The great majority of services tend to occur in the middle of the spectrum, and these are heavily under-reported.

Fraudulent reviews, both good and bad, are self-explanatory attempts to game the system and are the cause of much ill-feeling among restaurateurs, hoteliers, hairdressers and the like.

Demographics are interesting. Studies have indicated that reviews tend to be posted disproportionately more by educated, wealthy women than by other demographic groups.

To these three, I would add a fourth. The greatest factor motivating reviews, especially negative ones, is whether there has been a significant degree of human interaction in the experience. Reviews of objects such as computers, cars, nasal hair trimmers or intimate vibrators can be quantified objectively. Indeed, they can frequently be reduced to numerical values. Such reviews are generally more reliable and can be trusted to a greater degree.

On the other hand, service industry reviews, such as those of hotels, restaurants, hairdressers, dentists, complimentary therapists and snake-oil salesmen are different. They are primarily driven by the subjective experience of the human relationships involved. This is particularly the case with one or no star reviews. After all, nothing motivates a scathing, spluttering outburst of apoplectic indignation more than does the belief that one has not been treated with the level of respect to which one feels entitled. There's not that much difference between the reaction of an affronted middle-class restaurant patron who considers the waiter to have been somewhat over familiar and that of a teenage gang member who thinks he's been 'dissed'. It's only a matter of style and degree. And available weaponry.

Many reviews, therefore, especially the very negative, probably tell us more about the reviewer than they do about the thing reviewed and this, I submit, is the case with many reports on the yottie grapevine. I suspect that the sources of the reports alleging obstructiveness on the part of the Pylos Port Police had experienced delays for the same reason that we had but had reacted differently.

Ill temper, curtness, impatience and downright rudeness are very effective at putting noses out of joint, irrespective of whether that nose belongs to a waiter or a Port Policeman. There does seem to be a tendency for adverse reviews, especially those alleging rudeness or poor service, to come disproportionately from the same groups of individuals, whether on trip advisor or the yottie fora.

The first five stops after Kalamata were all small, quiet fishing villages with slowly dwindling populations, ranging from just over 2000 at Pylos to an almost extinct 58 in the case of Kyparrisia. They all exuded an air of gentle decline.

Katakolon, on the other hand, is qualitatively different. It's no bigger than the others, with the town proper having a resident population of only 600 but it's not in gentle decline – it's the second busiest cruise port in Greece, after Piraeus, which serves Athens. For this it has ancient Olympia to thank (or curse).

We arrived just after the 2012 Olympics finished. All had been done and dusted. London's transport system was back to merely the usual chaos and maybe just the odd missile launcher had been accidentally left on a rooftop in Hackney. Inspired by *Citius, altius, fortius* and all that, we called in to Katakolon in order to take the train to ancient Olympia, the cradle of The Games and the seedbed of physical excellence, good sportsmanship and international co-operation.

It was looking a bit tired. Mind you, it was getting on a bit, seeing as the first Olympic games were supposed to have been held there around 1100 B.C., a time when we Brits were running around getting absolutely plastered on cheap booze, painting ourselves blue and knocking seven bales of shit out of the neighbours on a Saturday night.

How we have progressed in the intervening 3000 years.

In Greece, though, things were considerably more civilised. They were just segueing effortlessly from Bronze to Iron Age technology while we were still trying to blunder our way through the previous transition.

That's not to say, of course, that Hellenic culture and society was a lost democratic arcadia of reciprocal support and respect. The much-vaunted Athenian Democracy, for example, was hardly a shining paragon of universal suffrage. Out of a population of around half a million, around 20% were slaves and so had no vote, despite doing nearly all the work. Roughly 40% were not born in Athens, and so also had no vote. The remaining 40% were free born Athenians. Knocking out the roughly half of these who were children this cut the available pool of voters down to about 100 000 people.

Unfortunately, around half of these turned out to be women and so, obviously, could not be trusted with making reasoned decisions on important matters such as whether or not to get rat-arsed and knock seven bales of shit out of the neighbours next Saturday. They were therefore excluded from the electoral roll so they could concentrate on having babies, doing their nails and talking about kittens. By the time you then weeded out convicted felons, the clinically insane and those with highly suspect views, such as Aristotle, this left the fate of the city state in the hands of about 1/10 of the population - 50 000 blokes who would have all been contenders for the local golf club, had such an institution been invented. The State of Florida appears to be moving toward this classical interpretation of democracy.

However, back to the games.

Every year, there seem to be some nit-picking malcontents who complain that the inclusion of activities such as a bunch of women wearing nose-clips and rictus grins while making star formations in a swimming pool, or someone sitting on a horse while it walks sideways are not really sports at all and make a mockery of the spirit of the games.

There is some support for this view if one looks back to the very origins of the Olympics. The first ones consisted of a single foot race over a distance of about 200 metres. Even allowing for the opening and closing ceremonies the whole shebang would have been over in forty minutes.

"Is that it then?"

"Yup - time to go home."

"But I've travelled from Macedonia to see this – it took me three weeks."

"We've had your money. Go on - bugger off."

Seeing that their current business plan was somewhat lacking, and that future income was likely to fall, the Elisians, who ran the show, decided to expand. The 200 metres was supplemented by the 400 metres and the 5 000 metres. Hot on their heels came the jumping, discus and javelin which, with the combined foot races, made up the pentathlon. The mathematically ept among you will have realised that this totals four classes of event, while the classical scholars among you will pedantically point out that the root of 'pentathlon' is the Greek πεηδε (pende), meaning 'five'. The Stephen Fry wannabees will then smugly don their polymath hats and point out that the two are internally inconsistent. This apparent solecism is explained by the fact that the aforementioned four events were used to whittle the contestants down to a final pair who faced off in a fairly brutal wrestling cum boxing finale called the *Pancratium*.

This brought the crowds in. Nothing like a bit of blood and gore to whip the punters into a buying frenzy. Working on the principal that more is better, they introduced chariot racing, which was a good spectator sport, there being only 5% of the competitors completing the course without (frequently fatal) mishap. Formula 1 is a pussy cat by comparison.

The *pièce de résistance*, though, was the Pancratium. Carl Von Clausewitz argued that war is politics continued by other means. The pancratium was psychopathic brutality continued by sporting means. Two unarmed naked, oiled contestants set about each other until one was either unconscious or (preferably) dead. That's not to say that it was completely uncivilised of course. Oh no. There were rules. Two, in fact: no biting, and no gouging out the eyes. Ripping off the goolies is fine, but mind the eyes.

As if to compensate for these gruesome displays of gratuitous violence, all the Greek states observed a sacred truce for the duration of the games. The various warring city states would temporarily stop butchering each other on their own doorsteps and instead send representatives to butcher each other at Olympia. Once that minor distraction was out of the way they'd go back and take up where they left off.

"Right, where were we? If I remember correctly, you were laying down there while I had my sword at your throat."

"Far from it my dear chap. I fear your memory betrays you. You were lying face down over there with a large bruise on the back of your head, while I had my spear poised at your bottom. I remember it distinctly."

As all this developed, Olympia during the games became somewhat like Lisbon during WWII. Because it was neutral it was a hotbed of spying, intrigue, assassinations, black marketeering and other nefarious activities.

All this power, glory and money, of course, compromised the Olympic ideal. In the beginning the strict rules on participation ensured that honour and amateurism reigned. Entry was restricted to free born male Greeks. The 'male' bit was easy to verify seeing as all contestants had to take part naked. The rewards for victory were purely symbolic. A palm was given to the victor once his particular contest was over, and he got a whole olive branch in the closing ceremony.

Of course, this happy state of affairs couldn't last. The rules were relaxed to allow entry from any part of the Greek and Roman worlds and athletes became progressively more professional and corrupt, as did their sponsors. The games became a sounding board for nationalistic tin-drum bashing and contestants were heavily, and surreptitiously, subsidised and assisted by their home states. Ring any bells, Vlad?

As if this wasn't bad enough, then the Romans came along. Their arrival was the equivalent of taking a mildly corrupt organisation such as the IOC and handing it over to a consortium of FIFA, Bernie Madoff, Sylvio Berlusconni and an assortment of bank CEOs, then saying they could write their own rules. Only in this case, in 67 A.D. it was handed into the tender care of Nero.

Now, say what you like about Nero, but he knew what he wanted. And what he wanted, was everything - including winning the Olympics. In person. Nero makes Vladimir Putin look like Rolf Harris on oxytocin.[82]

The trouble was, he was crap at sport (Nero, that is, not Rolf Harris. Rolf was actually a pretty mean swimmer in his day). This, however, was no barrier to perfidy for a man of his talents and tendencies (Nero's, not Rolf's, although given subsequent revelations I'm not so sure).

Firstly, he advanced the games by two years so that he could take part at a convenient time. Then he added two new events that only he stood a chance of winning, namely the physically strenuous sports of singing and lyre playing. To be honest, there were probably a great many better singers and lyre players than Nero, but I suspect that they were all well aware of his stance on human rights, fair competition and the rule of law and sent in an apologetic note saying they'd love to take part, but they had to stay in and wash their hair and anyway, they had a bit of a cold.

This, though, was still not enough. He wanted to win the chariot race, which he duly did. The judges wisely declared him the winner even though he fell off twice and failed to finish. He rewarded them for their tactful decision by very kindly refraining from having them each nailed to a couple of planks.

So let's not hear any more moaning Minnies wittering on about how the Olympics nowadays are a sham, lacking in true sporting values and selling out to commercial and political interests.

Compared with the originals they're purity incarnate. If only the ancients had had access to modern pharmaceuticals. The pancratium on PCP - now that would capture the Grand

Theft Auto demographic.

The games lasted for just over a thousand years until 393 CE when the Emperor Theodosius was overcome by a fit of Christian piety and decreed that all such *pagan cults* be banned. The site was abandoned and slowly reclaimed by nature until it was incorporated into the modern Olympic Games.

This did not happen immediately, though. Although Baron Pierre de Coubertin founded the International Olympic Committee in 1894, the tradition of carrying the flame from Olympia to the games' stadium was introduced for the 1936 Summer Olympics held in Berlin, overseen by Joseph Goebbels. So the whole business has a heritage to be proud of.[83]

Ancient Olympia is only 40 kilometres from Katakolon and is served by bus or train (or taxi, of course, if you're willing to pay 60 euros as opposed to the ten euros for the train). We opted for the train, newly modernised as it happens, which was more than could be said for the track or stations.

Greek culture has an interesting attitude to timetabling, be it for bus or train. Or anything really. They consider a timetable to be more on a par with an intellectual puzzle like sudoku rather than a logistical aid to efficient transportation and planning. They are pinned up proudly in communal areas for the cerebral stimulation of the admiring public. The publication of a new bus or train timetable is an event awaited with keen anticipation by the Greek cognoscenti. They gather round the display board and crane their necks in order to fully apprehend its intricate complexity and infinite subtlety. The admiration is accompanied by much beard stroking and murmurs of awed appreciation:

"Look at the eloquent way the 10:27 from Pyrgos dovetails with 11:43 to Patras without disrupting the 09:11 Corinth to Kalamata!"

"I agree – exquisite! And behold the subtle elegance of making the 14:55 Larissa wait at the station for 11 minutes 33 seconds, thus stopping it from impeding the 17:23 Athens

to Thessaloniki."

Unfortunately for the weary traveller, Greek timetables, like much in the intellectual and artistic spheres, have a correlation with reality that is tenuous at best. It is an affront to public decency for a train or bus to leave at the scheduled time. Late is common, very late even more so, but early is best – that really throws a spanner in the works. Greek timetables are not an accurate representation of reality but more a sort of Hellenistic I Ching needing expert interpretation to divine the future movements of the relevant vehicles from the vague and contradictory omens, a bit like a haruspex having a rummage through the entrails of a recently slaughtered goat.[84]

The previous afternoon I had consulted the timetables and concluded that the most suitable train left at 09:00. Just to be on the safe side I enlisted the expertise of three adepts well versed in the arcane convolutions of Greek timetables, namely the woman behind the counter in the ticket office, a waiter from a nearby café and some bloke having a fag on one of the station benches. After much consultation of the timetables, muttering of incantations and scattering of runes they all three came to the same verdict as me – nine o' clock.

I was encouraged by their consistency but not completely won over. I'd been in Greece too long to fall for that. I awoke the next morning and decided to nip over to the station at eight o' clock and double check, just to be on the safe side. I was surprised to find the train there waiting with its motor ticking over.

"Are you going to Olympia?" I asked in pigeon Greek.

"Yes" he replied, only in proper Greek.

"What time do you leave?"

"Eight thirty"

"Buggeration!" said I in colloquial English and dashed across to the boat where I found Liz halfway through her morning ablutions. These were peremptorily curtailed, and I dragged her protesting to the train, the traces of foaming toothpaste around her mouth lending her a rather threateningly rabid air.

We got to Olympia about the same time as the train was scheduled to leave Katakolon.

I mentioned, did I not, that Katakolon is the second busiest cruise ship stop in Greece? There's a reason for that, and it's not the dusty, sun-baked laid-back charm of the town. Gigantic cruise ships call in here on a daily basis, sometimes more than one at a time, which can get a tad tight as it's not a very big port. They call in, as one would expect, because Ancient Olympia is the third most visited ancient classical site in Greece, on a par with Delphi and beaten only by The Parthenon and Knossos on Crete. In peak season tourists flock here in their thousands.

So why is there only one ticket booth and, even more pertinently, only one toilet block?

Things weren't too bad for our visit, mainly as a result of the vagaries of Greek timetables. The unexpectedly early departure of our train had served to give us a head start on most of the over two thousand mainly American tourists on the cruise ship tied up at Katakolon, most of whom had sauntered up to the station just in time to see the train cresting the ridge in the distance. There wasn't another train for over an hour, so that gave us about 90 minutes to get the tickets, visit the toilet (note use of the singular), and make a start on taking a gander at the ruins.[85]

It took me most of that 90 minutes to buy our entrance tickets. Bewildered tourists milled around looking for an entrance building containing ticket booths and turnstiles. What they should have been looking for was a small timber garden shed with a flap-down shutter that doubled as a counter. Behind the counter sat a single, flustered-looking woman and pinned to the wall was a tattered notice saying *εκδοτήριο εισιτηρίων. Ενήλικες 12 ευρώ.* Those blessed with a smattering of Greek eventually worked out that this said *'Ticket office. Adults 12 euros'* and promptly formed a queue in front of it. Well, I say 'queue' but it was more of an exact halfway point between a queue and a scrum.

This alerted the non griegophones who all pitched in and tipped the balance more to the scrum end of the spectrum. We tagged along at the back.

It took me three quarters of an hour to elbow my way to the front and buy a couple of tickets. This was partially due to my British reserve and reluctance to use my elbows and cause a scene, but most of the delay was caused by the tour guides from the endless coaches that steamed into the car park at five-minute intervals. They seemed to have *an arrangement*. The tour guide would chivvy her charges off the coach and kettle them in a *cul de sac* in the carpark. After severe admonitions not to wander off in search of a toilet, she left them in the charge of her deputy and headed for the ticket booth.

On arrival she would walk directly to the counter, brushing past the assembled sweaty, dusty tourists and shove her way in front of whoever was at the head of the queue. She would then slap the money on the counter and demand however many tickets she needed for her coachload. The harassed woman in the ticket booth would meekly comply.

Ignoring the muttered protestations and threats of physical violence the tour guide would then march imperiously to her crowd of punters, dole out the tickets and lead them off to the ruins, leaving the queue of pleb tourists to fantasise wildly about lynch mobs and tickets smeared with novichok. This scenario played out at two to three-minute intervals as the seemingly endless stream of coaches pulled into the car park.

Once I had bought the tickets, though, the site of Ancient Olympia itself was, despite our many fellow tourists, an atmospheric haven of peace and tranquillity. Unlike the sun-blasted furnaces of Knossos and Delphi, it was made up of an archipelago of shady oases, perfect for sitting and absorbing the atmosphere of the place. We sat in the balmy, airy sites and imagined the goings on at the stadium, the colonnaded pathways and the temples of Hera and Zeus.

There wasn't so much as a café though, but they did have the foresight to provide a vending machine dispensing such wholesome delights as crisps, chocolate bars and sugary, tooth-rotting biscuits.

Then the punters from the cruise ships arrived on the

second train, overwhelming the place and outnumbering us independents and bus tour plebs by a factor of around ten. We were finished anyway and took the train back to a spookily deserted Katakolon. This was unexpected as there were, as I mentioned, two cruise ships in. These things are huge, around 300 metres long and weighing up to 100,000 tonnes. Typical of these, and by no means the largest, is the MSC Orchestra, which was one of the two moored up while we were there. It can carry over 3000 passengers along with the just under a thousand crew necessary to service them and the boat.

It has five restaurants and ten bar/cafes. Having loaded the punters up with calories it then helps them get rid of the same by providing five swimming pools, along with four Jacuzzis, a gym, an aerobics studio, a sports court, a sauna and a steam room. These are topped off with a spa, a beauty salon, a mini golf course and a medical centre to deal with the inevitable fallout from all that overindulgence and unprecedented exercise.

For the survivors it has two entertainment lounges (with dance floors), a theatre, an internet café, a virtual games room and a library (How charmingly quaint). Then, just in case any of the passengers manage to run this gauntlet and still manage to have some money left, there is a casino to help rectify this anomaly.[86]

There were two ships of this sort of size in Katakolon, prompting the peculiar phenomenon of *déja vu*. We had seen an almost identical situation in Kuşadası when we went to see Ephesus. Both instances gave a disturbing insight into the way large cruise ships such as these can distort local economies.

The town proper, with its population of around 600 cannot support much in the way of businesses and services. A complement of 6000 from a couple of cruise ships, though, is another matter. That's an extra ten free-spending tourists for every man, woman and child resident in the town. On the surface one would have thought that such a huge influx of spending power would have increased demand by such an extent that the residents of Katakolon would have benefitted from a cornucopia of choice as far as shopping opportunities were concerned.

The problem with this simplistic deduction is that it fails to take into account *when* the demand is there, and what the demand is *for*. The residents want access to the essentials of life; they need food shops, pharmacies, hardware stores and the like. Clothes shops and electrical retailers would come in handy; a medical centre would be nice. Cruise passengers need little of this. For them the essential infrastructure of modern life, from food and drink through entertainment and general housekeeping to medical care is all provided by the mother ship. They don't need to buy ingredients for tonight's supper, or replacement light bulbs for the *en suite* bathroom. No, what they want is tat, and loads of it.

And if that's what they want then that's what they'll get – especially at the prices they seem willing to pay. The iron law of supply and demand comes in to play. Vendors are tuned in to the cruise ship schedules. When there are no cruise ships in port, Katakolon, Kuşadası and the like are sleepy backwaters, shuttered and boarded up against the searing sun. The dusty streets are deserted except for the occasional mongrel lying panting in the odd patch of shade provided by one the scattered stunted bushes.

When a ship is due, however, a total and radical transformation takes place. Restaurants set out their tables under swiftly unrolled awnings. Gift and souvenir shops open their shutters and doors. Aluminium-framed canvas stalls are slickly erected in serried ranks lining the road from the liner dock to the train and bus stations, corralling their prey into the economic killing zone like a tuna trap.

The tourists stream off the boat and descend on the stalls like a swarm of locusts, frantically buying vast quantities of stuff they don't need and will almost certainly never use, before trooping back to the ship, proudly carrying their booty like foraging ants returning to the nest.

Half the shops and stalls were piled high with the most appalling examples of cheaply made, mass produced, mainly plastic, ultra-kitsch, churned-out-in-China crap it has ever been my misfortune to behold. The first contact any of these so-called 'souvenirs' of Greece or Turkey had with the country in question was when the container from China was offloaded at Piraeus or Izmir.

The other half were stacked to eye level with what purport to be high end designer clothes, jewellery, handbags, shoes, watches, luggage, pens and perfumes (Sorry *fragrances*), but are, in fact, cheap knock-offs, turned out in their thousands by South East Asian sweatshops.

This is big business on a global scale, worth over 460 billion dollars a year according to the OECD. That's about 2.5% of world trade, or roughly equivalent to the entire economy of Austria.

Counterintuitively, (to me, at least) the most knocked off item is shoes. This is followed by clothing, leather goods and then techie stuff. China generally gets the blame for the most of this. On the surface this dubious honour is justified, as the most reliable estimate I could get hold of reckoned that China accounted for 63% of global trade in this sector. Turkey limped in a poor second with 3.3%.

On reflection, though, those figures don't show the whole picture. You'd expect China to rank highly, it's the most populous country on the planet. There are 1500 million of them. Turkey pitches in with barely a twentieth of that. Interestingly, if you work out their *per capita* contribution to the global knock-off trade you get exactly the same figure. On the *per capita* basis, the worst offender is Singapore, whose contribution is ten times that of China or Turkey.

The Turks, however, seem to take pride in their contribution to the global knock-off economy. Throughout the country, in markets, shops and street-side stalls, you will see large signs proudly advertising *'Genuine Fakes'*. On the surface this appears to be a mere contradiction in terms, but it is, in reality, a true oxymoron. The counterfeiting industry has its status order as does any other human construct. At the bottom are those ultra-cheap, tatty, slapdash, sloppy imitations that would be recognised as such even by a cursory glance from an ascetic with advanced cataracts. At the other end of the scale are genuine fakes. These are made with much more care and attention to detail; so much so, in fact, that it is difficult for even the well-trained eye to be certain of their true provenance.[87] As you would expect, these are much costlier than their equivalents from the other end of the scale.

By way of comparison, take a Breitling Avenger watch. If you buy one of these legitimately it will set you back in the region of five thousand quid. A cheaper end copy will cost you anything up to twenty quid and, if you're lucky, will last for up to two whole weeks before it falls to pieces. A genuine fake will command a price of between one hundred and two hundred pounds and will perform as well as, and for as long as, an original. This is no surprise as it is, to all intents and purposes, identical to an original.

When people are first made aware of this, their first reaction is to ask why the copy is so much cheaper. Perhaps the question should really have been *"Why are the originals so much more expensive?"*

The legitimate trademark holders will argue, with some justification, that they incur costs such as design, advertising and testing that the counterfeiters do not. They will also argue that they have a reputation that has taken many years to build up.

It is this last that covers the real reason designer goods cost so much. Being expensive is their *raison d'etre*, their Unique Selling Point. People do not buy designer dresses, handbags and sunglasses because they are elegant, beautiful, well designed and well-constructed. Some are, but others are crass, hideous, pretentious and knocked up on the cheap. In support of this potentially contentious assertion, and to pre-empt any subsequent heated justifications from the glitterati, I submit the seventeen hundred quid Balenciaga tote bag that was virtually identical in design to a 40p IKEA bag. Don't tell me that was a triumph of style and practicality. No, people buy this overpriced, shallow, ostentatious dross precisely *because* it is expensive. They are paying for the name. They are buying status. In this they are no different from the Russian gangster with his bling, or the merchant banker with his Porche, or indeed the yottie who demonstrates his authenticity by buying a fiendishly expensive pair of Dubarry boots and proceeds to splatter them with antifoul and gloss paint.[88]

I plead guilty as charged.

The hop across the Southern Peloponnese was also noticeable for the number of times we moored alongside. This is generally rare in the Med, where space restrictions encourage the authorities to insist on Med-mooring, bows or stern to. The Southern Peloponnese, though, are much less frequented by yachts, most of which transit the gulf of Corinth and the Corinth canal on their way between the Ionian and the Aegean. Relatively few take the much longer route around the outside. As a result, mooring space is not at such a premium and alongside mooring is more available.

Each of these two mooring techniques has its pros & cons. Alongside mooring is more secure as the bow, stern and midships are securely tied to a sodding great concrete breakwater – you don't have to rely on an anchor to hold one end in place. On the other hand, if the weather is grinding you abrasively up and down against the aforementioned great concrete breakwater, you may need one or more anchors to try to hold you off it.

Access is easier with alongside mooring, especially if heavy items such as gas bottles, batteries or crates of beer need to be hauled on or off. The corollary to this is that it is easier for vermin, thieves and other undesirables to get aboard. And, of course, it's easier for them to get off again along with your chart plotter, radar, electric folding bikes, wallet, credit cards and passports. It is also easier for the cat to jump ship.

We know of several boats that carry a ship's cat (or cats). Most of them take the balanced and sensible view that cats are essentially totally self-centred wild animals who happen to know a cushy number when they see one. In keeping with this eminently astute and practical attitude they give their cats free rein to go ashore at will, safe in the knowledge that selfish little bastards will be back on board at the first twinge of hunger, duplicitously proclaiming their undying and selfless love for you by curling round your ankles and purring.

Not so Einstein.

Her name, as most of you will remember, was bestowed with an air of extreme irony. She has none of the skills necessary for survival in the wild. Balance and feline grace? Hah! She can't make her way along a two-metre-wide pontoon without falling off. Agility, speed and endurance? Give me strength. She's got more bellies than a professional darts player and despite being nominally an ambush hunter she has the acceleration of a moribund slug.

As for territorial mapping and defence, she labours under delusions of competence. Because we are constantly on the move, she is unable to establish a recognised territory beyond the confines of the boat. To compensate for this, she reserves her bitterest bile for any other cat who has the temerity to even approach *Birvidik*. This, she sees as a direct threat to her supply from the Biscuit Fairy. Should an inquisitive cat decide to investigate this new object that has suddenly appeared in his territory he is met by a banshee howling towards him with claws flailing and fur standing out as if she has just been plugged into the mains. Luckily, the usual response here is to turn and run like Hell.

This is fortunate because should he decide to turn and fight, she wouldn't stand a chance. All she's got going for her is a significant weight advantage. She could be outrun by a banana slug and her reflexes rival those of a three-toed sloth. After about forty-five seconds of anaerobic burst she grinds to an asthmatic halt and lays prostrate and panting on the quay.

It is at this point that she looks around and realises that although her adversary is nowhere to be seen, she is unable to savour this victory as she has no idea where she is or how to get back to the boat, despite it sitting no more than fifty metres away. At this, panic sets in and she looks frantically around for somewhere to hide. Her favourite tactic in circumstances such as this is to crawl under the nearest motor vehicle she can find and to worm her way into the most restricted cavity available, usually in the engine compartment.

This presents us with the challenge of finding her, retrieving her and luring her back to the boat. To facilitate this, we have employed our usual technique when confronted with a difficulty, namely to throw money and technology at it. At night in port she is fitted with a harness and collar festooned with flashing, multi-coloured LEDs. These aid search & rescue and have the added advantage of causing her acute embarrassment in front of the local ferals, who give her the sort of reception that Quentin Crisp would get if he decided to take a stroll down Clavers Street in Montego Bay on a Friday night.

The lights are supplemented by a radio direction finder transmitter on her collar. We retain the receiver antenna. Pressing a button on this activates her transmitter which sends out a homing signal. Our unit picks up this signal and starts flashing and beeping like something out of an early episode of Doctor Who. We wave this around like some deranged Harry Potter and home in on her using the colour of the light and the pitch and frequency of the beeps.

This worked a dream and so we, of course became blasé. Until we moored up in the northern harbour in Ermioni. This comprised a long stone breakwater with three restaurants situated at the root. The base of the breakwater served as a car park for the restaurants, whose lights shone out and illuminated the quay. We were sitting in the cockpit enjoying a post-prandial drink when Einstein shot past us onto the quay to see off a local tom who had unwisely decided to pay a social call.

We smiled indulgently, put down our drinks, picked up the antenna and stepped ashore. After a couple of false leads from the RDF, we homed in on a Volkswagen parked outside one of the restaurants. Pitiful cries could be heard emanating from the engine compartment. Pleas, calls, threats and even a trail of cat biscuits all failed to entice her out. I went back to the boat for technical backup and returned armed with a headlight, a torch, the birdie whistle and a packet of cat treats.

I prostrated myself in front of the VW and used the headlight and torch to search underneath. No luck. Plenty of noise but no visuals. I rolled on to my back and pulled myself under the car – it was a tight fit.

We were starting to get an audience by now.

By the time I had wriggled into position under the car I could just make out a paw and one ear in the engine compartment. She had managed to squeeze herself in, but she couldn't turn around to get back the way she came, and she couldn't get out forwards because the fan belt and skid pan were in the way. I tried to squeeze my arm in to turn her around, but all this succeeded in doing was to make her even more distressed. The pitiful wails became louder, higher pitched and more frequent.

I squeezed out and we took stock. There didn't seem to be any way we could get her out from below. If we could get the bonnet open it should have been relatively easy to get her out from the top. Rather than incur the wrath of the car's owner by taking a jemmy to the bonnet I went round every table in the three cafés, asking if they owned a white VW, registration APN-2614. No luck.

This left us in a bit of a quandary. Breaking in was out of the question. Leaving her there risked the owner coming back and starting the engine, which raised the spectre of whistling fan belts, whirling pulley wheels and finely chopped cat. I did consider leaving an explanatory note under his wiper blade, but there was no guarantee that he'd see it, or read it if he did notice it.

In the end, I went for the middle path. I went back to the boat and picked up my socket set. Much to the interest of the assembled onlookers I crawled back under the car and proceeded to remove the skid plate.

Throughout this manoeuvre I was waiting for irate shouts in Greek, something which roughly translates along the lines of "*What in fuck's name are you doing dismantling my new car. Put that fucking spanner down before I shove it up your arse.*"

Having removed the skid plate, I peered inside and could just see a bedraggled Einstein looking at me reprovingly. I cooed encouragement to her and tried to tempt her out using the cat treats. Even these failed.[89] In the end I crawled back under the car, stuck my arm through the gap where the skid pan used to be, grabbed hold of her harness and yanked. This was met by a crescendo of protestations and a digging in of claws. Luckily, claws don't provide much traction on steel and I managed to pull her out. She did lose a dew claw in the process though.

I passed a chastened but still complaining Einstein to Liz, who murmured soothingly to her and carried her back to the boat. A ripple of applause came from the watching diners and I set about trying to put the car back together before I was set about by an irate Greek.

Back on *Birvidik* we agreed an official change to Standard Operating Procedures. Henceforth, whenever we were moored up, especially alongside, Einstein would have to be in one of three conditions: Locked below, securely attached to the boat or under direct and close supervision. By this we hoped to avoid her jumping ship again. Fat chance.

Theft was less of a worry than escaping cats. We had been concerned about it when we first set off from Jersey, given the vulnerability of mooring up at public quays and harbours with the associated exposure to inquisitive glances from passers-by at all hours of the day and night. We took stringent precautions at first, especially in the light of yottie grapevine reports of rampant thievery in France, Spain and Italy. When moored overnight, or if we left the boat for any length of time, we demounted all the electronics from the cockpit – chartplotter, radar, depth sounder, VHF etc. and hid them away in the saloon. We locked the folding bikes away in the capacious cockpit locker. The outboard was chained and padlocked to the guard rail. The dinghy was secured to the davits with 10 mm stainless steel chain. Winch handles and tools were transferred to the deck lockers, which were then securely padlocked. In our more paranoid moments we even tied down the boathooks and deck brushes.

Needless to say, all this was inordinately inconvenient and time consuming and therefore unsustainable. A balance had to be struck. If we took all the necessary precautions, we ended up spending a substantial proportion of our lives locking stuff away and then taking it all out again. This left little time for the essential joys of the cruising life, such as exploring the surroundings or sampling the delights of local restaurants. If, on the other hand, we took a chance, our enjoyment was dulled by the nagging worry that we would return to find *Birvidik* a hollow shell, with anything of the faintest value stripped out and already on its way to the nearest fence. In the face of this conflict we gradually became more relaxed and insouciant about anti-theft precautions

This tendency increased as we travelled further south and east, as dishonesty in general, and theft in particular, seemed to pose progressively less of a problem.[90] Indeed, by the time we got to Greece and Turkey it appeared to hardly exist at all. Bicycles and our canoe were left on deck in full view. Padlocks lay open and useless on the hasps of the deck lockers. The dinghy, complete with outboard, slopped lazily against the stern platform to which it was casually tied. We never had a thing stolen.

It seemed to be a cultural phenomenon; with the possible exceptions of the very big cities, theft and assaults just didn't seem to happen. We got the impression that the possibility didn't even cross people's minds, neither as potential victim nor as potential perpetrator. We spent nearly six years in the Eastern Med, taking minimum precautions throughout, and we didn't get taken for as much as a plastic bucket. Nor did we meet anyone first hand who had had stuff stolen. There were reports at third or fourth-hand on the Yottie grapevine but these are to be taken with a complete cellar-full of salt.

Although theft and assault are invisible or non-existent in Greece and Turkey, the same cannot be said, unfortunately, for corruption.

I don't know if corruption is more prevalent in Mediterranean countries than in Northern Europe or whether it is merely more blatant. It is certainly more noticeable, and the further East you go, the more noticeable it becomes. By the time you get to Greece and Turkey the tendrils of corruption and nest feathering seem to have infiltrated every aspect of life, especially public life.

There is, for example, the Greek phenomenon of φακελακια (*fakelakia* in the latin alphabet), which translates literally as *little envelopes*, but is used in Greece to refer to the bribery of public servants and private companies by Greek citizens in order to 'expedite' service. For 'expedite service' read 'Get any bloody service at all'. *Fakelakia* is also linked to a cultural perception (promulgated by those who benefit from it) that the various documents issued by authorities, such as a driving licence or planning permission for example, are 'papers' you need to 'buy'.

Although the pervasive nature of *fakelakia* means that its pernicious effects contaminate all aspects of life, perhaps the most telling occur in the field of medicine.

Before everything went belly-up in 2008, Greece had a pretty good health service – culturally very different from the NHS, but pretty good, nevertheless. Indeed, Greece has the highest number of doctors per 1000 people of all the OECD countries.[91]

Perhaps the most striking difference to Brits is that public hospitals provide medical and nursing care, but not hotel services. Relatives are expected to provide food and do personal laundry.

This, of course could prove a little trying for those living alone with no extant family, or for hospitalised tourists or ex-pats. Fortunately another Greek custom, ξενοφιλια (*xenophilia*), comes to their aid. *Xenophilia* is usually translated as 'hospitality. But it is more than that. The *xeno* part of the word means both 'guest; and 'stranger or foreigner'. *Xenophilia* imposes a social obligation to help and succor guests in the widest sense of the word. Almost invariably, an unsupported patient will find that the friends or relatives of those in nearby beds will extend honorary membership of their social group and provide food and other services.

However, it is in the getting access to medical treatment in the first place that *fakelakia* raises its ugly head. We have no first-hand experience of this. Coming from Jersey we do not qualify for treatment under the Greek health service and so have to pay privately for medical treatment. We do, however, have second hand experience.

A friend of ours needed an eye operation, and was entitled, through the EHIC, to have this on the Greek equivalent of the NHS. He saw the consultant, who agreed that the procedure was suitable and that he could have it on the Greek Health Service. There was, however, a problem. The waiting list, apparently, was so long that he would have to wait nearly a year for the operation. Paul accepted this, resigned himself to a long delay and said nothing. There was an awkward pause and the specialist said then he should come back in a couple of days for a further consultation.

When Paul relayed this story to some of our Greek friends, they just laughed at his naïvety. The surgeon was giving him a second chance to pay a fakelaki. They patiently explained to him that he needed to put about 300 euros in an envelope and hand it to the consultant at his next meeting.

"What, blatantly?" Paul asked.

"Oh yes. Just hand it over."

Of course, being British Paul couldn't carry off such bare-faced bribery. Emanating embarrassment, he shuffled into the consulting room and held out the envelope mumbling something pathetically unbelievable like *"A friend of mine asked me to pass this to you"*.

He never even felt it go. It was gone from his hand and in the doctor's back pocket in a flash. That surgeon could have moonlighted as a successful stage magician. Both professions require a high degree of manual dexterity. He bade Paul sit down and opened his diary.

"Can you come in tomorrow at nine a.m.?"

Speechless, Paul gaped, open mouthed, and nodded.

"OK – we'll do the op then."

That 300 euros seems to be about the standard *fakelaki*. This is a relatively small amount and before the crash of 2007/8 most Greeks seemed to accept this as an integral part of life. Now, though, many cannot afford even such small sums whilst at the same time the squeeze on the living standards of medical staff has increased the pressure on them to require *fakelakia*.

As a result, there is a growing groundswell of anger and resistance to the endemic levels of corruption. One of the leading lights in this movement is the website edosafakelaki.org, which was set up by Kristina Tremonti after a traumatic episode she experienced when her war veteran grandfather needed urgent treatment at a public hospital in Kalamata. He had terminal prostate cancer and suffered a sudden onset of profuse bleeding.

In an interview with the BBC, she explained: *"... we had to rush him to hospital. We were faced with absolute negligence. Nobody gave us the time of day - they were very disrespectful and basically ignored my grandfather."*

"We sort of picked up the cue that they were expecting a bribe, so as soon as my mother reached into her purse and gave them the amount - which I believe now was 300 euros (£240; $395) - he was submitted to the operating room within an hour."

This corruption is not confined to the Greek medical sector. It permeates almost every corner of civil, political and business life in Italy, Greece and Turkey. Jobs for the boys (and girls) is a fundamental tenet of local and national government. If the local mayor changes then it's all change for almost the entire local government workforce. The new incumbent's supporters and election workers call in their markers. He pays his debts by firing virtually everyone who served under the previous administration, from the highest civil servant to the lowliest road sweeper and then filling the newly created vacancies with his family, friends, supporters and other cronies.

We have several first-hand experiences of this, but one in particular comes vividly to mind. While we were in the Saronic we ploughed the same furrows repeatedly, visiting the same harbours several times. One of our favourites was Epidavros, where we became friends with several people, notably the charming and elegant young woman who looked after the quay, collected mooring fees and organised water and electricity supplies. On the morning of one of our departures, I went over to her kiosk to pay.

"See you in about ten days." I said cheerily

"No you won't. I've been fired" she replied.

This surprised me – she was an excellent worker; cheerful, friendly, helpful and efficient. She was also fluent in English, French and German. Did she want me to write a letter to her boss extolling her virtues and questioning the wisdom of sacking her? I asked.

"Won't be any use", she said, *"He's been fired too."*

My mind conjured up several salacious explanations for this dual sacking, but I kept them to myself.

"The municipality has just elected a new mayor." she volunteered. *"He's putting all his people into the municipal jobs."*

I was outraged at this, in stark contrast to her matter-of-fact approach. I was so incandescent with self-righteous indignation that I almost went out and bought a Daily Mail. Wasn't she angry? I asked. I bloody was and it wasn't even my job. She smiled.

"I can't be, really. I only got this job in the first place because my uncle was the previous mayor's election agent."

Before we wallow too much in righteous indignation and a sense of superiority of our own systems, perhaps we should reflect on such venal matters as taxpayer funded duck ponds and brown envelopes full of cash handed to the likes of Neil Hamilton.

Or MPs prostituting themselves in cash-for-questions.

Or senior HMRC civil servants being criticized for clearing cozy deals with tax-dodging companies and then whizzing through the revolving door to end up working for just such companies as lucrative 'tax advisors'.

Or senior army officers, previously responsible for agreeing contracts for millions of pounds worth of defence equipment, ending up being paid a fortune for a couple of days' *consultancy* work for arms companies?

Oh don't get me started.

Killini was the last port of call on our trip round the Peloponnese and had little to commend it. Its sole *raison d'etre* seems to be to serve as an embarkation point for the ferries to Zante, Ithaca and Cephalonia. It is a place that people travel through, rather than to. No-one actually stays there. In fact, no-one seems to even live there. The only time you see any human activity at all is when there is a ferry on turn around. Apart from that it's a ghost town. We explored the whole place on foot in twenty minutes. Needless to say, we moved on the next day.

We set off for Missolonghi and in so doing, crossed our wake. Well, I say 'crossed our wake' but it is a tad pretentious and grandiose of me to use the term, which is usually reserved for those hardy souls who have sailed right around the world. It defines the point at which the boat is exactly coincident with where it had passed on the way round, thus marking the completion of a successful circumnavigation. Far from having girdled the globe we had merely managed to blunder our way to Turkey and back.

Nevertheless, it kindled a mix of psychological responses. On the one hand it was nice to relax in attractive, interesting and familiar surroundings. We knew and liked the Ionian and it promised an enjoyable, stress-free and relaxing end to the season. On the other hand, however, we felt a bit flat, a bit back into a routine instead of feeling the excitement of moving on and discovery. A bit like the end of an adventure.

We had enjoyed the Ionian and were looking forward to revisiting our old haunts, this time with the benefit of experience and local knowledge, but we couldn't easily shake off the feeling that the edge of the cruising experience had been slightly dulled, especially when we thought back and compared it to the elation and sense of achievement we felt when we first arrived in Greece an eventful five years earlier.

This bittersweet reverie was interrupted by the roar of a couple of Pratt & Whitney R2800's as a firefighting plane skimmed overhead, closely followed by three more. The Greek authorities had another major wildfire on their hands.

During the hot, dry summers, the heat, the sun and the unkempt forests make these fires inevitable. According to the Greek Fire Department there are an average of over 4500 wildfires every summer. These planes are one of the major weapons at their disposal in the constant battle against incinerating the countryside, each capable of dumping nearly six tonnes of water at a time onto the parched inferno below.

We had witnessed these tactics in action in Spain years earlier and had marveled at the courage and skill of the pilots as they scooped up the water and maneuvered in tight turns before releasing their loads. The Greek pilots demonstrated equal skill and nerve. This is necessary as the activity is extremely hazardous. Between 1975 and 1990 the Greek Government bought sixteen of these aircraft. Over that time eight were lost.

It's bad enough trying to compensate for the sudden deceleration when the scoop hits the water and then having to make tight, low altitude turns in confined spaces, but there are other difficulties. They can only fly in good visibility, so cloud's out, and they face problems at take-off when the ambient temperature hits 38 degrees C. As most of the fires occur at the height of the summer, this is a significant limitation.

Soon after the impromptu fly-over a general call came on channel 16 from marine traffic control on the Antirio bridge. It gave a general alert as to the presence of firefighting planes (not strictly necessary I would have thought; they're difficult to miss) and instructed all marine traffic to keep out of their way. They didn't, however, give any indication of where their scoop zones were likely to be. I was tempted to call up traffic control and ask exactly how I was supposed to keep out of the scoopers' way, given that they were doing about 160 knots while the most I could squeeze out of poor old *Birvidik* was about eight knots. I decided against in the end. I reckoned they had enough on their plate without have to deal with smart-arse comments on an open channel from know-it-all yotties.

We managed to avoid being scooped up and deposited unceremoniously on the smouldering hillside and arrived safely in Missolonghi, which had changed beyond all recognition. Those blessed souls who have read the first book in the series[92] will remember my scornful and cynical remarks on the likelihood of the planned marina coming to fruition in the timescale indicated. Indeed, I scoffed that it was probably unlikely to come to fruition at all. I stand partially corrected.

The leaflet we had been handed four years previously had confidently predicted that two blokes armed only with a scratty broom and a shovel were going to transform the dusty backwater that was Missolonghi into a fully-functioning, state of the art marina in a mere two months. And by George, my cynicism notwithstanding, it looked like they'd done it. OK, four years later they were just putting in the finishing touches, so it had taken them a smidgen longer than originally forecast but it was done.

The transformation was staggering. A network of pontoons had been put in place and the service pods connected up. A spanking new building housed a modern office and reception in addition to a shiny new sanitary block with well-designed toilets and showers and a utility room equipped with new, large capacity washing machines. There was a large chandlery, not open yet but in the process of being stocked up. The lifting bay was completed and boasted a travel lift and a crane. The hard standing was rough and unsurfaced in places, but it looked like they were working on that. At the root of the main pontoons was a restaurant and bar. A basic grocery shop was on the way. It provided almost everything the visiting yottie could desire.

It did, however, have one big drawback. It was stifling. Missolonghi was an 800-metre-wide salt water lagoon, surrounded by low-lying marshland, which itself was girded by high limestone mountains. Access from the sea was via a four-kilometer channel dredged through the marsh. Any breeze didn't stand a chance of working its way in there.

The heat was debilitating, even after Turkey. The mercury hit over 40 degrees C in the afternoons, which precluded any activity other than turning on every fan on the boat and lolling around listlessly like beached walruses. At intervals we would shuffle our way across to the sanitary block and stand under the cold shower in shorts and t-shirt for twenty minutes before squelching our way back to the boat. This only took four minutes, but we were almost dry by the time we got back on board.

By eight in the evening it dropped to a slightly more manageable 34 degrees, in which we could just about drag ourselves down the pontoon to the bar for a cold beer.

Overnight wasn't much cooler and as a result we slept fitfully. It was too hot for bedclothes, even for a single thin sheet. As a result, there was no respite or escape from the mosquitoes that migrated over in their hordes from the nearby marshland. Early morning was the only time we could attempt any physical activity. We took to going for walks at seven in the morning so that we could be back on the boat being blasted by the fans for 9:30.

We lasted in this heat for three days before heading for the island of Trizonia in the gulf of Corinth. It was here that we were subject to the only instance of aggressive behaviour we have ever experienced on our travels.

Apart from Mijnheer en Mevrouw Klootzak in Fiskardo, of course, and they weren't so much aggressive as just downright rude, unco-operative and bloody minded.[93]

The evening had started off well. We were just finishing dinner, seated at a waterside table and savouring the atmosphere when a series of small boats brought a wedding party over from the mainland. It was apparent from the seating layouts that the celebrations were due to take place at the restaurant adjacent to ours.

Greek weddings are sumptuous, extravagant, joyous, over-the-top affairs, as much spectacle as celebration and ceremony. The singing, dancing and laughter spread outwards like ripples from a stone in water, enveloping and involving everyone in the area. We paid up and stood watching the extravaganza. Enthusiastic dancing spread in waves. Onlookers joined in, joyfully waving their arms in the air. Even I couldn't help jigging self-consciously from foot to foot. Happiness, fellow-feeling and bonhomie encompassed all present.

Except the bastard on the table about twenty metres behind us.

Although he had nothing to do with the wedding, in

fact he was at a different restaurant on the other side of the quay, he decided that people in general, and we in particular, were blocking his God-decreed view of the proceedings.

The first we knew about it was when he raised his considerable bulk from his seat, waddled across the quay and, without warning, gave me an almighty shove from the side, sending me flying into Liz before I stumbled prostrate on the cobbles. Liz, meanwhile, ricocheted off me and into a table, sending drinks flying, before ending up on her bum beside me.

All of this came as a bit of a surprise to me, but what came as more of a surprise was my reaction. Most ethologists contend that there are two basic types of response to aggression, namely *fight or flight* and *tend and befriend*. The former tends to be the male response and the latter tends to be the female response. They are mediated by a slightly different balance in the cocktail of hormones that are released into the bloodstream[94] when subjected to an aggressive attack such as, for example, having some retarded lard-arse send you and your wife sprawling to the floor in front of a couple of hundred people.

Being a fully paid-up Guardianista I fully expected to overcome my genetic and cultural inheritance and go into tend and befriend mode. I expected to get myself up, ensure Liz was OK and help her to her feet, before looking upon my attacker with sympathetic disapproval and asking him in a calm and civilised manner if his was a proportionate response under the circumstances. Then I would utilise the social power of peer pressure by enlisting the assembled onlookers in expressing their deep disapproval of his totally unreasonable behaviour, resulting is his being shamed into making a grovelling and heartfelt apology. Thus would I demonstrate the ability of man to overcome his baser instincts and his biology and raise himself to the civilised heights of reason, compassion and co-operation. I would demonstrate by my reserve and restraint that *Homo Guardianarius* could rise above his squalid biological and cultural heritage.

Did I bollocks.

I went straight into fight or flight mode before my knees hit the floor. By the time I got back up on one knee I was glaring the bastard viciously in the eye while I decided whether the response was going to be fight or whether it was going to be flight. By the time I was upright I had the measure of him physically. He was probably a few years younger than me and he had a definite weight advantage, but that's where it stopped. His weight was nearly all blubber and his complexion suggested that he drank even more than I did. His already laboured breathing indicated that he had about as much stamina as 60 a day man on the north face of the Eiger. I also reckoned from his stance and movement that it was unlikely he could match my brown belt in Kenpo. My male pride had been severely dented. Fight was starting to look odds-on favourite.

We squared up to each other where it became apparent that he was going through the same thought processes, though probably more slowly. He backed off, turned, and waddled back towards his seat with as much dignity as he could muster. My decision now was whether to leave it at that and retire with some shred of self-respect, or to go after him, shout at him and shove him around a bit until he reacted and then use that as an excuse to beat shit out of him.

Beating the shit out of him was winning hands down. I looked around and suddenly realised that the music was still playing, but the laughter and dancing had stopped. Everyone was motionless, watching in silence. The bride was standing with a look of shock on her face. As were most of the other guests. They seemed to have a pretty good idea what was going through my mind.

As far as I could see through the red mist, my decision was dependent on two factors in play here. On the one hand, this incident had severely compromised what should have been a joyous celebration and a memorable time in the couple's lives. Beating wobble-bottom to a pulp in front of everyone wouldn't have really enhanced the experience for them. It would, though, have made it a day to remember.

The second factor came in to play when I looked

around me. I was one foreigner amongst about a hundred Greek blokes, a number of whom were quite likely to be relatives of Dogbreath over there. I also had no idea of my quarry's status in the community. Was he the mayor with the associated power, influence and status that entailed, or was he the local n'er-do-well, the town drunk, an irritant and embarrassment to the entire village? I could hope for the latter, but I certainly couldn't rule out the former. All in all, I couldn't even begin to guess what the reaction of the assembled company would have been had I followed through with my barbarous intentions. And that was before factoring in the possibility of having to account for my actions in the local nick.

I turned, took Liz by the arm and we walked away with as much dignity as we could summon. I'd like to think that my tactical withdrawal was primarily driven by moral convictions and respect for the wedding guests, but I have a nagging feeling that it was the odds calculation and the possibility of being banged up in a Greek jail for GBH that tipped the balance.

Another revelation to me was the length of time it took for the effects of the incident to wear off. My craving for revenge, for recompense for the public humiliation[95] he had inflicted upon us, continued for several days afterwards. I would suddenly come out of reveries to find myself vividly fantasising about beating the living daylights out of him. These fantasies evoked physiological responses; I could feel my blood pressure going up and the atrial fibrillation went apeshit. All of this was just the result of a mere affront to my dignity, there was no actual physical damage done. How the Hell do combat veterans or sexual assault victims cope? It's a thin veneer of civilisation we wear.

We decided that remaining in a small community like Trizonia after an incident such as that could be likely to lead to a degree of social awkwardness, so we set off early the next morning for the island of Meganisi.

This is another favoured spot for the yottie. 'Meganisi' translates as 'big island'. Big compared to what? It's ten kilometres long by five kilometres across at its widest point, but even those measurements are deceptive. On the chart it looks like a giant, scrofulous, mutated sperm, with a 250-metre-wide tail taking up over half of its 10-kilometre length. It's got three villages, one primary school and not a solitary ATM. Secondary school pupils have to go over to Lefkas on the car ferry, as do yotties if they've run out of readies.

The northern coast, though, is a sailor's paradise, or rather it would be if there weren't so many bloody sailors. It boasts a multitude of crenelated inlets, giving good anchorage protection from most wind directions. In addition, there are two long bays containing laid moorings with lazylines. Porto Spilia, overlooked by the village of Spartahori, was one of them. I called Babis, the local restaurateur, who doubled quite prosperously as berthing master. He saved us a place on the main quay, complete with lazyline. We moored up, plugged in, and settled into caravan mode, looking forward to a relaxing couple of days.

You know that uneasy feeling you sometimes get - you can't quite put your finger on it, but something's definitely not quite right. I had that feeling in spades at Porto Spilia.

We had moored up bows-to the key with the stern tied to a sodding great concrete block and light southerlies forecast. It should have been the cruising idyll personified, but I definitely wasn't happy. To make matters worse my feelings of unease steadily increased over the course of the day, but I was damned if I could work out why. I suspect that it was an accumulation of almost subconscious cues. The air didn't feel quite right, the sky didn't look quite right, the sea state wasn't quite right - I don't know, for all I could tell the local strays might have been having trouble with their sciatica and the seagulls were flying in a foreboding pattern while the crows made those Hammer Horror noises. Whatever it was, I didn't like it.

Usually in these circumstances I keep my feelings to myself. Not being able to give an opinion supported by evidence, I keep shtum for fear of making a complete tit of myself. It's one thing to sagely pronounce "*Oo-arr! D'ye see that - a slight mackerel sky accompanied by a faint haze over the hilltops and the wind backing to NE. We're in for a fearful blow from the South, you mark my words Me Hearties!"* This sort of thing is very impressive, especially if it comes true.

You're unlikely to earn the respect of big hairy sailors and have the local female population gazing wide-eyed at you with ovaries aquiver if the best you can come up with is "*Ooh - I don't know why, but I feel a bit frit*".

In the end though I gave in to my inner wuss, blew up the big sausage fender and stuck it on the bow. After that I went around checking and adjusting the lines and positioning anti-chafe. Then I checked all the systems, disconnected the electrics, made sure our masts were out of line with those of the boats either side and finally sat in the cockpit to work myself into a barely disguised lather of apprehension. This behaviour did not go unnoticed by Liz. Neither did it escape the attention of the skippers of neighbouring boats. Quizzical eyebrows were raised in my direction. I was asked pointed questions about which weather forecast I used, and did I have a tame professional meteorologist on board. I mumbled some pathetic drivel about routine precautions and hid in the saloon.

I should have had the courage of my convictions. The sky steadily darkened into lowering anvil heads. Lightning flashed with increased frequency and thunder growled in the distance. The wind increased and backed to the east. Then it increased again and backed to the north east.

Porto Spilia is well sheltered from all directions except one, namely a tiny little ten degree sector.

From the north east.

So the wind, of course, stayed in the north east and blew up to a nice gale force eight. This built up a substantial seaway of 1 - 2 metre waves, which it proceeded to shove into the harbour. The boats rolled alarmingly from side to side and pitched viciously fore and aft, which made them lurch, snatch and strain at their lines. The waves came straight on the sterns of the boats on our quay, stretching the lines holding them off and surging them perilously close to the rough concrete.

Then the rain started. Not gradually, but straight in at

full whack as if someone had emptied a swimming pool over the boat. The scuppers couldn't cope, and the side decks filled with water. At times we couldn't see the bow, so we had no idea how far off the quay we were. At this point the lightning and thunder were simultaneous and the wind increased again, accompanied by bigger waves and vicious gusts. The highest recorded was 45 knots (severe gale nine). The rain eased but the wind and waves hung on in there.

If we thought we had it bad, our predicament was nothing compared with the boats on the pontoon slightly further down. The wind and waves were hitting them on the beam, and they were rolling alarmingly. The shrieks and howls of the wind were occasionally interspersed with the sickening crash of masts clashing. Several boats snapped mooring lines and had to leave the pontoon and circle forlornly through the white water of the bay. Even without the load of the departed boats, the pontoon fixings started to give way and the main section threatened to snap off and drift away with boats still attached to it.

Panos, the berthing master, earned his corn that night. It took him and nine others to restrain the pontoon with extra ropes. Despite this one boat still ended up on the beach. That night, he said afterwards, was the first time he had prayed in twenty years. His brother, Babis, commented that it was only the third time in 36 years working there that he had seen it as bad as that.

After it had been going on for about four hours nerves were getting a little frayed. "*Don't worry*" I said in a vain attempt to restore morale, "*These systems don't last more than a few hours and there's got to be a wind shift soon - it always changes through 180 degrees in these*". I looked around to be greeted with looks of suspicious disbelief. In truth, I have to admit that the statement was made more in hope than conviction.

I should have had more faith. The words were hardly out of my mouth when it did just as I predicted. In less than a minute the wind fell to flat calm and then blasted in at force eight from the opposite direction. From this we were well protected and the waves died to almost flat. You could almost hear the collective sigh of relief from the whole bay.

What didn't stop for the next couple of hours was the rain. This didn't discourage the assembled yotties, who togged themselves up in foul-weather gear and repaired *en masse* to Babis's restaurant in a state of manic excitement and relief, where they demanded vast quantities of food and even vaster quantities of alcohol.

We, of course, were in the vanguard.

It was a short hop from Meganisi to Vlicho Bay on the island of Lefkas. Once Vlicho has ensnared a yottie with its siren call, it can be difficult for him to tear himself or his boat away from it. For that reason, it is often referred to by yotties as Velcro Bay.

This is hardly surprising, as Vlicho has a lot going for it. It is a large, enclosed bay, only accessed by a narrow channel near the resort town of Nidri. Depths are around five metres and most of the bottom is good holding – thick, glutinous mud. It also boasts a wide range of good tavernas and Vlicho Yacht Club, which is an institution famed throughout yottiedom.

Although some of the more hardcore, hair-shirt, gone-native, self-righteously prissy-knickered cruisers pooh-pooh it for being too ex-pat orientated, Vlicho Yacht Club is a boon to yotties of all nationalities. OK its ultimate purpose is to make money, but that's to be expected – it's a business, not a bloody charity.

Its owners, Ruairi and Vicky have equipped it with all the facilities the wandering yottie could dream of. It serves as an information and advice centre, a social hub and a library. It has a convivial bar and restaurant and provides a range of services from the technical to the domestic. Our yottie can get a hot shower there and check out the bus timetables (assuming the bus company hasn't changed them without telling anyone). He can log on to the internet and get the boarding cards printed off for his flights from Preveza airport if circumstances dictate that he has to hurry back home. Should such an eventuality arise, Ruairi will arrange gardiennage and keep an eye on the boat. The club has a library for the exchange of books and DVDs and a bought and sold facility.[96]

It also has a washing machine.

Ah yes, a washing machine. Few non-cruisers fully appreciate how limited are the home comforts available to the standard yottie. Many everyday tasks, that the average landlubber wouldn't give a second thought to, are so time-consuming and physically strenuous to the yottie that they become bugbears, dreaded out of all proportion to their importance. Prime among these is laundry.

Very few sailing yachts are fitted with washing machines, mainly for reasons of space, cost, water capacity and electrical load. There *are* small lightweight plastic washing machines on the market, but these try to be all things to all men and so end up being nothing to anybody. Every yottie tries one at some stage and every yottie either throws it away or deviously manages to flog it to some trusting, gullible ingénue.

The options available to deal with this lack boil down to find a laundry, find a washing machine or do it by hand. There is a fourth option, which is not to wash clothes, towels and linen at all. This option is frequently advocated by Mr. Yottie but Mrs Yottie invariably exercises her veto and over-rules him.

Most of the time in the summer, things are not too too[97] bad. Everyday clothing usually consists of just light shorts, t-shirts and swimming costumes, all of which can be given a swift jiggle in a bucket of soapy water and will then dry in microseconds when pinned out on the rigging in the sun and breeze. There comes a point, though, when even the least fastidious yottie will be forced to admit that the bed linen and the towels really do need to be washed. Mrs Yottie usually drives this point home by pointing out that the sheet looks like camouflage fabric and is so stiff that it can be leant against the bulkhead like a sheet of five mm plywood. She presses this home by demonstrating that the bath towels are by this stage so encrusted with salt and crud that they could double as breakfast trays. And from the look of them probably have. In cooler periods, jeans and fleeces are worn which further exacerbate things. It is instructive, therefore, to compare the technique of doing the laundry yottie-style with its more common domestic counterpart.[98]

Doing the washing in the average suburban semi is a piece of piss. Even blokes can do it. Well, almost. Admittedly they fail to turn the jeans inside out. OK, they leave the socks screwed up in impermeable balls and signally fail to go through the pockets and remove paper tissues, ball point pens, open packets of chewing gum and old lipsticks before shoving it all in. Granted, they put Mrs Yottie's best angora jumper through on boil, ensuring that it comes out the size of a postage stamp, and see no problem in mixing newly bought cheap black jeans with her delicate white bras and her favourite chiffon top, but they *can* do it. After a fashion.

All that's involved is to sort the load, stick it in the machine, sling in one of those clever, squidgy detergent capsule jobbies, close the door, twiddle a knob, press a button and leave it to it. After a couple of strenuous hours on the sofa, come back, take it out, give it a shake and hang it up. Job done.

Now compare that with the Herculean task facing the yotties on wash day. Handwashing heavier items is so laborious that it is avoided except in dire emergencies, but eventually they are going to have to bite the bullet.

In the first place, there is absolutely no point in sorting it into loads as you're only able to wash one heavy item at a time.

Let us say that, in a fit of masochistic optimism, it is decided to start with a pair of Mr Yottie's jeans. These always pose a challenge as they will have:

a) almost certainly not been washed for at least six months.

b) usually been liberally coated with engine oil, sticky glutinous mud, seagull shit, gravy, marmite, chocolate and egg mayonnaise

c) probably been left to moulder in a damp locker for about two months before being taken out and left in bright sunlight to bake the coatings mentioned in (b) above to a toughened crust hard enough to stop an armour-piercing shell.

Let us also assume that we are in the fortunate position of having access to electricity and water. If you're not, then you're on a hiding to nothing. The first task is to heat up significant quantities of water. An immersion heater is good, but a kettle will do at a pinch. Half fill your bucket with boiling water and add twice the recommended amount of the most powerful detergent you can lay your hands on, along with a kilogram of washing soda and half a litre of bleach. Add the jeans, poke them about a bit with a stick and leave to stew for about an hour, giving them a bit of a poke every ten minutes or so.

Remove the jeans from the water and carry them up on deck, dripping a trail of dark grey, greasy water all over the saloon floor. Lay the jeans flat on the deck and identify the most offensive and intransigent stains. Put a spoonful of biological washing power on each stain and scrub with a nail brush until your knuckles are raw from catching them on the treadmaster. Double the jeans back over the guard rail and twist them together into a Spanish windlass. Wring two-handed until you have got out as much water as possible, which won't be a lot.

Empty the bucket over the side, refill with boiling water and repeat the process until either the water comes out a slightly lighter grey or the irritant dermatitis in your hands starts to be mistaken for leprosy.

The washing phase is now over. All you have to do now is rinse it. Swirl the jeans around in half a bucket of hot water and repeat the Spanish windlass trick. Inspect the colour of the water. Continue repeating the rinse cycle until the water comes out light grey, you run out of water or exhaustion sets in.

Congratulations. Your knuckles and finger tips may be rubbed raw, but you have now washed a pair of jeans. In doing so you have gone through an entire packet of washing powder, several litres of bleach, a five kilogram pack of washing soda, four kilowatt hours of electricity and about forty litres of water. All for one pair of jeans. Using this method, a reasonable load of a couple of pairs of jeans, two medium towels and one set of bedding will gulp its way through about 250 litres of water or about a third of *Birvidik*'s water capacity. A modern high-efficiency washing machine will wash that load using only one KwH and fifteen litres of water.

Most of the water is used in trying to rinse the industrial quantities of detergent out of the items. In the very early days, we did try fitting a mangle[99] to the guard rail on the aft deck. This had two drawbacks. The first was the looks of wide-eyed disbelief and shock on the faces of the male French passers-by as they stared with horror and disdain at me wringing out Liz's knickers on the aft deck. Obviously, the concept of the sensitive Metrosexual New Man, of which I am the classic exemplar, the defining archetype, had yet to cross the channel to our continental cousins. The open disdain, the disconcerted, incredulous murmurings, the *sotto voce "Mais non! Une telle chose, comment est-elle possible?"* – all of these I could cope with. I'm confident in my sexuality. It was the second drawback that meant the mangle had to go. It didn't bloody work.

Well, OK, that's not strictly true. It did work on some items, such as silk handkerchiefs, nylon pop socks and shoelaces. You know, the sort of thing that you virtually never wash in the first place, and if you do wash them, they can be wrung to arid dryness in the palm of your hand in microseconds. Give the thing a pair of jeans, though, and it failed miserably. In fact, give it anything that's thick and/or uneven and it fails miserably. Either the rollers jam on the thick bits like seams or zips or, if the rollers are far enough apart to let the seams pass between them, the thinner bits sail through still sopping wet.

You can see why most yotties seek out laundries or washing machines.

Despite the attractions listed above, Vlicho is not without its problems. The surrounding mountains frequently protect the area from nasty weather, but they can also trap small, intense storm cells in their confines. This is not a particularly rare phenomenon, occurring two or three times a year, at differing strengths. When one of these buggers hits, everyone is better off out of Vlicho. Unfortunately, these microbursts as they are known, tend to be small-scale local phenomena and are almost impossible to forecast.

The absolute mother of these hit suddenly on the 20th September 2011. Luckily, we weren't there, but we know several people who were. The forecast was for a force five to six and there were a hundred or so boats anchored in Vlicho. At ten to six in the evening it was hit by a microburst producing 60 to 100 knot winds. That's force 11 to 12 Beaufort or the sort of speed you'll come across if you're unlucky enough to be caught out in a category 2-3 hurricane.

It was an extremely localised phenomenon. Less than two kilometres down the road at Nidri there was virtually no wind and just a few desultory thunderclaps. Even at the epicentre in Vlicho it was very short lived. Everything was done and dusted in just over half an hour.

Short it may have been, but it was long enough. It was carnage. Boats at anchor dragged. Sails, despite being tightly furled, blew out and promptly shredded in seconds. Several boats were driven ashore and more were knocked down flat on their sides, many of them more than once.

Being out of the water was no better. At the local boatyard the propped-up boats went down like dominos, twisting and breaking masts, splitting hulls and springing decks. Luckily, these were unoccupied, which wasn't the case with most of those in the water. A French skipper drowned, having knocked his head when he slipped between his boat and the quay with which it had collided.

A large catamaran had been blown over into a complete capsize, dismasting it and leaving it upside down in the water. The skipper, Dr Clive Probert, was thrown out of the cockpit. Luckily, he managed to scramble back on to the upturned hull, where he was horrified to discover that his wife Norma, a non-swimmer, was nowhere to be seen. She had been carried below by the rush of water when the boat flipped, so it had to be assumed that she was trapped in the upturned hull.

The wind dropped as suddenly as it had struck, and Ruairi came out in his RIB to see what could be done. He rushed over to the upturned cat and was brought up to date by the distraught skipper. The two of them rapped on the hull, listening, without great hope, for a return knock or call. It came. The skipper described the layout of the boat and where he thought the knocking was coming from.

Ruairi tied off the RIB and slipped into the water. He took a deep breath and dived under the cat. His first challenge was to negotiate the tangled rigging and the sections of broken mast and spreaders that enveloped the submerged cockpit area. This must have been challenge enough as it was. Good, clear visibility is not among Vlicho's many siren charms. I have dived there to check on my anchor. It was like trying to dive through mulligatawny. If I put my arm out straight ahead of me, I couldn't see my hand.

Despite these obstacles, Ruairi made his way into the boat and came across Norma's legs. She was standing on the cabin headlining (ceiling) and was breathing from a small air pocket. Ruairi joined her, gasping for breath.

He explained to her that she would need to take a deep breath and hold it for about five seconds, during which time, he would do the same and guide her out. Norma was no water baby. She said afterwards that she didn't even like getting water on her face in the shower. Despite her apprehension, she did as Ruairi asked, and he took her down and led her out and through the tangle of rigging. She almost lost it at one point and gripped the companionway in panic. Ruairi prised her grip free and led her through the rest of the rigging to the surface and her waiting husband.

For this unparalleled bravery[100] (or lunacy, depending on how you look at it) Ruairi was awarded the Royal Humane Society's bronze medal.

BRONZE?!

What the fuck do you have to do to get a silver? Cut your right leg off with a rusty pruning saw, lightly sauté it and then feed it to a starving baby?

And as for a Gold, I'd have thought that dying horribly was the minimum qualification. Preferably by sacrificing yourself to a pack of ravenous hyenas or something equally unpleasant.[101]

Parts of Vlicho also serve as examples of another well-known yachting curiosity, namely the Boat Graveyard. These can be found all over the Med, but they are especially common in Greece. They are where boats come to moulder and die. Every one of the boats has a story and they are almost invariably desperately sad. Perhaps the saddest situation all round is when the skipper has died and none of his heirs have the slightest interest in the boat.

Typically, these places symbolise the end of a dream. Boats are usually brought to them when their owners are not willing or able to carry on cruising. This is usually for reasons of being too old, too decrepit, too ill, too skint, too generally pissed off with the whole business or too dead.

When a yottie reaches the end of his cruising life and returns to the land, either on it or under it, he is said in yottie parlance to *swallow the anchor*. Irrespective of whether he does this by inclination or circumstance, he will still be confronted with the same problem; namely what to do about the boat. To the untrained mind, the answer is obvious – sell the bloody thing. This, though, fails to take into account the harsh and esoteric realities of the world of the yottie.

Cruising boats are not impulse buys. Well, not at first. They can take years to sell. To compound the problem, while they are in the process of being sold, they have to be somewhere.[102] The ideal would be to have them safely laid up ashore and supervised by a gardienne. For a 12.5 metre boat this will cost around 4000 quid a year for the mooring alone, with gardiennage on top, and that's if you take out an annual contract.

Yotties are notoriously tight so that option is obviously a non-starter. They are so tight, in fact, that paying anything is completely out of the question. They therefore seek out moorings such as those in Vlicho and Trizonia which are without official ownership or supervision, without water or electricity, without security and most importantly without charge. The details of these sites are promulgated on the yottie grapevine and resigned skippers cajole their aging boats there like mahouts on mythical expiring elephants.

Most skippers at least start off under the delusion that this is just a temporary state of affairs; an interim holding action to give things a chance to get sorted out and put on a more seamanlike basis.

This, of course, is complete crap. Once the boat has been tied up and left, and the skipper has decamped back home to sleep on his eldest daughter's sofa in exchange for babysitting the grandkids six days a week, the boat will move inexorably down the priority list. Human psychology comes into play here. The importance we assign to tasks, and therefore the likelihood of their actually getting done, depend on a number of factors, very few of which are logical. The consensus[103] seems to be that there are six prime factors; immediacy, proximity, threat, reward, perceived likelihood of success and cost (in time or money).

Sorting out a boat half a world away in the Med doesn't score well on any of these:

Immediacy – are you being hassled today, and thereafter on a daily basis? No – you might get the odd snotty email or an unintelligible fax in faded Greek.

Proximity - Is the source of irritation next door? Are you kidding? It's in Greece for Christ's sake

Threat - Are you likely to have a couple of goons knocking on your door? Unlikely. Greek municipalities are not known for their close business links with the successors to the Kray twins. If you left the boat in Spain, however, watch out. You'd have the likes of Kenneth Noye rearranging your anatomy before you could say 'Ouch'.

Reward – will completing this task result in large deposits winging their way to your current account, or in your being showered with underwear by hordes of fragrant, wide-eyed, admiring women? Not even worth asking the question. Give it a number between 0 and 5 though.

Perceived likelihood of success (PLS)– On a scale of 0 to ten. Negative numbers are not permitted. (But probably should be)

Cost – Multiply the estimated number of hours required to complete the task by the estimated expenditure in pounds. Divide the product by 100 and then divide the result by your PLS and then your reward to get your Cost Effectiveness Quotient. Any CEQ above 5 hasn't got a snowball's.

The inevitable consequence of all this is that, despite the best of intentions, nothing gets done. Quickly or slowly, the boat goes the way of all flesh and succumbs to the inevitability of the laws of thermodynamics. Varnish crazes and peels under the relentless U.V. searing down on it. Water then gets into the wood forming ideal conditions for rot and algae. The same fate awaits any exposed canvas work. Metalwork corrodes and flakes. Ropes rub and saw against the rough quay, then fray and part. Fenders get nicked, or they rot, puncture and burst, leaving the hull to grate against the jagged concrete, taking off any remaining paint and gouging great furrows in the fibreglass. Rats, mice and cockroaches colonise the inside. Eventually the seacocks fail and water floods through the rodent-chewed hoses and sinks the boat. At least the sails and the electronics in the saloon are spared a watery grave as the local and transient ne'er-do-wells clocked the boat after the first month, broke in, and stripped it of anything even remotely valuable. Forlorn, abandoned and unloved, the once cherished vessel finally gives up waiting for its skipper to come back, quietly surrenders to the waves and settles gently on the bottom.

I really should stop being anthropomorphic about boats.

The problems don't stop there though. Available quay space is in danger of being taken up completely by rotting or sunken wrecks. Other cruisers and charter boats can't get to the quay. This is bad news for the local businesses, many of whom rely on visiting boats for a substantial proportion of their livelihood. They, in turn, make their displeasure known to the local municipality who, needing to cement their voting base, find themselves pressured into doing something about it. This is fraught with legal, logistical, technical and financial ramifications. Even in Greece the authorities can't just appropriate someone's property and then dump or flog it. In Russia, possibly, but not in Greece. First, they have to make *reasonable* [104] efforts to identify, contact and inform the owner.

The authorities first step, therefore, is to find out who owns the boat. Then they can send him a nice, official, letter telling him to get his finger out and either make the boat seaworthy or dump the thing. This, though, requires that you know who the owner is and where he lives. This can be done *via* the ship's name and registration number, assuming the skipper hasn't surreptitiously scraped them off before departing. This is on a par with removing the number plates when fly-dumping a car. It does indicate a degree of premeditation.

Even if the authorities do manage to get a name and address for the owner it won't get them very far, as their missives will just get filed and conveniently forgotten. In the end, the local mayor's office will file an affidavit saying that they have tried on multiple occasions to contact the owner, all without response. The court then gives the municipality authority to confiscate the vessel and dispose of it as they see fit.

A copy of this, in faded Greek, is sent to the owner who files and ignores it. The mayor then either arranges for the disposal of the boat at municipal expense or flogs it at a knock-down price to one of his mates. The quay space thus created is available to visiting boats for about three days until it is filled by the next moribund hulk and the cycle starts over again. There is a sort of comforting circularity about the whole process.

Another bonus to being in Vlicho is the regular bus access to Lefkas town. This is a reasonably large community of nearly 14000 people and so has all the facilities and services the yottie is likely to need. He shouldn't get carried away, though. Greek services are services, Jim, but not as we know it. This was exemplified by our trip into Lefkas to sort out some paperwork and do a few jobs, among them to visit the main Post Office.

The Greeks have a (generally undeserved) reputation for idleness and profligacy. This is especially noticeable in the more rabidly xenophobic reaches of the British press. Here, the poor Bubbles are frequently accused of being work-shy parasites, sitting on their arses all day and living the high life at the expense of the poor, hardworking, Northern European taxpayer.

Contrary to these assertions, the Greeks (at least those few of them lucky enough to actually have a job) work the longest hours in the EU, well ahead of the UK and Germany (or behind of course, depending on how you look at it).

The sting in the tail, though, comes when you consider how productive they are. They may work all the hours God sends and then some, but they don't seem to get a lot actually done. If you order the EU countries by productivity the Greeks are well down - 21st out of 28 in fact.

The only countries less productive (and the more geographically ept amongst you may see a pattern develop here) are Bulgaria, The Czech Republic, Estonia, Hungary, Latvia, Poland and Romania. This lack of productivity is hardly surprising. Workers in all these countries work far fewer hours per week than the Greeks. In addition, most of the Poles' productive work takes place outside Poland anyway, mostly in propping up the British and German economies and helping to pay my pension.

I have a theory about this. Like most of my theories it is almost completely unsubstantiated by fact or evidence. It also shamelessly panders to my prejudices and preconceptions, but it's my book and my theory so you're going to get it anyway.

I contend that, despite the received wisdom on the combined effects of globalization and the EU, European culture is far from becoming homogenous. On top of the myriad extant national cultural quirks, Europe is divided into two opposing world views or *Weltanschauungen* if you want to show off and come over all intellectual. These are characterised by attitudes to work and rules.

On the one hand there is the Protestant work-ethic model which emphasizes individual responsibility and views work and obeying rules as an over-riding duty if not a sacred obligation. Such societies tend to cluster in the North and West of the continent.

The alternative view is the Catholic-fatalist model. This

sees work as a heavy burden imposed by fate, and rule breaking as an intrinsic and generally unavoidable part of the human condition, which can be forgiven in return for penitence. These underlying assumptions permeate through most aspects of a society's culture, but if you really want to see it in action take a butcher's at a post office in action.

The initial impression on entering a Greek post office is that you've wandered into an amalgam of a refugee camp, a trading-floor bear pit and a run on a bank. Virtually every aspect of civil life takes place in a post office. Money and paperwork fly in all directions. Ever-diminishing pensions are paid out (avoid all Mondays in general and the first Monday of the month in particular). Permits and licences are obtained. Bills are paid in, as are taxes, the last-mentioned only on rare occasions and then only by those without enough money to avoid having to pay them. Which is most Greeks. Conversations are held across the mêlée at shout-level and people mill about waving forms, hands and money around like a convention of demented tic-tac men.

At the far side of this seething mass of humanity, dwarfed and overwhelmed by the chaotic free-for-all, sit two isolated female desk clerks. The scene resembles newsreel footage of famine relief efforts where heavily outnumbered volunteers gallantly fail to stave off the frantic predations of the desperate and dispossessed.

At first sight, you would expect them to be at their wits' end, run ragged and verging on total nervous collapse. You would be wrong. They have been doing this for years and have developed a coping mechanism. They appear to have entered a deep, Zen-like state and carry out their duties calmly, deliberately and infuriatingly slowly.

Their attention to detail is legendary. This, I suspect, explains their Zen state. Meditation at such an advanced level requires a mantra. Their mantra is probably all 27 volumes of the *Greek Postal Service Rules & Procedures Manual*. Every transaction in a Greek post office (and there are *thousands* of different ones) **must** be carried out exactly in accordance with a detailed procedure. Failure on the most minor point invalidates the entire process and you have to start over again.

As a result, the length of the average visit to a Greek post office is usually measured in geological time. Most Greeks therefore take food with them when they visit the post office and the Greek postal service recognizes this by supplying seats and tables. It also explains why almost all Greek men sport beards. Most of them grew to their current luxuriant fullness while the owner was waiting in a post office queue.

The first reaction of the foreigner on encountering this phenomenon is to venture the opinion that the office is horrendously understaffed. Closer inspection though puts the lie to this judgment. Our gallant clerks are not alone. For a start, there is Mrs Overall.

Mrs. Overall is not noticed at first as she is very highly trained to blend in with her background. She can be recognized, despite her chameleon-like qualities, by her faded floral pinafore. Her primary task seems to consist of listlessly flicking an ancient and battered broom into random and disjointed spots amongst the scattered boxes and files behind the clerks. Her trance-like reverie is occasionally interrupted by being asked for coffee or being dispatched to find someone's glasses. From observation, her entire day's workload could be completed in about half an hour by a semi-comatose three-toed sloth. However, she probably gets paid diddley-squat so it's not a problem in the grand scheme of things.

At least Mrs. Overall can be seen to be doing something useful, however small. This is more than can be said for the other three employees who become apparent on more detailed observation. These are all men of a certain age. One looks like a shelled tortoise. The second is seriously overweight and has thinning, wiry, salt & pepper hair tied back in a pony tail. The third is rotund with a bushy white beard. I mentally filed them as 'Gollum', 'Sleazebag' and 'Bagpuss'.

At first glance their primary task appears to involve flitting between computers, one in the tiny office and the others scattered strategically throughout the desks cluttering the work area behind the clerks. Once at a computer, they sit down, frown at the screen, waggle the mouse around a bit and make a few desultory clicks. Then they frown at the screen again, walk over to the next computer and repeat the process.

After you have watched them for a while it becomes clear that this is a feint, a cover for their true purpose which is to hinder the clerks and slow them down from a plod to an amoebic slither.

It soon becomes apparent that the three musketeers here, despite their seeming seniority, don't have the slightest idea of how to carry out even the most basic tasks associated with running a post office. As a result, they frequently interrupt the clerks with queries, waving a piece of paper under their noses and demanding its immediate completion. The clerk then loses her concentration. Her Zen-like repose shatters and she has to go back to the beginning of the interrupted process. Her current customer seriously considers strangling himself with his own small intestine.

That is not to say that the three musketeers here do no useful work at all. They serve a very valuable purpose for their friends and relations. These favoured few breeze in, elbow their way through the assembled hordes, and cheerfully hail their chosen musketeer. After an animated few minutes of handshakes and conversation, the interloper hands over his or her paperwork to the musketeer, who looks at it, decides he has no idea how to process it, and promptly hands it to one of the clerks and gets it sorted out on the spot. The clerk then goes back to square one of her interrupted procedure. Her interrupter triumphantly returns it to his friend with an air of indulgent magnanimity, smug in the knowledge of yet another favour notched up on the social balance sheet. The assembled *hoi polloi*[105] seem hardly fazed by this brazen favouritism and can't even be bothered to raise a resigned sigh.

It did, however, give me an idea for a business plan. I shall set up franchise for a stall in every post office. It will sell wax effigies of the three musketeers or their equivalents and long, sharp pins. Not only will I make a shedload of money, but if the voodoo actually works then the productivity of the Greek postal system will quadruple overnight.

It was experiences like being in Greek post offices that sensitised me to relative queuing techniques in Greece and the UK.

George Mikes (1912 - 1987) was a Hungarian émigré and an acute observer of British life. In 'How to be an Alien', published in 1946, he noted that "*An Englishman, even if he is alone, forms an orderly queue of one.*" Today, over seventy years later, he's still spot on the money. Attitudes to queuing are another of the psychological markers that delineate and define the underlying cultural differences between the British (especially the English) and Mediterranean societies (especially the Greeks).

To the British, the queue is sacrosanct, the epitome of all that is fair, proper, decent and right. Queue-jumping is considered absolutely beyond the pale and the queue-jumper is, in British estimation, about on a par with a child molester. The Greeks take a far more relaxed approach to the whole queueing business. In fact, if you go back to Classical Greece, they took a far more relaxed attitude to child molesting as well.

A British queue is a rigid, organized structure governed by strict, though unspoken, rules and conventions. A Greek queue is a more fluid, creative and organic structure, a constantly mutating mélange of people and interactions. Mix the two cultures and there will frequently be tears before bed-time. Or at the very least some bad-tempered muttering.

To understand this, it is necessary to appreciate the underlying British rules that apply to queuing. Paradoxically, this is more difficult for a native Brit than it is for an outsider such as Mikes. We natives have been immersed in these conventions since birth and have become so accustomed to them that they are invisible to us - until they are broken. Trying to recognize them is akin to a goldfish trying to recognize water. It only comes to his notice when it's not there.

In Britain, well defined queues are almost never jumped. No-one would walk up to the front of a long, intact queue and insert himself at its head. To do so would be unthinkable to most Brits. If you don't believe me, try it. The mere thought of the mass opprobrium it would engender makes the act psychologically impossible. Even *thinking* of doing it produces all the physiological signs of stress - raised heartrate, fine motor tremor, shivers, goose bumps, butterflies in the stomach and mild to moderate nausea.

Ironically, should you succeed in overcoming these inhibitions then the worst you are likely to receive from those you have gazumped is a raised eyebrow, a *sotto voce* 'harrumph' or at worst an almost inaudible *'Well! - Really!'* The real barrier to queue jumping has been drilled into your subconscious since early childhood. In fact, the idea is so unthinkable to the English psyche that, if actually confronted with it, most of us would assume a truly life-threatening emergency or that the perpetrator must be an ignorant foreigner who knows no better. No Englishman, not even a hedge fund manager, could be enough of an absolute cad as to act in such an unseemly manner.

It is when circumstances conspire to create a degree of ambiguity in the queue that the English queue-jumping early warning antennae switch to high sensitivity. Such ambiguity occurs where the structure of the queue is disrupted by obstacles, or the necessity to leave a gap to allow others to pass. Sometimes two queues meet or conversely one queue divides to service two or more different counters.

It is in circumstances such as these that the English anti-jumping charade kicks off. This dance has two essential underlying principles: *Don't make eye-contact* and *Don't, whatever you do, make a scene.* If a potential queue-jumper is spotted in the peripheral vision, a subtle mime of passive-aggressive body language comes into play. Its primary task is to let the potential jumper know that he has been spotted and that the potential jumpees are on to his little game.

This responsibility falls primarily to the person immediately behind the ambiguity and the first step is to reduce the gap as much as possible given the circumstances.

This is usually achieved by shuffling forwards and, if possible, claiming the space in front with any available territorial blocking device, such as a supermarket trolley, push-chair, invalided war veteran or small child. If jumpee number one is a little slow in initiating this ploy, those behind exert a subtle pressure on her in turn by shuffling forwards themselves, resulting in her being inadvertently goosed by the bunch of leeks carried by jumpee number two behind her. If the trolley or similar had been turned at 90 degrees to the direction of the queue (e.g. to let cross-traffic pass) it is now casually turned and pointed directly in the direction of the claimed space.

It is important to note that eye-contact between jumper and jumpee must be avoided at all costs. To make her message plain while still avoiding eye contact, the jumpee will turn her back and shoulders so that they are square on to the potential jumper, thus psychologically blocking his path. Rucksacks are a very effective accessory for this tactic. The strategy can be enhanced by leaning forward on the trolley and psychologically claiming the disputed gap in the queue. Generally, mere bulk makes the blocking technique more effective if done by a man. Reluctant husbands are frequently employed for this purpose.

In the vast majority of cases, these subtle postures and hints succeed in shaming our potential jumper into calling the whole thing off and retiring to his rightful place at the back of the queue. This, if God were an Englishman, would now be out of the door and halfway down the road, about fifty places further back than would have been the case had he not wasted everybody's time with his attempted queue-jumping shenanigans in the first place.

However, the key adjective applied to all the above tactics is *subtle*. These manoeuvres are glaringly apparent to Brits, whose antennae are finely tuned to them, but they pass completely unnoticed by a Greek. It is not that they are seen and deliberately ignored - they are just not seen.

Thus, an Englishman in a Greek post office, doctor's waiting room or bus stop finds himself in a state of shocked disorientation and mute apoplectic rage. He also finds himself at the back of the queue. Locals push in front of him. They walk straight to the front of the queue to ask the employee a long-winded and complex question. They call over relatives and friends from the other side of the room, hold long and animated conversation with them and then insert them into the queue at their side. They park Grandma in the queue as soon as they walk in the door and then go off to do their shopping, returning in dribs and drabs and holding up the whole queue in the process. Old ladies walk to the cash desk ostentatiously holding a solitary bag of flour aloft and then magically produce a full basket from beneath their voluminous shawls. Or, even worse, our old lady then beckons the rest of the family who suddenly appear with two trolleys loaded to overflowing with enough supplies to provision a full-scale assault on the summit of Annapurna.

It is absolutely inconceivable to the English that such behaviour can be anything other than a crass personal affront and a deliberate display of disrespect. How could they possibly have missed those narrowed eyes, those suspicious glances and obvious shuffles? What about the raised single eyebrow, the turned shoulder and the territorial claim staked by the precisely positioned trolley? Are these people blind?

Well, yes. In this case they are. To these unspoken messages at least. The English tendency to understatement extends even into the realms of body language. The Greeks' body language is as loud, expansive and expressive as their spoken communication. In such an environment our underplayed anti queue-jumping nudges and winks impinge upon their consciousness about as noticeably as a fart in a sewage works.

That is not to say that a Greek queue is a totally unregulated free-for-all, untrammelled by rules or social conventions. It just looks that way to the untrained eye. They have their cultural expectations and conventions like any society. They're just different ones from ours.

We caught the bus back to Vlicho and set off back to *Birvidik* in the dinghy. In our brief absence it had been all-change in the anchorage. About half the boats had left, to be replaced by about the same number of new arrivals. Amongst the new arrivals were five boats that we knew well, including three who had overwintered in Agios Nikolaos with us, *Rosa de Venti, Wilde Thyme* and *Kiara*. In addition we spotted *Pulsar* and *Aquatint* with whom we had overwintered in Malta. Further across were *Wave Dancer* and *Ride of a Lifetime* (winter in Marmaris). There were also several others with whom we were on nodding terms.

A new recruit to cruising would have thought this a remarkable coincidence. Not so a couple of seasoned old-timers like us. There are relatively few cruising routes through the Med and even fewer really popular ones. Most cruisers pass through this area on their way to, and back from, the eastern Med. Lefkas, especially Vlicho, is a bottleneck on this well-trodden path. It's unusual to pole up here and *not* find someone you know.

We circled the new arrivals and said our hellos. In the process we and *Wild Thyme* were invited to drinks on *Rosa di Venti* where we were told by Peter and Kaye on *Wild Thyme* that they were swallowing the anchor. They had arranged to have their boat lifted at Preveza in five days' time and so the coming Monday would be their last night as liveaboards. We all agreed to sail to Preveza and see them off in style.

Well, we sailed to Preveza and saw them off, but it wasn't a raucous affair. There's always a slightly melancholy undercurrent to these occasions, a sense of 'end of an era'. We rowed back to our respective boats not long after midnight and got up the next morning to wave them off as they lifted their anchor and made their final voyage – a short hop to the lifting bay.

Feeling slightly pensive and deflated we sailed a short run across the Gulf of Amphilakia to an anchorage off the village of Vonitsa. It was a beautiful spot, a long narrow inlet with an island in the middle. It had good depths and holding and was accessed through a narrow channel from the North. It was well protected from every direction except for a 10-degree sector from dead North. The wind was forecast to be light, and from the South West. Is this starting to ring any bells?

We anchored in eight metres and bit it in at 1000 revs. It was a fine, calm sunny day and we relaxed in the cockpit reading. After about an hour I caught a zephyr of wind on my face and the sun went out. I looked around and was not impressed. Out across the gulf, directly to the North as it happens, thunderclouds were gathering. Threatening blue-black anvil heads spread across the sky. The wind, as you have probably predicted, strengthened. It backed to northerly and started to send a swell into the anchorage.

The chop increased and several other boats up-anchored and left. We had to make a decision; should we stay where we were and sit it out, or should we weigh anchor and hack across the bay to Preveza town quay? We decided to stay. I let out another twenty metres of chain and checked that lifejackets, fleeces and waterproofs were ready to hand.

We waited with the usual build-up of tension, at which point it cleared up a bit. So we relaxed. At which point it started up again. So we tensed up. This *pas de deux* continued on and off for the next eighteen hours and we had to take turns on anchor watch overnight.

It finally cleared about two days later. It had been nothing serious, but neither of us had felt comfortable about going ashore and leaving the boat unattended. As it started to ease, we looked at each other across the cockpit and both blurted out simultaneously "*I don't think I want to do this anymore!*" Peter and Kaye swallowing the anchor may have given things a subconscious nudge, but this moment had been brewing for some time.

We're like a pair of bloody adolescents. ten years we planned and prepared for this liveaboard life and now, after a mere eight years, we wanted a change.

Bored.

Fed up.

'ad enough

Don't wanna do sailin' no more.

Wanna do somefing diff'rent.

Why do we 'ave to do sailin' alla time.

Other people don't have to do sailin' alla time.

S'not fair.

We'd been as far east as we had originally intended and were now going back over old ground. This was nice enough in its way. We knew the harbours and anchorages so there were no nasty surprises lurking round corners. In addition, we knew where the supermarkets, laundries, water and 'leccy points, decent cheap restaurants and other necessities were, so life was far more efficient, but it lacked novelty.

And we do like our novelty.

We considered our options. We still wanted to cruise the Adriatic and see Albania, Croatia and Venice, but after that, what was there? North Africa was as yet unvisited, but more and more of it was becoming just a teensy bit iffy. Cross the Atlantic? Nah - either too boring or too terrifying or both. We've never really been enthusiastic about the prospect of ocean crossing.

At the root, though, was the fact that, fascinating as the whole experience has been, there is an element of sameness about always seeing a place from the perspective of its coastal zones. Inland is a completely different experience as we noticed in our short trip up the Guardiana river five years earlier. So the obvious answer was to go inland.

There was, however, one tiny problem to this *eureka* moment. *Birvidik*, despite being an extremely seaworthy boat and an ideal liveaboard, is far from suited to the canals and rivers of inland waterways. The masts are too tall to get under the bridges and through tunnels. She draws 1.8 metres, which is too deep for many canals, and she is made of GRP which would last about three weeks in the rough and tumble of rivers and locks.

And so the plan was hatched.

The first task was the hardest - we would need to sell *Birvidik*. This posed several difficulties. Firstly, after many years we had finally adapted her almost exactly to our requirements. On top of that, she had been an integral and important part of our life for eighteen years. Leaving her would produce emotions akin to bereavement.

Secondly, we had timed it perfectly by deciding to try and sell a boat in the middle of a recession.

Having sold her, we would need to buy a suitable boat for the inland waterways, namely a steel barge. Most of these are found (at the best prices anyway) in Holland.

In between these two tasks we would face another problem. Once *Birvidik* was sold we would be homeless. And so would the cat. We would then need transport and accommodation, as well as storage for our meagre personal belongings, which currently fill every crook and nanny of *Birvidik*.

Finally, we would need to equip the new boat to meet Liz's exacting standards.

Well - that's not much of a challenge is it? We decided to give it a go.

So, The Plan was devised along the following lines:

1. Put *Birvidik* on the Market.

2. When (if?) she sells, look for a cheap second hand campervan.

3. Move selves, belongings and cat into campervan.

4. Look for surplus-to-requirements aircraft hangar for all those items that will not fit in campervan.

5. Drive to Holland and search for suitable canal boat.

6. Buy suitable canal boat, hopefully for around the price we get for *Birvidik*.

7. Equip aforementioned canal boat to Liz's aforementioned exacting standards.

8. Go on expensive course to learn how to deal with inland waterways of Europe.

9. Transport stored items from Greece to Holland and secrete away in crooks and nannies of new boat.

10. Sell campervan.

Piece of piss.

What could *possibly* go wrong?

And so it was resolved to spend what was left of that season pottering around the Ionian before checking in to Lefkas marina for the winter. Once snugged up in there we would put *Birvidik* on the market and see what happened.

Going on what had happened with other sellers to whom we had spoken, this could take up to three or four years. That wasn't a problem. We still had the Adriatic to explore; Albania, Montenegro, Bosnia-Herzegovina, Croatia, Slovenia, Venice and the East coast of Italy. We hadn't been there before.[106]

Watch this space.

If you have enjoyed this book, please consider nipping over to Amazon and leaving a review. I'm not too proud to grovel.

You might also want to keep an eye out for the third book in the trilogy, which is currently underway.

You can send any comments, observations, diatribes or glaring typos that I've missed to me at:

birvidikpersonal@gmail.com

Bob Newbury
Jersey
April 2019

¹ I told you it would make things a lot easier if you bought the previous book.

² Actually, that statement is complete bollocks. The Grand Tour ran from the mid-1600s to about the mid-1800s and was restricted to those awash with wealth and social status, which effectively meant the scions of the nobility and the wealthier of the landed gentry. It was usually undertaken post-Oxbridge, which made it an early fore-runner of the modern gap year.

³ This is a direct lift from the last page of 'An Idiot Aboard'. I know it looks like blatant lazy self-plagiarisation, but I'm pleading it as an aid to continuity.

⁴ *"What the bloody Hell's a gulet?"*, I hear you cry. Don't worry your pretty little head about it at the moment. It's just a type of boat. All will be explained later.

⁵ Trigger warning: Bowdlerisation facility will be disabled from now on. Just thought I'd break you in gently.

⁶ This is the interesting phenomenon whereby toxins and pollutants that are present at very low levels in the environment become more concentrated as they move up the food chain. Mercury is a good example. It is present in very low levels in plankton, but by the time it has been carried up the food chain to the tuna it is present at potentially hazardous concentrations.

⁷ No-one does, believe me. I have first-hand experience of this, as will be graphically described further on in the book.

⁸ Anachronistic slang shows one's age, does it not? It's not as cringe-inducing, though, as the pathetically risible attempts of those well old enough to know better to casually drop modern youth argot into their everyday conversation. It doesn't make them look or sound 'down with the kids'. It makes them look, and sound, like posing, self-conscious twats.

⁹ I'm going to keep hassling you until you buy the bloody thing. There's no escape.

¹⁰ 'Passarelle' is a posh word for 'gangplank'. It frequently, but not always, has a hand rail for added security.

¹¹ It is interesting to note that whereas most English chants are of the *"here we go, here we go, here we go"* genre, the equally violent but far more stylish Italians co-opt operatic arias from the likes of Verdi and Puccini.

[12] Pedant's corner: The correct and seamanlike term is *faked*, but virtually everyone nowadays uses *flaked* so I've gone along with it, under protest. I know that language is an organic, mutable phenomenon in a constant state of evolutionary flux, but that doesn't mean that I have to like the idea. I'm still fighting a valiant rear-guard against misplaced apostrophes and the conflation of 'less' and 'fewer'.

[13] A heavy weight. Its operation is explained in more detail later.

[14] These subconscious decision-making processes come up again later, but if you want a more detailed, well-written and erudite analysis I can heartily recommend *Thinking, Fast and Slow* by Daniel Kahneman

[15] As far as possible, I try not to make topical references as they date the book so much, but I couldn't resist this one. At least I've managed to avoid Brexit (so far).

[16] This is probably just as well, as posing, preening, swaggering and strutting are usually remarkably ineffective tactics for impressing women. I just wish I'd known that in my twenties. If youth only knew, if age only could.

[17] *"It is not enough that I succeed. One's friends must also fail"* Attributed to Somerset Maugham (1874 – 1965), probably inspired by François Duc de la Rochefoucauld (1613 – 1680)

[18] I appreciate that superstitions such as this sit uneasily with my professed scientific rationalism, but I'm in good company. Niels Bohr, the Nobel-laureate physicist and philosopher used to have a horse shoe nailed to his door.

A visitor asked Bohr about the purpose of the horseshoe, expressing incredulity that a man of science could possibly be swayed by a simple-minded folk belief. The physicist replied:

"Of course I don't believe in it, but I understand it brings you luck, whether you believe in it or not."

[19] There has been a lot of research showing this phenomenon. It shows that the least knowledgeable on a subject tend to be most certain of their opinion, whereas the most knowledgeable show the greatest uncertainty in their conclusions and beliefs. It even has a name *The Dunning-Kruger effect*.

[20] The Appian Way is just over 60 kilometres long, so that's one slave nailed up every ten metres. (or every twenty metres if

they used both sides of the road)

²¹ All musicians do this to some degree but modern Jazz players take it to ludicrous extremes, especially sodding saxophonists.

²² Despite this, in the 60s, like everyone else of my age, I slavishly followed the Beatles' example and professed admiration for Ravi Shankar and all things spiritual and Indian. If truth be told, it all sounded horrible to me, but I didn't have the nerve to admit it. It's a powerful thing, peer pressure.

²³ The female keeps up a call throughout this exhibition. I suspect she's either screaming out *"Leave 'im Darren – 'e ain't worf it'* in camel, or she's getting her rocks off like a certain category of female pro boxing fan.

²⁴ In common with most areas in the Mediterranean with a significant Northern European population, Finike has an animal welfare charity dedicated to rounding up feral cats and dogs, treating them for any ailments and having them sterilised. Most of these organisations are run and staffed by women, mainly Dutch and British. The Finike Group is no exception. They do sterling work, but it's ultimately doomed, You can't swim against the tide of natural selection.

²⁵ This is the only word I've come across that requires two hyphens to make it intelligible.

²⁶ Yeah – OK. It's closer to sarcasm than it is to irony.

²⁷ A quick and dirty application of Stoke's Law suggests a terminal velocity of around 160 kph – 100 mph in old money. That's about the speed of a stone from a sling, which was enough to take Goliath out of the game.

²⁸ These are not synonymous, but both apply in this case.

²⁹ Legal advice is recommended before undertaking this course of action.

³⁰ Or around five kilometres if we drag ourselves out of the 10th century.

³¹ The turkey is not native to the middle east, having first been domesticated in Mexico. It is thought to have acquired its name from its being imported into Europe via merchantmen based in the middle east, much of which was in the Ottoman empire. They were originally known as *'turkey coqs'*, shortened to *'turkeys'*.

³² Before some smart-arse pedant jumps in with *"Cockroaches **are** beetles"*, they're not. They're in the order

blattodea, which includes termites. So there. Mind you, I thought they were beetles until I looked them up.

33 This would not have been a good idea. Galatasaray are one of the most popular clubs in Turkey and have supporters everywhere. Galatasaray supporters have a reputation for defending their club's honour with, let us say, *vigour*.

34 Interestingly, although boric acid is highly toxic to most insects, it is relatively benign to humans. It is worth remembering that many of the things we regularly eat are poisonous if taken in excess. Caffeine, for example is almost 14 times more toxic to humans than is boric acid.

35 Most motion sickness medications are antihistamines, and cats' brains, apparently, do not possess the histamine receptors that humans' brains do. Differences such as this make you question the justification for compulsory testing on animals, especially the notorious LD50 test.

36 Einstein didn't need a visa, she was born in Turkey.

37 I make no apologies for lifting this verbatim from the previous book. They're my books; I can do what I like with them.

38 Well, it would be the Italians, wouldn't it – with a sentiment like that

39 These are minibuses that act as shared taxis. They leave when they're absolutely jammed full, which explains their name, derived from the Turkish for 'stuffed'.

40 '*Mr* Yottie', note. The gene for this trait is situated on the Y chromosome.

41 There's always a temptation to massage the figures, whether you're an individual with a tax return, a company with an annual report, a scientist with a study to publish or a country reporting economic data. Luckily, there's a clever little tool that can check large data sets for fiddling; it's called *Benford's Law*. When the Greek national accounts, as submitted to the EU, were checked for conformity with Benford's Law they failed spectacularly.

http://www.badscience.net/2011/09/benfords-law-using-stats-to-bust-an-entire-nation-for-naughtiness/

42 I wouldn't bet the farm on this being an accurate and universal representation of reality. It has come in for some heavy-duty criticism.

43 "Nothing is certain in this life except Death and Taxes."

Benjamin Franklin 1705 – 1790.

44 I don't know if this is related to the apocryphal penchant some women are reputed to have for perching themselves on the corner of the washing machine during the spin cycle.

45 Don't. This is a statistical misunderstanding commonly known as the Texas Sharpshooter Fallacy. The question you should be asking is not *'What are the odds against inverting the screen occurring by chance?'*, but *'What are the odds of three keys being pressed at random having any effect?'*

46 There are a lot of rules of thumb in this sailing lark.

47 It's surprising how often this happens, with the foredeck hand gaping disbelievingly as the last of the anchor chain shoots over the bow roller and into the briny. If you're in any depth of water and you don't have dive gear aboard, it's an expensive mistake to make.

48 Don't fall into the trap of thinking that if a boat is twice as long then it's twice as big. To keep things in proportion, if you double the length you need to double the width and double the height. 2 x 2 x 2 = eight times as big.

49 Why are so many aphorisms inaccurately attributed to Einstein? Is there a feeling that his near-mythical status will lend more authority to it? The earliest reliable attribution to this quote that I can find is in a Narcotics Anonymous pamphlet from 1981

50 Derivatives of this in Spanish and Portuguese are hangovers of the Moorish occupation of much of the Iberian peninsula from 711 to 1492. *Ojalá* (pronounced *o-ha-la* in Spanish) and *Oxalá* (pronounced *oo-sha-la* in Portuguese) both translate as *let's hope so* or *God willing*.

51 This seems almost abstemious in comparison with the Royal Navy where, traditionally, the first alcoholic drink of the day was taken when the sun rose over the topmost yardarm. In summer in the northern latitudes, where the phrase originated, this would have been about 11 a.m.

52 I am one of the few people on the planet who actually knows what seagull shit tastes like. I was lying on the beach after a particularly heavy night and had fallen asleep with my mouth open when I was dive-bombed with pinpoint accuracy by a seagull. Straight into the back of the throat. It doesn't taste as bad as you think. It tastes worse.

And before the pedants start wittering, I know it's really concentrated urine, not shit. The knowledge doesn't make it taste any better.

⁵³ A strange phenomenon, common to most Turkish supermarkets, is the inordinate amount of shelf space dedicated to adult nappies. These are extremely useful for mopping up spillages in the engine bay but buying them in large quantities lays oneself open to suspicions of chronic incontinence.

⁵⁴ Most modern antifouls are copper based. Symptoms of copper toxicity include vomiting, haematemesis (vomiting of blood), hypotension (low blood pressure), melena (black, tarry faeces), coma, jaundice and generalised gastrointestinal distress. It is thought to predispose towards Alzheimer's. You also get a brown ring around the outside of the iris which can just ruin your selfies.

⁵⁵ A medical acronym, no longer used now that patients have access to their notes. It stands for *Totally Fucked But Unfortunately Not Dead Yet.*

⁵⁶ The laws of thermodynamics are totally unforgiving bastards and are behind most of the misery in the Universe. There will be more on these later.

⁵⁷ Well, no Brit in his right mind – which is by no means all of them.

⁵⁸ I know, I know. Turkey's capital is Ankara. Istanbul's still the biggest city, though. By far.

⁵⁹ He also liked a drink and was reputed to have downed a litre of raki every day of his adult life. That's about 350 units a week – makes me feel quite restrained. Mind you, he did die at 57 from chronic liver disease.

⁶⁰ One can justifiably question his methods, but I would also question his timing. If the deed had been done twelve years earlier, Kemal wouldn't have sired Osman Johnson who in turn would not have sired Stanley Johnson. Which in turn means we wouldn't have had to suffer Boris.

⁶¹ Recep Tayyip Erdoğan has played a clever long game, culminating in the failed coup in 2016, the first time such a coup has failed in Turkey. At the time of writing, though, it looks as if the consequences of his hubris might be coming home to roost.

⁶² The BFQ is the animal's bite force in Newtons divided by its body mass in Kilograms. The cat's BFQ is 58. The only carnivores I could find with a lower BFQ were the Cape Genet (whatever that is) on 48 and, surprisingly, the Asiatic Black Bear

on 44. Mind you, with teeth as sharp as a cat's you don't need much force.

63 Chums, also known as 'angels', are heavy weights (ours are 15kg each) with fittings that enable them to be slid down the anchor chain. They serve two purposes; they keep the pull on the anchor more horizontal and they act as shock absorbers, reducing the snatch load on the anchor.

64 German, since you ask.

65 These seem to have acquired cult status in yottiedom, but why anyone should ever want to eat something that tastes mainly of piss is beyond me.

66 Eyesight deteriorates so gradually with age that you don't appreciate the degree to which you are making educated guesses as to what the letters actually are. This becomes suddenly and glaringly apparent when you try to read something in an alphabet to which you are not accustomed – like Greek or Cyrillic.

67 All these judgements are anecdotal and totally unsubstantiated by objective evidence.

68 Names have been changed to protect the guilty and to avoid libel proceedings.

69 It's oxytocin yet again. Bloody stuff gets everywhere.

70 The Greeks change their bus timetables without notice or explanation. No attempt is made to advise users of the new arrangements, they are just expected to know, to absorb the knowledge by some form of cultural osmosis. The locals seem to be able to do this, but the practice leaves expats and visitors totally bewildered. I suspect it is a means of asserting local identity in the face of the onslaught of tourists.

71 As I have mentioned before, the conventional wisdom is that every equation inserted in a book halves its sales, with the exception of $e=mc^2$, which inexplicably doubles them. So ignore the equation – I only put it in to show off.

72 Bloody thermodynamics again.

73 This sort of stress can even extend to whole organisations as in the case of the NHS and Local Government struggling to meet the impossible demands placed on them by politicians and career bureaucrats who simultaneously refuse to give them the resources necessary to meet those demands.

⁷⁴ Amygdala is Greek for 'almond'. Medical jargon, like any argot, is designed to facilitate communication within the in-group while being impenetrable to outsiders. It does that by roping in words from Latin. If Latin fails to confuse and obscure enough then it falls back on Greek. Preferably in the Greek alphabet if some had their way. Got to keep the oiks out.

⁷⁵ If you have read homoerotic undertones into this, you're spot on the money. Homosexual relationships were encouraged among these groups to enhance loyalty and self-sacrifice should a lover be threatened in battle.

⁷⁶ Early artillery was notoriously inaccurate. Things didn't really start to improve until the introduction of rifling for artillery pieces in 1855.

⁷⁷ This may sound a strange sentiment to modern ears, but languages are constantly evolving. In the English of 1805, '*England confides*' meant '*England is confident that*'.

⁷⁸ Difficult but not impossible. Take, for example, panicking Tory politicians who fear their seats may be at risk. OK, *any* politician who fears his seat may be at risk, but allow me to indulge my prejudices

⁷⁹ What is it with Man U? They are incomprehensibly popular throughout the world and are supported by thousands of people who couldn't pinpoint Manchester on a map if it had a pin in it and a bloody great arrow pointing to Old Trafford. First thing many foreigners say when encountering an Englishman is "*Ah – English! Manchester United!*" followed by the most recent manager but one and the name of some player I've never heard of.

⁸⁰ The Duchenne smile is what is generally looked upon as a genuine smile as opposed to a 'Say Cheese' smile. Both involve raising the corners of the mouth by contracting the zygomatic major muscles, but in the Duchenne smile the muscles around the eyes also contract, raising the cheeks and producing crows' feet round the eyes. Conventional wisdom has it that the Duchenne smile is purely involuntary and cannot be convincingly mimicked, but I never seem to have much trouble.

⁸¹Cognitive dissonance is the mental discomfort triggered by simultaneously holding two or more contradictory beliefs, values or ideas. Normal human behaviour, then.

⁸² Ah, yes - Rolf Harris. The draft of this was written before his arrest, conviction & slamming up. I left it in because I couldn't

think of a better example of apparent benign avuncularity. I always had a bit of a soft spot for Rolf, despite his being a bit on the naff, non-hip side. Who can forget his seminal version of *Stairway to Heaven*? It brought tears to Robert Plant's and Jimmy Page's eyes. Savile made my flesh creep from the very start, but not Rolf. When he was first mentioned in connection with operation yewtree, my first reaction was *"Oh no, not Rolf!- if he's a bad'un then who can we trust?"*

83 I know this ends a sentence with a preposition, but it's better than tortuous constructions such as *"This is something up with which I shall not put."*

84 In his infinite insecurity, Man has used many omens in an ultimately futile attempt to predict the future, from inspecting tea leaves to boiling a donkey's head (cephalonomancy, since you ask).

Haruspicy is probably one of the least tasteful. It is beaten only by anthropomancy, which is having a poke and a sniff around the entrails of dead or dying sacrificed humans, preferably young, virgin female children. Nice, huh?

85 Following the financial crisis, the Greek Railway Service has broken with tradition and abolished timetables for this route entirely. Train times are determined daily on an *ad hoc* basis following a consultation of the cruise ship schedules (and probably a touch of cephalonomancy). Nothing is published and the only way to determine train times for a particular day is to ask at the ticket office that morning and hope it hasn't already left.

86 Nevertheless, ships such as these are dwarfed into insignificance by the latest generation of super liners. At the time of writing, the largest cruise ship in the world is the Symphony of the Seas. This behemoth is nearly 400 metres long and weighs in at a quarter of a million tonnes. It can carry just under 7000 passengers, served by just over 2000 crew, giving it a population on a par with a small town, such as Shanklin on the Isle of Wight.

87 In some instances, so scurrilous rumour has it, the local mafia wait until the legitimate staff knock off for the day and then they move their own workforce in for an unofficial night shift that knocks out branded copies using the same plant and raw materials.

88 *"It is only shallow people who do not judge by appearances."* Oscar Wilde

89 This is unheard of. They're usually fool-proof. I'm sure the makers put something addictive in them.

90 Italy is an exception to this general rule. Bill and Laurel

Cooper in *Sell up and sail* posit that theft is the state religion in Italy and many yotties would agree with them.

[91] And most of them seem to display a pragmatic disregard for procedure. I needed some blood tests done and phoned up the doctor. He said that to save me coming out, he'd call in the marina on his way home. He took the samples sitting in his car in the carpark. We got some funny looks from passers-by, who obviously thought we were a couple of junkies shooting up.

[92] Just thought I'd throw in another shameless plug.

[93] As reported in *An Idiot Aboard*.

[94] It's our old friends testosterone and oxytocin again. The former triggers the fight response and the latter the 'Tend & Befriend'.

[95] Humiliation cuts deep, sometimes deeper than physical attack. In severe cases it can completely destroy the sense of self. That is why ritual humiliation is often deployed to reinforce social mores and punish those who are judged to pose a threat to the established social order. Thinks of the stocks and pillory, tarring and feathering and shaving the hair off women who are thought to have had liaisons with enemy soldiers.

[96] I've just read this through, and it sounds like a typical, emetically gushing advertising puff masquerading as a trip advisor review, but it's all true. Despite my generally cynical outlook, some places do hit the spot, and this is one of them

[97] This is a useful Jersey dialect term which fills a semantic gap in standard English. It denotes a position that is worse than 'not too bad' but isn't quite bad enough for the epithet 'bad'.

[98] I bet that when you acquired this book you had no idea you were in for the fascinating treat of a whole, riveting section on doing the washing.

[99] A *wringer* to our transatlantic cousins.

[100] Ruairi has been reported as having said afterwards that he just didn't think about it and that, had he stopped and thought, he would probably not have done it.

[101] Yeah, I know. The collective noun for hyenas is a *cackle* or a *clan*, but *pack* sounds more threatening.

[102] During WW2, Spike Milligan was marched into his CO's office on defaulter's parade. He stood to attention and saluted. The CO looked up, surprised. *"Milligan – what are you doing here?"*

"Everybody's got to be somewhere, Sir" Replied Spike.

103 Well, I say *'consensus'* but in truth I just made most of this up.

104 Ah yes, that lovely little word *'reasonable'*. So beloved of lawyers, so open to interpretation, so wonderfully effective at keeping them in clover indefinitely

105 Before the pedants start off again, I know that this is a tautology, as *'hoi'* means 'the'. I just can't find an alternative construction that isn't gratingly clumsy.

106 Well, we had actually. Some of it, anyway. We travelled down the coast of Yugoslavia by motor bike in the 1970s. Enver Hoxha made sure that Albania was safe from corrupting influences like us though.

41583182R00177

Printed in Poland
by Amazon Fulfillment
Poland Sp. z o.o., Wrocław